MURDER MOST QUEER

TRIANGULATIONS

Lesbian/Gay/Queer ▲ Theater/Drama/Performance

Series Editors
Jill Dolan, Princeton University
David Román, University of Southern California

TITLES IN THE SERIES:

Passing Performances: Queer Readings of Leading Players in American Theater History edited by Robert A. Schanke and Kim Marra

When Romeo Was a Woman: Charlotte Cushman and Her Circle of Female Spectators by Lisa Merrill

Camp: Queer Aesthetics and the Performing Subject edited by Fabio Cleto

Staging Desire: Queer Readings of American Theater History edited by Kim Marra and Robert A. Schanke

A Problem Like Maria: Gender and Sexuality in the American Musical by Stacy Wolf

A Queer Sort of Materialism: Recontextualizing American Theater by David Savran

Margaret Webster: A Life in the Theater by Milly S. Barranger

The Gay and Lesbian Theatrical Legacy: A Biographical Dictionary of Major Figures in American Stage History edited by Billy J. Harbin, Kim Marra, and Robert A. Schanke

Cast Out: Queer Lives in Theater edited by Robin Bernstein

Queering Mestizaje: Transculturation and Performance by Alicia Arrizón

Bulldaggers, Pansies, and Chocolate Babies: Performance, Race, and Sexuality in the Harlem Renaissance by James F. Wilson

Lady Dicks and Lesbian Brothers: Staging the Unimaginable at the WOW Café Theatre by Kate Davy

A Menopausal Gentleman: The Solo Performances of Peggy Shaw edited by Jill Dolan

Performing Queer Latinidad: Dance, Sexuality, Politics by Ramón H. Rivera-Servera

Acts of Gaiety: LGBT Performance and the Politics of Pleasure by Sara Warner

Butch Queens Up in Pumps: Gender, Performance, and Ballroom Culture in Detroit by Marlon M. Bailey

Murder Most Queer: The Homicidal Homosexual in the American Theater by Jordan Schildcrout

MURDER MOST QUEER

The Homicidal Homosexual in the American Theater

Jordan Schildcrout

THE UNIVERSITY OF MICHIGAN PRESS

Ann Arbor

Published in the United States of America by
The University of Michigan Press
Manufactured in the United States of America
♾ Printed on acid-free paper

2017 2016 2015 2014 4 3 2 1

A CIP catalog record for this book is available from the British Library.

ISBN 978-0-472-07232-3 (cloth : alk. paper)

ISBN 978-0-472-05232-5 (pbk. : alk. paper)

ISBN 978-0-472-12052-9 (e-book)

Contents

Acknowledgments

The journey of writing *Murder Most Queer* began during my gay adolescence in the 1980s, which coincided with the emergence of the AIDS crisis and the rise to power of conservative movements that vilified queer people. Throughout my teens and twenties, my anxiety and anger over these circumstances found expression in the political rage of LGBT activism, the robust rebellion of the queer punk subculture, the shimmering darkness of queer goths and new romantics, the vibrant violence and passion of gay novels by authors ranging from James Baldwin to Dennis Cooper, the ironic nihilism of New Queer Cinema—and the surprising number of homicidal homosexuals I found flourishing onstage in the American theater. I continued to stalk these characters into the twenty-first century because I found them beautiful and horrible, abject and empowered, ridiculous and profound, virtuous and sinister. The contradictions and ambiguities intrigued me, and at times frightened me, and this book is the result of my need to peer into the darkness and wrestle with the monstrous and the marvelous.

Many mentors, colleagues, and friends have aided me in my work on *Murder Most Queer*, and I'm especially grateful to professors David Savran, Judith Milhous, and Alisa Solomon, who guided this project through its initial incarnation as a dissertation at the Graduate Center of the City University of New York. The CUNY Graduate Center provided an excellent home for those of us working at the intersection of theater studies and queer studies, and I consider myself fortunate to have also studied with Jill Dolan and Marvin Carlson, as well as the late George Custen and Eve Kosofsky Sedgwick. The Vera Roberts Dissertation Award, generously endowed by Professor Roberts, offered crucial financial support during the dissertation process. My fellow students at the Graduate Center were constantly engaged in the exchange of ideas and perspectives, and being part of this community of emerging scholars was crucial to the creation of this book. The Graduate Center is also the home of the Center for Lesbian and Gay Studies (CLAGS), where I had the good fortune to work for many years under the directorships of Jill Dolan, Alisa Solomon, and Paisley Currah. In addition to much-needed support from the Monette-Horowitz Dissertation Award, CLAGS also offered me a vital home in the field of queer studies, invaluable mentorship and scholarly opportunities, and an incomparable team of coworkers and comrades, including Preston Bautista, Rachel Cohen, Heidi Coleman, Sara Ganter, Claudia Moreno Parsons, and Lavelle Porter.

Portions of *Murder Most Queer* benefited greatly from being presented in public forums, and I'm obliged to the organizations and individuals who invited me to present my work, including the LGBTQ Focus Group of the Association for Theatre in Higher Education (ATHE); the Mid-America Theatre Conference (MATC); the American Society for Theatre Research (ASTR); the Queer Matters Conference in London; Sue-Ellen Case, David Román, and James Schultz at the QGrad Conference at the University of California, Los Angeles; and Paisley Currah at the CLAGS Colloquium Series. The editors and anonymous peer reviewers who guided the development of portions of this book for publication in other venues also played an important role. Thanks to Gretchen Sommerfeld and Amy Dudley for shepherding an early version of chapter 2 that appeared as "Queer Justice: The Retrials of Leopold and Loeb" in the *Journal of American Culture* 34, no. 2 (June 2011): 175-188. I'm grateful to Catherine Schuler and Bob Kowkabany for their invaluable input on an early version of chapter 3 that appeared as "The Closet Is a Deathtrap: Bisexuality, Duplicity, and the Dangers of the Closet in the Postmodern Thriller" in *Theatre Journal* 63, no. 1 (March 2011): 43-59. Many thanks also to James Fisher who published an early version of a section of chapter 6 as "No Tragedy: Queer Evil in the Metaphysical Comedies of Nicky Silver" in his edited volume *"We Will be Citizens": New Essays on Gay and Lesbian Theatre* (Jefferson, NC: McFarland, 2008).

Many of my thoughts about the theater in general and queer killers in particular were explored in the vibrant exchange of ideas that occurs in the classroom, and this work would not have been possible without the intelligence, creativity, and engagement of all those who have been my students. I'm much obliged to the colleagues who gave me the opportunity to create and teach courses in theater history and dramatic literature during the early part of my career: Alisa Solomon (CLAGS Seminars in the City), Mira Felner and Jonathan Kalb (Hunter College), George Custen and Maurya Wickstrom (College of Staten Island), Colette Brooks (Eugene Lang College, The New School), and Mary Fleischer (Marymount Manhattan College).

Much of *Murder Most Queer* came to fruition during my years at Ohio University's School of Theater in Athens, Ohio, and I'm deeply indebted to the excellent people who sustain this vibrant artistic and scholarly community, particularly my colleagues in theater history and playwriting, William Condee, Erik Ramsey, and Charles Smith, as well as the school's directors, Robert St. Lawrence, William Fisher, and Madeleine Scott. My scholarship was immensely enriched by working with Merri Biechler, Holly Cole, Shelley Delaney, Dennis Delaney, Daniel Denhart, Brian Evans, Barbara Fiocchi, Tom Fiocchi, Ledger Free, David Haugen, Lowell Jacobs, Kjersten Lester-Moratzka, Michael Lincoln, Treva Nichols, Laura Parotti, C. David Russell, Rebecca VerNooy, and Robert Winters. In addition, Jeanette Buck, Mateo Galvano, Maureen Wagner, and Lorraine Wochna were constant sources of personal and professional support. I completed *Murder Most Queer* while in my current position in the Theatre and Performance Program at Purchase College, State University of New York, and I'm grateful for the support of wonderful colleagues, including David Bassuk, Kay Capo, Lenora Champagne, Rachel Dickstein, Shaka McGlotten, Lisa Jean Moore, Sylvan Oswald, Lenka Pichlikova, Peter Sprague, Greg Taylor, Kathleen Tolan, and Gary Waller.

I'm thankful for the intellectual and creative community consisting of friends and colleagues outside my home institutions. *Murder Most Queer* benefited from substantial critical analysis and feedback from Sam Buggeln, David Foley, Libby Garland, Sharon Green, Sara Warner, James Wilson, and Constance Zaytoun. I'm also grateful to those who engaged in fruitful conversations about this project, including Mia Barron, Keith Bunin, Joshua Furst, Doni Gewirtzman, Holly Hughes, Susan Kim, Laurence Klavan, Chris Menna, Tim Miller, Marilyn Neimark, Joshua Price, Bob Putnam, Richard Renfro, Stan Richardson, Nick Salvato, Bruce Whitacre, Marion Wilson, and Joe Zellnik.

I owe special thanks to LeAnn Fields, Jill Dolan, David Román, the board of editors, the anonymous readers, and the entire team at the University of Michigan Press, including Alexa Ducsay, Marcia LaBrenz, and Janet Opdyke. My work has been deeply influenced by the scholarship produced by the Triangulations Series, and I'm honored to have this book be part of that series. LeAnn Fields supported this project from its inception, and I'm extremely grateful for her encouragement and support throughout the entire process.

Murder Most Queer exists because of the theater artists whose work inspired and provoked me to write this book, and I offer particular thanks to those who generously offered to share their unpublished plays with me. The American theater is a better place because of their challenging and exciting plays and performances. Images of those productions appear in this book thanks to the generosity and permission of Charles Busch, Gerry Goodstein, Richard Hamburger, Joan Marcus, Alain Monot, Dixie Sheridan, Kathy Sova, Frank "Fraver" Verlizzo, and Amy Webber. I'm also indebted to Thomas Lisanti and the staff of the New York Public Library for the Performing Arts.

Finally, I consider myself truly fortunate to have such a loving and supportive family. My parents, Steve and Toni Schildcrout, continue to inspire me with their passion for knowledge, appreciation of the arts, and commitment to justice and equality. I'm grateful to all my family members, including Barbara Schildcrout, Debra Gold, and Alan Vaughn, who set an example by pursuing the arts in their own lives, and then welcomed me into their homes so I might do the same. Doug and Abi Schildcrout made me an uncle to three amazing nephews, now all teenagers, who help me appreciate the degree to which our culture has—and hasn't—changed for the next generation.

This book is dedicated with love to my partner in crime, David Zellnik.

Introduction

Beyond Queer Villainy

The villainous homosexual has a long and terrible history in America. Colonial authorities criminalized same-sex relations, which were—along with treason, murder, and witchcraft—punishable by death.[1] Every state in the United States adopted sodomy laws that made same-sex sexual relations a felony, and in some states the maximum punishment was life imprisonment. In 1962 Illinois became the first state to decriminalize homosexuality, and many other states followed, while some kept sodomy laws on the books into the twenty-first century. Even when such laws were not enforced, they were used as justification for discrimination against lesbian, gay, bisexual, and transgender (LGBT) people, limiting civil rights and stigmatizing queer people as criminal. The link between sexual difference and criminal deviance created the "homosexual villain" as an archetype in our social discourse that persists to this day. Significant changes in the legal status of LGBT people—including the Supreme Court's 2003 *Lawrence v. Texas* decision, which decriminalized homosexuality in every state, and the 2013 *United States v. Windsor* decision, which dismantled the discriminatory Defense of Marriage Act—have not eliminated the social forces and ideologies that insist on the inherent criminality of the queer.[2] Opponents of LGBT equality, including politicians, pundits, and certain religious leaders, continue to raise the specter of the villainous queer who threatens families, social institutions, and national security. This antigay rhetoric imagines LGBT citizens as sinister threats who must be combated and defeated.

The representation of the villainous homosexual also has a long history within American entertainment. Our popular culture has often depicted queer characters who are threatening, murderous, and, in some cases, categorically evil. Cultural scholars have explored the queerness—sometimes covert and sometimes overt—of the vampire, the Nazi, and the serial killer in Hollywood films.[3] Even Disney's cartoon villains are often marked by gender nonconformity, instilling a fear of the masculine woman and feminine man as a deadly threat.[4] It should come as no surprise that the political realities surrounding same-sex relations influence the depiction of queer people within our cultural narratives. Such representations have long served to reaffirm the ideologies that criminalize the queer in the American imagination.

One of the ways in which a stigmatized minority fights against its oppression in American society is by attempting to control or influence the representation of members of that minority within cultural discourse. Following the path established by the National Association for the Advancement of Colored People and the Jewish Anti-Defamation League, the Gay and Lesbian Alliance Against Defamation (GLAAD) was formed in 1985 to encourage fair representation and actively combat representations that the organization considers demeaning or derogatory, particularly within mass-produced popular culture such as mainstream cinema, television, and popular music.[5] If GLAAD deems a representation of a queer person to be detrimental to LGBT people, the organization can put pressure on creators, sponsors, and consumers to recognize and hopefully eliminate the defamatory representation. A standard narrative of the quest for positive gay representation is the journey from invisibility to villainy to humanity.[6] Representations of "normal" and even exemplary LGBT people are lauded and affirmed, and negative representations are thus positioned as hindrances to the goals of acceptance and assimilation.

In the rogues' gallery of negative representations, the homicidal homosexual is a key culprit. As the ne plus ultra of homophobia, the homicidal homosexual represents the sexual aggressor, duplicitous traitor, diseased corruptor, and evil destroyer of all that is good. In most narratives, these moral monsters exist in order to be eradicated, thus affirming the strength of traditional gender roles, heterosexuality, the family, and conservative values. The rhetoric of positive versus negative representation also calls for the eradication of these monstrous characters, supposedly because they impugn the goodness of all queer people and stand in the way of LGBT people achieving full acceptance and citizenship within our society. When gay and lesbian activists demonstrated against films with queer killers, such as *Cruising* (1980) and *Basic Instinct* (1992), they made national headlines and raised awareness about derogatory stereotypes.[7]

Throughout the 1980s and early 1990s, part of the argument of the gay rights movement against those homicidal characters is that they seemed to stand alone in the field of representation. When there were so few representations of any queer people in the media, the negative examples seemed all the more universal and therefore defamatory. Also significant was the function of the queer villain within these narratives, usually pitted against a heteronormative hero. Both of these dynamics were examined in Vito Russo's *The Celluloid Closet*, first published in 1981 and revised in 1987, which offered a powerful critique of Hollywood's construction of queer villainy.[8] Years later Russo's analysis is still influential, as evidenced in this entry on a popular blog about gay male culture, written by Brent Hartinger.

> Literally all the big-budget Hollywood movies until, perhaps, *Philadelphia* in 1993 that featured major gay male characters portrayed them as insane villains and serial killers. Worse, these movies often played on the audience's fears of gay people and discomfort with behaviors that violate gender norms, using people's prejudice to make them hate the villain more, and make the audience feel better when the hero finally vanquishes them (usually violently killing them).[9]

Yet Hollywood cinema is not the only cultural venue, and this particular scenario for the homicidal homosexual is not the only script.

One of the key venues in which LGBT people have played a major role is on the stages of the American theater. More than many other venues over the past century, the theater has offered representations of queer lives that are diverse and complex—and it has offered them frequently and to popular and critical acclaim.[10] While gay and lesbian activists staged protests against queer killers in American cinema, the American stage has been home to dozens of homicidal homosexuals, many of them created by queer theater artists, who have enlisted this archetype in the fight against homophobia. In the American theater, the homicidal homosexual has played a very different role, going beyond queer villainy.

Murder Most Queer reclaims the homicidal homosexual as a figure that must be interrogated rather than simply condemned. By more fully analyzing key examples of murderous queer characters who have populated the American theater for nearly a century, this book has two major goals. One is to expose the forces that create the homophobic paradigm that imagines sexual and gender nonconformity as dangerous and destructive. The second is to explore the ways in which theater artists—and, for the most part, *queer* theater artists—have rewritten and radically altered the significance of the homicidal homosexual. Far from being simple reiterations of a homophobic archetype, these homicidal homosexuals are complex and challenging characters who enact trenchant fantasies of empowerment, replacing the shame and stigma of the abject with the defiance and freedom of the outlaw, giving voice to rage and resistance, even to vengeance. These bold characters also probe the darker anxieties and fears that can affect queer lives and relationships, including victimization from homophobia, the oppression of the closet, and the devastation of AIDS. In doing so, these dramatic characters, even in their most fantastic or outrageous instances, also illuminate very real emotional, social, and political circumstances. Instead of sentencing these characters to the prison of negative representation, *Murder Most Queer* analyzes the meanings in their acts of murder, confronting the real fears and desires condensed in those dramatic acts and recognizing the potential value—and even pleasure—of violence in the theater.

"Monstrous and Marvelous": An Approach to Representation, Interpretation, and Violence

A discussion of plays that wrestle with murder, sexuality, and murderous sexuality raises intriguing challenges regarding the nature of identity, violence, and interpretation in the theater. Throughout this book, my goal in analyzing works of theater is not to expose the single true meaning "hidden" in these plays but to explore a variety of competing interpretations and reactions. The potential meaning of a dramatic text in performance can vary wildly depending on the artistic choices made by directors, actors, designers, and other members of the production team. A play, then, does not have a single secured meaning determined by the author, but rather is a site of many potential meanings.[11] Additionally, while performances may address spectators as a group, individual audience members can view the same performance but find different ideas, emotions, and meanings. Authorial intentions and social conventions may urge the audience member toward a *dominant* reading, that is, a reading based on the assumption of shared social values and acceptance of dominant ideology as expressed through narrative conventions. Yet *resistant* readings can run rampant in the theater, especially among queer audience members who refuse to submit to "normal" social structures and interpretive practices.[12]

Thus my task here is not to determine the "correct" reaction to a play but to explore, through a close analysis of texts and contexts, possible reactions, interpretations, and experiences that I hope will make the plays more interesting, exciting, and challenging. My goal is not to reduce these plays but to enlarge them.

Beyond this fundamental method of interpretation, theatrical acts of murder raise more complex ethical and aesthetic questions. How can I argue that audiences should find value or take pleasure in murder on the stage, when in real life such violence is unambiguously abhorrent? Why should a group that is often accused of villainy in real life take pleasure in watching a fictional character enact that villainy onstage? Plato condemned the ancient Greek theater because he distrusted the unruly emotions stirred by spectacles of violence and suffering, while Aristotle defended theatrical representation with his notion of *catharsis:* the purgation of pity and fear experienced by the audience when viewing tragedy. More recently the philosopher Stanley Cavell has argued that in our modern era the purpose of tragedy "is not to purge us of pity and terror, but to make us capable of feeling them again."[13] When it comes to spectacles of violence, the aesthetic qualities of the theater—beauty, eloquence, magnitude, and so on—can engage and provoke an audience, both intellectually and emotionally. Theatrical violence, then, allows us to confront and wrestle with the causes, effects, and significance of violence.

Oscar Wilde, as a chief proponent of the Aesthetic Movement, celebrated extraordinary fictional characters who expressed extremes of sorrow, joy, and rage, "who had monstrous and marvelous sins, monstrous and marvelous virtues." Wilde recognized that in the realm of art, one can see the monstrous and the marvelous in the same instance, both in the good and in the bad. Wilde embraces these contradictions when he claims that "the object of Art is not simple truth but complex beauty."[14] The French psychoanalytic philosopher Georges Bataille also identifies the audience's desire to witness the monstrous and the marvelous when he writes that "men are swayed by two simultaneous emotions: they are driven away by terror and drawn by an awed fascination."[15] Furthermore, Bataille cites the novels of the Marquis de Sade when he argues that "sexual activity is a form of violence," a form of physical violation "bordering on murder," which is why our society's strongest taboos are against murder and certain sexual activities.[16] Sex and murder, then, are twin taboos that are often interchanged, both in the subconscious and in works of fiction, and eroticized as acts of transgression.

Both murder and eroticism are highly dramatic subjects, involving physical and emotional tensions and confrontations. Plays with queer killers can be especially powerful because they confront both social taboos with the fantasy of transgression, and these fantasies can speak to the difficult realities faced by LGBT people in a society that vacillates between acceptance and rejection. Even the most well-adjusted gay person may struggle with the stigma connected to same-sex desire in a homophobic culture. And even the gentlest person may imagine the possibility of committing murder, recognizing the potential for destruction that all human beings possess. In reality, of course, most people do not commit murder, but we are fascinated by those who do, perhaps because they allow us to recognize, exercise, and potentially exorcise, the part of ourselves that has the ability to commit monstrous acts. The homicidal homosexual is not the villain among us but the potential villain within us.

The function of drama is not necessarily to reflect our dark capacities realistically but to express them beautifully, shockingly, and trenchantly as only artistic creations can. There is pleasure to be found in plays that cause us to experience our emotional capacity as humans, especially if that capacity is rarely exercised in our daily lives. The artistic representation of violence, coupled with a sensitive imagination, creates a situation in which ordinary people can have the pleasure of experiencing the magnificent potential, including the magnificently monstrous potential, of our own lives. We may be fascinated by our own capacity for destruction, even our potential for evil—especially if one happens to inhabit an identity often accused of being destructive or evil—and these fictional representations allow us to indulge in that fascination in a way that is thrilling, challenging, and ultimately enriching.

Transgressive characters (as opposed to happy, well-adjusted, moral people who live in harmony) make for great drama because their actions speak to our fears and fantasies surrounding taboos. Many of the "great plays" of western culture feature characters who have the ability to fascinate us with their breaking of taboos: Oedipus, Medea, Lucifer, Richard III, Shylock, Othello, Don Juan, Phaedra, Mack the Knife, and Sweeney Todd. These villain-heroes reject social norms, discarding repression and boldly pursuing their goals and their own satisfaction. Such characters are often, in a word, sexy—attractive to us because they embody the fantasy of our own forbidden desires and potentials. The character who is monstrous and marvelous makes for good drama, and the homicidal homosexual participates in this esteemed tradition.

The homicidal homosexual, however, is more than the inevitable byproduct of standard dramatic plotting and the abundance of murderous acts in the theater. The murderous queer character occupies a distinctive position among theatrical representations due to four related factors: (1) the construction of "the homosexual" and "the murderer" in medical and legal discourse as parallel, and sometimes twinned, identities; (2) the stigma and abject social status shared by both the murderer and the homosexual as criminals and "moral monsters"; (3) the homophobic rhetoric that imagines homosexuality as a murderous "death style," especially in the era of AIDS, that threatens individual lives, as well as the social order; and (4) the importance of secrecy, deception, and revelation (i.e., the closet) in structuring narratives about murderers and homosexuals. All these factors contribute to the prevalence and relevance of the homicidal homosexual, beyond the usual appearance of murderers in dramatic plots.

A current argument against the representation of violence is that it causes those who view it to act violently themselves. Generally, those who speak out against a culture of violence are concerned with video games and Hollywood films, not with Sophocles, Shakespeare, or the plays under discussion in the following chapters. Yet the point usually missing in arguments against violence in mass-produced media is helpful to remember when discussing theater as well: the effect of violence on an audience does not depend only on *what* we view but on *how* we view it.[17] The danger lies not in the representations themselves but in what we as viewers make of them—or in how we passively neglect to make anything of them at all. Granted, in our modern culture we generally assume that theatergoers are more sophisticated and engaged than the audience for *Saw VI,* but one can easily sit passively and wallow in the sensational gore of *Titus Andronicus,* just as one can interrogate *Saw VI* with intellectual rigor. Like all works of entertainment, the plays under discussion in this book are sites filled with potential meanings, and my goal is to provide analyses that will make them more emotionally and intellectually interesting to the reader or audience member—not despite their violence but because of it.

While emphasizing audience reception and multiple potential meanings, it is also worth addressing the question of motive in the creation of art. *Murder Most Queer* does not render verdicts on those who create plays with homicidal homosexuals, judging them to be homophobic if they are straight, or "self-hating" if they are queer. Such dismissals cut short the conversation and diminish the potential meaning of these rich plays. In *Fatal Women: Lesbian Sexuality and the Mark of Aggression* (1994), Lynda

Hart cites Freud's analysis of "people who are paradoxically guilty *before* a misdeed occurs, and thus commit crimes in order to assuage their guilt."[18] Perhaps this dynamic applies to the LGBT artist, who feels the stigma of being queer in a homophobic society and therefore "enacts" the crimes of queer villainy on the stage to achieve a sort of catharsis. Yet the artist's motive might be more conscious, based on a desire to wrest the homicidal homosexual out of the hands of the homophobes and to rewrite him or her according to the artist's own desires. By reclaiming and reforming a homophobic archetype, the artist might destabilize the homicidal homosexual's significance and redirect him or her within a new script. Finally, the prevalence of violent bias crimes against LGBT people can burden queer people with the fearful passivity of victimization.[19] By romanticizing criminal transgression, LGBT artists can exchange the role of victim for the empowering fantasy of the queer killer, combating violent persecution with violent action and replacing shame with a defiant pride. Even if these motives play some role in the creation of these plays, however, the plays themselves remain complex and contradictory works, and it is not always so easy to disentangle victim and perpetrator, power and abjection, shame and pride.

Even as I argue for the multiple, unstable, and even contradictory meanings to be found in various homicidal homosexuals, *Murder Most Queer* does not detach these dramatic representations from any foundation in reality. My readings are grounded in three elements that I consider crucial to an understanding of these dramatic works: LGBT history, theater history, and genre. The history of LGBT people in America includes the ideologies that constructed queer identity and experience, the forces that implemented and resisted queer oppression, and the events and movements that helped change the status of queer people. Plays, which exist before an audience in time, cannot separate themselves from the social context in which they are created and performed, whether that context is the emergence and suppression of a gay subculture in the 1920s, the Cold War paranoia of the 1950s, the gay liberation movement of the 1970s, or the devastation and rage surrounding the AIDS crisis. Just as history is an important lens through which to view a play, so a play can shed light on its historical moment, reflecting the social and political perspectives of its time while, in some cases, resisting the dominant discourse. The social and political status of queer people has changed radically over the past hundred years, and these plays must be understood in relation to that history.

In addition to queer history, theater history also provides an important basis for interpreting plays with homicidal homosexuals. Engaging with this history illuminates how different systems of production operate in creating theater, attracting different audiences and occupying different positions on the cultural and ideological landscape. Plays in this study are performed in different theaters, including commercial Broadway, not for profit off-Broadway and regional theaters, off-off-Broadway and "fringe" theaters, and gay theaters that exist to produce gay plays for predominantly gay audiences. Differences among these theaters include the size of the venue, ticket prices, the social identity (including class, race, gender, and sexual orientation) of most audience members, wages for the artists, celebrity of the actors, number of performances, degree of censorship, critical reception, and place in theater history. Often an individual play is performed in more than one realm of production, and when possible I take these variations, including revivals and film adaptations, into account. This study includes information on theaters, producers, playwrights, directors, actors, critics, and audiences since all of these participants play a role in constructing the meaning of a play in performance.

Third, genre plays an important role in my interpretations, since genre conventions inform both the creation and reception of any given performance. Just as a play does not exist outside its historical context, so a character like the homicidal homosexual does not exist outside his or her particular theatrical genre. The dramatic function of the murderer and the significance of the act of murder can vary widely, depending on whether that act occurs in a play that is (or borrows the conventions of) a melodrama, opera, thriller, romance, courtroom drama, musical, comedy, or satire. Dramatic structure and performance style also inform the creation and interpretation of any given work, ranging from linear realism to fragmented surrealism, from stark minimalism to grand spectacles of camp. Of course, these three elements—queer history, theater history, and genre—are usually intertwined: particular genres rise and fall in particular theatrical venues in tandem with (or in opposition to) the ideologies surrounding sexuality and sexual identity at a particular moment. History, ideology, and theatricality thus illuminate our understanding of the plays, at the same time that the plays illuminate our understanding of history, ideology, and theatricality.

While exploring plays for their historical, ideological, and aesthetic underpinnings, I also consider resistant readings, hypothesizing why a queer or queer-friendly audience may still find interest and even pleasure in a play that is ostensibly homophobic. Similarly, I investigate what may be disturbing or upsetting in a play that is ostensibly not homophobic. In order to do so, I resist the temptation to judge whether a particular play is "good for the gays" or "bad for the gays." Such debates, which dominate much recent critical discourse around culture, especially on blogs where fans argue the political merit or efficacy of everything from gay advertising to gay zoology, certainly can be an engaging and productive exercise. My project here, however, is to explore complex works of art that generate contradictions and elude a simple good/bad dichotomy. This study does not argue against or demand change from theater artists or producers who present homicidal homosexuals. Rather, I am arguing for a change in how we interpret this particular archetype, and I hope that *Murder Most Queer* contributes to a more intricate and nuanced understanding of precisely how works of theatrical art explore our fantasies and nightmares of violence and criminality, rage and despair.

How to Capture a Homicidal Homosexual

Any book dealing with representations of sexual identity must address its use of categories and labels, since words like *homosexual, gay, lesbian,* and *queer* have particular histories and implications within the discourse. *Homosexual* has a clinical connotation, based in nineteenth-century sexology, and is now often used by antigay forces to pathologize gay people and emphasize their sexual difference. *Gay* and *lesbian* are labels of self-identification that became more widely used during the gay liberation era of the late 1960s and 1970s and thus connote a conscious identity based on same-sex desire, as well as cultural and political affiliation with a minority community. *Queer,* which was popularized in part by the radicalized sexual politics and academic discourse of the late 1980s and 1990s, is often used to encompass all differences from the norm of monogamous heterosexuality. In response to a predominantly white and middle-class gay culture, scholars and activists have used *queer* to articulate and celebrate differences in gender, race, and class among LGBT people.[20] I use all these terms throughout this book, since they are useful in expressing the different understandings of identity that have existed over a century of American culture. For example, I employ the rather clinical *homicidal homosexual* in order to emphasize the legal, medical, and social construction of this archetype—while also taking advantage of the alliterative echo to acknowledge, with no small amount of critical irony, the twinning of these identities in the homophobic imagination.

The various identities often grouped under the rubric of *queer*—including not only gay, lesbian, bisexual, and transgender but also many other instances of gender and sexual nonconformity—may be collectively vilified as threats to the "normal," but each identity also bears a vilification uniquely its own. While gay men and lesbians, for example, may share certain villainous traits in the homophobic imagination, feminist scholars have shown how the murderous lesbian is the unique product of both sexism and homophobia.[21] Gay men, on the other hand, are potentially the most empowered subgroup among those comprising the queer collective, but they may be uniquely vilified because that very empowerment can also render them more threatening to social structures of masculinity and patriarchy. The strategy of this book, then, is to discern how different kinds of vilification coincide and intersect, not just in terms of sexuality but also in terms of gender, race, class, and other markers of identity.

Even when using terms that acknowledge the significance of collective social and political identities, it is important to recognize that these terms do not describe universal experiences. Eve Kosofsky Sedgwick, often considered one of the founders of queer theory, has argued eloquently and persuasively against a singular notion of "homosexuality as we conceive of it today" but rather for a "plural, multi-capillaried, argus-eyed, respectful, and endlessly cherished" understanding of queer existence.[22] In discussing plays, then, I do not attempt to apply a single understanding of "what it means to be queer" but rather to appreciate the particular existence of each individual character. At the same time, characters do not exist outside social and cultural realities, and these contexts inevitably inform our understanding of identities, relationships, and communities.[23]

In this study, I focus on theatrical characters who experience romantic or sexual desire for a person of the same sex. When establishing criteria for the inclusion of plays in this study, I took characters and plots at face value. In almost every case, the homicidal homosexuals are presented to the audience *as homosexual characters,* known as such because they express or act on their romantic or sexual feelings for a person of the same sex as themselves. Of course, different characters are drawn with different degrees of explicitness when it comes to sexuality, so this study will also examine a few instances of coded queerness, particularly since the closet is often a crucial link in the conflation of the queer and the killer. Similarly, murder is just that: the deliberate killing of another human being, usually through violence. I have avoided wildly metaphorical readings that allow almost any character to be read as "queer" and any dramatic action to be read as "murder." For example, it might be interesting to entertain the notion of Stanley Kowalski as the embodiment of homoerotic masculinity who "murders" Blanche DuBois in the final act of *A Streetcar Named Desire* by destroying her illusions about her identity. But such an interpretation will have no place in this study. I do not intend to "out" any characters or make accusations of murder heretofore unknown to the general audience.

Murder Most Queer focuses on American plays, since the United States has its own history and culture of queer vilification and representation and the American theater has played a unique role in that struggle. But national borders are not impermeable, and the American theater is deeply influenced by plays from other countries; American theatergoers regularly attend plays imported from abroad, especially from Britain, France, and Canada. In this study, then, I have included certain foreign plays that have had significant productions in the United States and influenced the American theater. It would be impossible, for example, to discuss the history of plays representing Nathan Leopold and Richard Loeb (lovers who became infamous for the murder they committed in Chicago in 1924) without discussing *Rope,* a play written by an Englishman but successfully produced on Broadway and frequently revived in the American theater. Similarly, an examination of the American thriller *Deathtrap* would be incomplete without citing the influence of English thrillers by Agatha Christie and Anthony Shaffer, as well as the French film *Diabolique.* In some cases, ascribing any single nationality to a play can be tricky: Chay Yew was born in Singapore, wrote *Porcelain* while a student in Boston, and now lives and works primarily in the United States. The play, set in London and commissioned and first produced by a British theater company, has had many productions in the United States and is one of the most prominent plays to examine the intersection of sexual and racial difference in the representation of the queer killer. Therefore, even though its characters exist in a very different cultural milieu, *Porcelain* is an important and unique play in the United States.

Plays and performances have their own systems of production, genres, and positions on the cultural landscape. Nevertheless, theater artists and audiences do not exist in a vacuum, and I believe that the theater has reciprocal (rather than strictly competitive) relationships with other media, particularly film. Therefore, when it is relevant, this study will consider movies that have a direct relationship with theatrical representations. Plays with well-known cinematic versions, such as *Rope* and *Deathtrap,* influence later revivals of those plays and potentially influence the way audiences view the theatrical experience. A theatrical parody of a famous film, such as *Carrie,* can queer the meanings of the original and is best read in relation to the original. In some cases, similar trends influence theater and cinema, so it can be helpful to consider, for example, the camp creations of Charles Ludlam in relation to the films of his contemporary, John Waters. In all these cases, however, my primary goal is to examine theatrical representation, with cinema as part of the larger cultural context for that examination.

I have tended to focus on plays that I judge to be significant in terms of their impact on other theater artists or their popularity with theater audiences. Therefore most of the plays in this study have been published, and many are regularly revived and occupy a position of relative prominence on the cultural landscape. The American theater, however, does not escape the sexism and racism that exist in the larger culture, and the result is a system of production in which representations of lesbians, bisexuals, transgender people, and people of color are not on an equal footing with representations of white gay men, which have dominated the American theater when it comes to the field of queer representation. Plays with white gay male characters who commit murder are more numerous and more often produced than plays with lesbian, bisexual, transgender, or queer people of color who commit murder. Despite this lack of equal representation in the theater, this book, while acknowledging the dominance of gay white male representation in this field, includes key examples of plays with killers who are lesbian, bisexual, transgender, and people of color. By recognizing the full diversity of the queer killer archetype, one can achieve a better understanding of how race, gender, and sexuality intersect in the construction of various kinds of queer villainy.

Murder Most Queer shows how representations of the homicidal homosexual have changed radically over the past century, so the book is arranged, for the most part, in chronological order, from the 1920s to the present, although some chapters stretch over more than one era as I trace the changes in a particular genre, contrasting performances in different decades. Chapter 1, "I Killed Him Because I Loved Him," examines the play many scholars consider to be America's first "gay play," which, not coincidentally, is also America's first play with a homicidal homosexual. I read *The Drag* (1927) by Mae West in relation to the history of gay culture in New York, the "homosexual types" delineated by the 1920s, and the forces of oppression that led to the censorship of the play. The homicidal homosexual plays a crucial function in this play, which, while billed as a "homosexual comedy," is in fact a romantic melodrama that aims to educate a female audience about the dangers of remaining ignorant of the existence of male homosexuality.

Chapter 2, "Queer Justice," looks at multiple plays based on the real murder committed by Nathan Leopold and Richard Loeb, beginning in the 1920s with Patrick Hamilton's *Rope*, and continuing through the 1950s (Meyer Levin's *Compulsion*), the 1990s (John Logan's *Never the Sinner*), and up to the current day (Stephen Dolginoff's *Thrill Me* and others). In this chapter, I show how differences in historical context, systems of theatrical production, and genre radically alter the construction and meaning of the homicidal homosexual, enacting different fantasies of justice.

Chapter 3, "The Closet Is a Deathtrap," focuses on thrillers, a Broadway genre that reached its height of popularity in the 1970s. I argue that Ira Levin's enormously successful *Deathtrap* (1978) uses the conventions of the thriller to wrestle with issues of the closet relevant to the gay liberation era and to exploit the decade's fascination with (and fear of) bisexuality.

Gaining prominence around this same time are queer theater companies that often existed in opposition to the commercial mainstream of Broadway, in terms of both aesthetics and ideology. Chapter 4, "Rage and Revelry," examines the bloody "excesses" and use of camp in the creation of homicidal homosexuals by queer theater artists from the gay liberation era to the present day. Examining the plays of Charles Ludlam, Charles Busch, Holly Hughes, the Five Lesbian Brothers, and others, I argue that these queer theater artists were instrumental in wresting homicidal homosexuals out of the hands of homophobes and giving them new, subversive, and provocative meanings.

Chapter 5, "Arias of Love and Death," contrasts two plays, *The Lisbon Traviata* (1985) by Terrence McNally and *Porcelain* (1992) by Chay Yew, both of which appropriate the conventions of tragic opera but employ very different theatrical styles to depict characters who occupy very different positions in terms of race and class. In particular, the struggles over McNally's play, which has at least three different published versions (with a murder, without a murder, and then with a murder again), reflect how gay playwrights and characters began to find homes in not for profit theaters during the 1980s, but the homicidal homosexual tested the limits of what was acceptable in mainstream theater.

Chapter 6, "Queer Evil," examines plays by Nicky Silver (*Pterodactyls*), George C. Wolfe ("The Gospel According to Miss Roj" from *The Colored Museum*), and Craig Lucas (*The Dying Gaul*), which depart from realism in order to confront the metaphysical implications of the rhetoric of "evil" surrounding queer subjects in contemporary discourse, as well as to express the cosmic rage engendered by the AIDS crisis of the 1980s and 1990s.

Chapter 7, "Serial Killers," discusses theatrical performances from the 1990s and the new millennium that interrogate America's fascination with queer serial killers—a persistent Hollywood stereotype that frames our understanding of real murderers like Jeffrey Dahmer and Aileen Wuornos. Theater artists have wrestled with and given new meaning to this notorious character in plays such as *The Law of Remains* (1992) by Reza Abdoh, *Self Defense* (2002) by Carson Kreitzer, and *Fascination* (2003) by Jim Grimsley, as well as solo performances adapted from *Zombie* (2008) by Joyce Carol Oates and *Jerk* (2010) by Dennis Cooper. This chapter, borrowing the tradition of the ancient Greeks, who always performed a brief comedy after a full day of tragedy, concludes with Christopher Durang's satirical portrait of a homicidal homosexual in *Betty's Summer Vacation* (1999).

In examining these plays, I do not seek to give a full pardon or excuse these dramatic killers in their fictional worlds, any more than my analysis of these characters should be misconstrued as somehow justifying actual acts of violence. Rather, my goal is to exonerate the plays themselves. Theater is one of the few venues in which it is both good and, for the most part, safe to express strong ideas, emotions, and actions—even when they may be unpleasant, threatening, or horrifying. My contention is that plays with homicidal homosexuals should not be dismissed simply as negative representations, and even plays that may be homophobic demand closer analysis for the ways in which they construct queer villainy and for the ways in which a resistant reading might combat such constructions. Rather than locking them up and throwing away the keys, the American theater has reclaimed these homicidal homosexuals through plays that wrestle with our fears and fantasies. By looking at them more closely, we can see the ways in which the darkness illuminates.

CHAPTER ONE

"I Killed Him Because I Loved Him"

The link between deviant sexuality and murderous criminality was evident on the American stage in 1927, when Mae West produced *The Drag*, her melodramatic play about a heartbroken fairy who murders his abandoning lover. Before the glamorous and sultry West was one of Hollywood's top box office attractions in the 1930s, before she was an international sex symbol, and long before she made her "comeback" as an older woman in atrociously campy movies in the 1970s, Mae West was a successful playwright and actress on Broadway in the 1920s. She wrote and starred in a play boldly entitled *Sex* for nearly a year before the New York City police raided the theater. Most historians agree that the impetus for this crackdown (so far into the run of the play) was in fact a second play that West planned to bring to Broadway. *The Drag* caused a sensation but was stopped before it could reach Broadway, and many historians credit this "homosexual play" as the cause of West's arrest, the closing of her long-running hit *Sex*, and the enactment of stage censorship laws in New York. *The Drag* moreover serves as the perfect play with which to begin an exploration of the amalgamation of homosexuality and homicide, especially in terms of medical, psychological, and legal discourses.

The Drag combines the melodrama of the spurned lover, the sentimental drama of the neglected wife, and the thrills of the murder mystery, along with a good dose cabaret-style drag entertainment.[1] Set in New York City, the play tells the story of Rolly Kingsbury, a wealthy and respected young man who, at the insistence of his father, has married Clair, the daughter of a prominent doctor who happens to be investigating the "problem" of homosexuality. Rolly secretly leads a double life, which includes a bevy of gay friends and an ex-lover named David who is crushed by Rolly's interest in a new man, one Allen Grayson. Meanwhile, hurt and confused by her husband's neglect, the innocent Clair falls in love with none other than Allen Grayson, creating further romantic intrigue. After hosting a drag party, Rolly is murdered, and the Inspector concludes that Grayson, wanting to have Clair for himself, committed the murder. At the last minute, however, David reveals himself as the true killer, having shot Rolly because he could not stand to lose his love.

"I Don't Get You Guys": Exposing the Inhabitants of the Gay Subculture

In order to understand the role of this homicidal homosexual, it is necessary to explore the ideologies that "construct" him, as well as the social milieu in which he exists. Mae West makes these ideologies explicit by framing her play with scenes of a Doctor (Clair's father) and a Judge (Rolly's father) arguing about the proper treatment of the homosexual, thus iterating many of the medical, psychological, and legal theories of the day. Throughout much of history, same-sex relations were punished as criminal acts, for example, sodomy, but in the late nineteenth century, as Michel Foucault points out in his influential *History of Sexuality,* medical and psychiatric models of "homosexuality" challenged this punitive legal model.[2] As early as 1864, the German lawyer Karl Heinrich Ulrichs argued against the prosecution of *Urnings* (his neologism for men who loved men), since their desires were "natural" to them, a normal variation and neither a crime nor a vice.[3] Ulrichs's argument was based in his understanding of an *Urning* as a person who has the body of a man but the mind of a woman, which Richard von Krafft-Ebing would later describe as "inversion" in his highly influential *Psychopathia Sexualis* (1886). Moreover, Krafft-Ebing distinguished these "inverts" from men who sought sex with other men not because of natural inclination but because of "acquired" perversion or debauchery. The inverts can't help themselves and deserve pity, while the perverts are deliberate libertines who deserve censure.[4] This notion was popular with psychiatrists, who could promote themselves as experts able to distinguish between the natural invert and the debauched pervert, as well as with homosexuals, who saw the sympathetic medical model as an improvement over the punitive legal model.[5]

Interestingly, this historical change in the classification of the homosexual is similar to the change in the classification of the murderous criminal. Historian Karen Halttunen explains that in colonial America "humankind was not divided into rigid categories of normalcy and deviancy, but strung out along a moral continuum, on which all were equally vulnerable to slippage in the direction of major transgressions such as murder."[6] But with the emergence of what she calls the "gothic imagination," the emphasis changed from the act of murder to the murderer as a distinct kind of person, separate from "normal" people. Like the homosexual, the murderer belongs to a "closed category of deviancy,"[7] explained in terms of a "criminal brain" and "criminal heredity" within medical and psychological discourses.[8] Psychological explanations for the murderer often sound surprisingly like those for the homosexual: "The answer typically involved childhood neglect, abandonment, and abuse, overbearing mothers and absent or inept fathers."[9]

As Eve Kosofsky Sedgwick has argued, new models for understanding homosexuality do not completely displace old ones, creating a multilayered and fluid discourse that incorporates a wide range of historical models.[10] Therefore, Mae West's play presents all these legal, psychological, and medical models as the general ideological framework for her exploration of the specific demimonde of New York's gay subculture in the 1920s. In *Gay New York: Gender, Urban Culture, and the Making of the Gay Male World, 1890–1940,* the historian George Chauncey explores the various social dynamics and the social positions available to gay men in New York between 1890 and 1940, debunking the myth that prior to the gay liberation era of the 1970s gay people were completely isolated, invisible, and uncritically internalizing society's hostility toward them.[11] For those "in the know," as Mae West demonstrates herself to be, some of the well-known types of homosexual during this period included the fairy, the queer, and trade.

In examining working-class New York culture, Chauncey focuses on the pairing of the fairy and trade, with fairies as highly effeminate men who offered themselves sexually to "normal" men. Wearing makeup, donning flamboyant clothing or drag, and behaving "as women," fairies inhabited the saloons, clubs, and streets of neighborhoods where laborers and sailors could seek their sexual services. As Chauncey explains, "Sexual desire for men was held to be inescapably a woman's desire, and the inverts' desire for men was not seen as an indication of their 'homosexuality' but as simply one more manifestation of their fundamentally womanlike character."[12] One of Chauncey's boldest claims, however, is that the fairy was not necessarily ostracized or criminalized in working-class culture.

> Much evidence suggests that the fairy, so long as he abided by the conventions of this cultural script [playing the feminine role], was tolerated in much of working-class society—regarded as an anomaly, certainly, but as more amusing than abhorrent, and only rarely a threat to gender order. He was so obviously a "third-sexer," a different species of human being, that his very effeminacy served to confirm rather than threaten the masculinity of other men.[13]

More than simply unthreatening to other men, the fairy could also be sexually enticing. Chauncey defines *trade* as "any 'straight' man who responded to a gay man's advances."[14] In the social structure, the fairy was in a social and sexual category similar to that of the female prostitute, and men could "use" him in similar ways without impugning their masculinity.[15]

West captures the relationship between fairy and trade in the very first appearance of a gay character in her play. Clem, a fairy who has brought the distraught David to the Doctor, negotiates a deal with a taxi driver in the following exchange.

Taxi-Driver:	Do you boys want me to wait?
Clem:	You better wait, you great, big, beautiful baby.
Taxi-Driver:	I don't get you guys.
Clem:	If you don't, you're the first taxi-driver that didn't.
Taxi-Driver:	What do you want me to do?
Clem:	Ride me around a while, dearie, and then come back for her, if you're so inclined.
Taxi-Driver:	O.K. with me. (*Exits.*)
Clem:	Rough trade, Davy. (101)

In this quick bout, Clem proves himself a highly skilled fairy, using a variety of techniques in order to seduce trade. As Chauncey points out, fairies did not perform "the sexual passivity expected of a respectable woman" but rather the sexual aggressiveness of a "tough girl" or prostitute.[16] Here Clem begins with an order, followed by flattery, a quip (which offers an "everybody does it" encouragement), and finally an offer couched in the obvious double entendre of "riding," complete with a campy "misuse" of a gendered pronoun. The forward technique works, the taxi driver "gets" and responds to Clem's invitation, and he will even accompany Clem to the drag party in act 3.

The fairy/trade schema, however, was largely a working-class phenomenon;[17] during this period, white middle-class gay men began to forge an exclusively "homosexual" or "queer" identity, making their sexual object choice rather than their gender behavior the defining element of their sexual identity. Chauncey argues that middle-class men, increasingly white collar and removed from more traditionally "masculine" occupations, feared effeminacy as the relinquishment of white masculine privilege. Shunning the stereotype of the fairy, middle-class gay men often passed as straight or, more accurately, constructed "multiple public identities."[18] The metaphor at the time was not "the closet," but the "double life."

> Leading a double life in which they often passed as straight (and sometimes married) allowed them to have jobs and status a queer would have been denied while still participating in what they called "homosexual society" or "the life." For some, the personal cost of "passing" was great. But for others it was minimal, and many men positively enjoyed having a "secret life" more complex and extensive than outsiders could imagine.[19]

A main impulse behind *The Drag* is to expose that secret life, putting it on view for the benefit of an audience. But whereas West seems to admire the brash fairy, she has little sympathy for the masculine homosexual who leads a secret life, especially when he deceives or exploits a woman. In *The Drag,* the duplicitous homosexual is Rolly Kingsbury, son of a judge and inheritor of the Kingsbury Iron Works, married to the innocent and virginal Clair, secretly cavorting with fairies, and intent on seducing Allen Grayson, a civil engineer who works for him. When Rolly makes a pass at Grayson, he reveals and discusses his "double life."

Rolly: Why do you think I've had you come here so often? Haven't you noticed the friendship I've had for you since the day you stepped into the office? All I could do was eat, drink, sleep, think of Allen Grayson.

Grayson: Why, Rolly, I'd hate to have you think of me in just that way. I've always looked at you as a he-man. God, this is—

Rolly: I thought you had some idea of how I felt toward you—my great interest in you.

Grayson: Yes, I did think it extraordinary. But what about your wife?

Rolly: You mean why I married?

Grayson: Yes.

Rolly: That is very easy to explain. Clair's dad and mine were very good friends, it was their one ambition that we should marry. It was practically arranged ever since we were children together and Clair is the same today as the day I married her, if you know what I mean.

Grayson: Why, I think that's the most contemptible thing you could do—marry a woman and use her as a cloak to cover up what you are. (123–24)

Rolly's seduction in act 2 is very different from Clem's in act 1. The taxi driver is relatively quick in picking up Clem's innuendo because (1) Clem is playing a feminine role, which is inherently viewed as sexual in its relationship to the masculine role, and (2) his offer to the taxi driver is more explicitly sexual, conveyed through seductive double entendres. Rolly, on the other hand, seems to inhabit a masculine role, so Grayson cannot understand how there might be a sexual relationship between them. Rolly's masculine role, then, must be a false mask that he wears in order to deceive others. Similarly, rather than directly offering sexual gratification, Rolly offers "friendship" to Grayson, but once the truth is revealed, the honesty of this friendship is also called into question. Note that Grayson is not really disgusted by what Rolly is—a homosexual—but by what Rolly is doing—wearing masks, covering up his "true nature," and deceiving other people, especially his wife. Secrecy, not sexuality, is at the root of Rolly's villainy.[20]

To be fair, there are many reasons why a gay man like Rolly in *The Drag* would feel the need to hide his homosexuality, especially in an era in which "coming out" to the straight world was not a central concept, let alone a virtue, of gay identity.[21] Despite a certain amount of tolerance in the 1920s in New York, and perhaps because of the emergence of the fairy as a well-known type, legal restrictions against gay people increased in the 1920s. Police raids on cafeterias, cabarets, speakeasies, and other meeting places frequented by homosexuals occurred often during the 1920s, usually employing the purposefully ambiguous charge of "disorderly conduct" since there was initially no law that specifically outlawed the assembly of gay people. The explicit criminalization of the gay male subculture occurred in 1923, when the New York state legislature criminalized "homosexual solicitation" and any other behavior that might lead to "committing a crime against nature or other lewdness." Chauncey notes that authorities "regularly used the statute to criminalize the assembly of gay men in a public place or their adoption of distinctive cultural styles, from camp behavior to dancing with people of the same gender or wearing clothes assigned to the other gender."[22]

In other words, men who behaved in a camp or effeminate manner could be arrested for disorderly conduct since nonmasculine behavior and dress were equated with the intent to engage in homosexual activity. It is also worth noting that arrests under the antisodomy statutes increased drastically during these years, with only 14 to 38 arrests per year in the 1890s increasing to 75 to 125 arrests in the 1920s.[23] The criminalization of gay sexuality and culture, along with the general antipathy felt for gay people in most segments of society, easily accounts for the desire of some gay men to create double lives, which allowed them to maintain the privileges of "normal" men. A statistic from Chauncey's research underlines this point: "A quarter of the men arrested for homosexual activity in 1920–21, for instance, were married."[24] While Mae West's play argues for the decriminalization of gay men, this does not alleviate her moral condemnation of men who deceive women by leading a double life.

"One of Those Damned Creatures": Introducing the Homicidal Homosexual

Into this moral landscape, West places the homicidal homosexual. David Caldwell, described in the dramatis personae as "an outcast," is neither a duplicitous queer leading a double life nor a camp fairy seeking copious sexual encounters. West presents David as an invert, a man with feminine passions, and therefore he is a victim—of nature, of society, and of love. When he first appears in the Doctor's office, he is nervous and weak, pacing the floor, claiming to be ill in both body and soul (101). He explains his problem to the Doctor in highly melodramatic terms: "I'm one of those damned creatures who are called degenerates and moral lepers for a thing they cannot help—a thing that has made me suffer—" (102). He confesses that from an early age he was aware of his feminine nature, and so he came to seek companionship and even love among "those of my own kind." David regards his abnormality as a "burden" and a "curse," yet he is surprisingly insistent about the happiness he has experienced in gay love.

> *David:* In time I met another like me. How can I tell you? We were attracted to each other. We loved each other. I worshipped

him. We lived together. We were happy. The curse didn't seem to matter so much. We lived our own life . . . lived it in our own way. No normally married couple were happier than we. Then—he married. [. . .] We drifted apart. It almost drove me mad. And then—somehow his wife didn't hurt me as much as—

Doctor: As what?

David: He has found another—a man—a normal man. He loves him. It's maddening.

Doctor: But, come, pull yourself together. There must be some way out of this.

David: I've tried to find it. I've tried doctor. I can't! I've thought of death—I haven't the courage to kill myself—I wish I had . . . I love him . . . (102–3)

What separates David from both the fairies and Rolly is that David is the only gay character who speaks about *love.*

Neither Clem with his taxi driver nor Rolly with Allen ever uses the word *love,* but David uses it repeatedly in his conversation with the Doctor, insisting on his love for Rolly and even comparing his relationship to that of a "normally married couple." He is a romantic, with love bringing him his greatest joy and also his greatest sorrow. It is worth noting that David has not reached his current state of suffering because Rolly married a woman. David knows that Rolly does not love his wife, and therefore she poses no threat to David. But Rolly's interest in Allen Grayson—a "normal" man—throws David into fits of despair because he recognizes that Allen is a viable contender for Rolly's love, leaving David well and truly abandoned. He turns to drugs in order to relieve his anxiety, and his current jitters may be attributed to withdrawal from both heroin and love.[25]

How might an audience in 1927 have responded to David's assertion of the legitimacy of same-sex love? Since David is not aggressively camp, he might be seen as less threatening and more sympathetic to an audience that finds fairies distasteful or offensive. David extols a bourgeois view of romance, with the shared life of domestic coupling as the goal of love rather than the "voracious" sexuality of the other fairies with their risqué double entendres and seduction of trade. David plays no role in the drag party in act 3—with a score of men in wigs and dresses singing, dancing, bitching, and cavorting—which was the main focus of outrage by self-appointed moralists and stage censors. But the vulgar fairy was a well-known, and in some parts well-loved, stereotype that may not have done much to threaten the social order of either gender or heterosexuality. David commits the less theatrical but more substantial transgression, defiantly equating homosexual with heterosexual love. Whether an audience member is more comforted or disturbed by David's bourgeois romance depends on whether one is more shocked by the notion that two men might have sex together or the notion that two men might deeply love each other. In either case, David's madness can serve as an escape hatch for an audience's potential anxiety around gay relationships: he may compare his love to "real" marriage, but he is a drug-addicted, hysterical outcast who will prove to be a murderer. An audience might respond to this "mad" defense of gay love any number of ways, from sympathy to dismissal to condemnation.

At the end of the first act, David reappears, and what follows is a brief scene that allows the audience, for the first and only time, to see these former lovers interact. Rolly is on edge because the Doctor, his father-in-law, has been questioning him about the problems in his marriage. David is disoriented due to the drug administered by the Doctor in an unsuccessful attempt to calm him down. Their scene together builds to an emotional and violent climax, as the act end of a modern melodrama should.

David: Doctor—Doctor—It's no use I can't—Rolly!
Rolly: You—What are you doing here? [. . .]
David: I couldn't stand it any longer—I came here to see the doctor—I thought—
Rolly: You came to tell him—
David: It's not so. I didn't tell him I so much as knew you. I came because I thought he could help me.
Rolly: You fool, he can do nothing for you—For any of us. (*Takes out his wallet.*) Here take this—and get out of here.
David: I don't want your money—Rolly please—
Rolly: Get out of here. I've had enough of you.
David: I've heard all about you and Grayson. He doesn't give a damn for you.
Rolly: Shut your mouth about Grayson—leave his name out of this.
David: It's true and you know it. He doesn't give a damn for you.
Rolly: Damn you—you—You—(*Grabs David by the throat and swings him onto divan.*) (*Doctor enters.*)

Doctor: Rolly!
Rolly: Who is this—this mad man—He tried to attack me. (115–16)

Because of this scene's position at the end of the act, and its climax in a physical attack, the obvious choice in playing the scene is a mounting emotional hysteria, with David's repeated cry—"He doesn't give a damn for you"—a vindictive attack by a distraught lover. But it is also possible to read David's line as more sympathetic: he knows that Grayson will not return Rolly's interest, and he is trying to warn Rolly that he will have his heart broken. The subtext can be concern and a desire to win back Rolly's heart, not just a petty jealousy. Similarly, it is obvious that Rolly is upset because he thinks David is going to expose his secret to his father-in-law. But it is also possible to read his apoplectic stutter—"you—you—You"—as the confusion and hesitation of a man who still has conflicting feelings about the lover he has abandoned. His physical attack on David ends up with both of them on the divan, Rolly on top of David, with Rolly's hands around David's neck. The line between passionate love and passionate hate is finely drawn, and at its best this scene can recognize the tension between the two emotions and the confusion between physical desire and physical violence.

The potential for sexual and romantic heat in this scene is made all the more dramatic because Rolly betrays and hurts David in so many ways. Expressing both his narcissism and his paranoia, Rolly assumes that David has come to the Doctor in order to expose Rolly's secret life. He belittles David's attempt to find any kind of solace, failing to express any sympathy for David's distraught state, then tries to pay him off, as one might a prostitute or a criminal accomplice—the strategy of a distinctly upper-class villain. He tries to get rid of David, to "cast out" this outcast, but finds himself physically entangled with him instead. When the Doctor enters to discover them together on the divan, Rolly disavows any knowledge of David, then accuses David of his own crime—"*He* tried to attack *me*." David makes no response to this double betrayal, keeping Rolly's secret even now. The Doctor, however, unwittingly expresses the possible response of the audience, leading David out of the room, calling him "poor boy" and "poor devil." West positions David as a character deserving of sympathy, a mistreated wretch who suffers for love, like many a melodramatic heroine before him, unjustly betrayed by a villainous man. Ironically, Rolly's false accusation of David will prove to be truthful foreshadowing by the third act.

David does not appear in the second act, but the other characters discuss his situation. During an afternoon visit at Rolly's home the next day, Clem tells the story of bringing David to the Doctor.

> Yesterday, you know Dave, that sentimental moll, the one who used to be crazy about you. Well, she calls me up and asked me to come right over, she's hysterical. Well, I goes over and there was the poor queen ready to jump out of the window. Of course, I knew what was the matter. She needed a jab. She's been taking heroin and morphine by the barrels. The trouble with her is she's sensitive of what she is. Now, I don't give a goddamn who knows it. Of course, I don't go flouncing my hips up and down Broadway picking up trade or with a sign on my back advertising it. (*Laughs.*) But of course, I don't pass anything up either, dearie. I'm out to have a good time as well as the next. (120–21)

This speech presents an interesting difference between David and the rest of the fairies. Whereas David expresses great anxiety and shame about his homosexuality, Clem refuses to accept stigmatization, asserting that the opinions of others have no effect on him. Whereas David is the suffering victim of romantic love, Clem believes in a universal desire to "have a good time." David's tone is emotional and serious, using bleak and old-fashioned phrases like "moral leprosy," while Clem's speech has the phrasing of Jazz Age New York, complete with camp argot and a "sophisticated" (i.e., unsentimental) attitude. Yet Clem is not unsympathetic. He does not hesitate to help David when he is in need, and he says, "I must call her up today and see how she is." As bitchy and competitive as the fairies can be, a sense of community binds them and makes them care for each other.

This community, minus the homicidal homosexual, comes together in all its glory during the drag party in act 3. To create this party, Mae West incorporated elements of the drag balls that were popular in Greenwich Village and Harlem, along with the sort of drag entertainment available at speakeasies and cabarets, in the 1920s.[26] The scene includes musical numbers, dancing, and comic bits and ends with a catfight—including the requisite pulling off of wigs. The festivities are cut short by the threat of a police raid, but still a general spirit of fun and frivolity pervades, with characters at the end of the evening declaring, "I had a gay time!" The police do not actually show up onstage, however, since Rolly "fix[es] everything all right"—meaning that he has bribed the police not to arrest him and his friends (134). The irony, of course, is that if Rolly had been arrested, he would not have been at home, and David would not have been able to sneak into his house through the garden and shoot him dead.

"What Some People Don't Know . . .": Heterosexual Women in a Homosexual Comedy

So far I have focused primarily on the gay male characters and relationships in *The Drag,* but in order to understand David's murder of Rolly and how it functions dramatically, it is also important to consider the play's female characters and heterosexual relationships. Just as many of the gay characters in the play seem to form an alliance against the dominant straight world, so do the women in the play support and nurture each other in a male-dominated world. When Clair admits that her marriage is making her unhappy, her father's response is hardly sympathetic: he questions her love for Rolly, accuses her of being spoiled, and then warns her against causing a scandal and harming the family name (111–12). Fortunately for Clair, she has two older women who show more concern and offer more support than the men in her life. Her Aunt Barbara never married, and she is a strong woman who expresses a wary distrust of men. Twice in the play's first act, she voices her skeptical view of husbands, giving what might be the play's credo: "A woman's never certain what she is marrying" (98). She reiterates her point when Clair opines, "You never know a man until you're married to him." Barbara's knowing response: "And sometimes, not then" (112).

In act 2, West introduces another "mature woman" to give comfort and advice to Clair. Marion appears only briefly, but she serves the crucial function of speaking candidly with Clair about sex. The most we know about this old friend of the family is that she has a happy and "active" relationship with her husband: "My husband likes to have me around. . . . He just runs me ragged" (125–26). As a married woman, Marion is in a better position than Barbara to give Clair direct advice on intimate matters.

Marion: I'll tell you what to do. When you're ready to retire, put on your smartest negligee. Be sure it's sheer, one you can see through.

Clair: I haven't any like that.

Marion: You should have. If you haven't, get one, get one. Put it on and drape it tight around you and sit on the end of his bed and cross your legs so, and of course, show as much as you can. Be sure you have a cigarette in your hand. It gives one poise. Then tell the boy a couple of bedstead stories.

Clair: I don't smoke and I don't know any stories and I never go to his room.

Marion: Well, when he comes to yours.

Clair: He never comes to my room.

Marion: What kind of a wife are you?

Clair: A wife and not a wife?

Marion: Why, Clair— (127–28)

In an era when women were often depicted as rivals for the affection or wealth of men, West presents women as comrades, able to provide assistance to each other by sharing their knowledge of sex and romance. Interestingly, at the beginning of the play, West shows how men conspire to keep women ignorant of such matters. When Aunt Barbara picks up the Doctor's copy of Ulrichs's book on "inverts," the Doctor rips it out of her hands and recommends that she read love stories instead.

Doctor: No more of those books for you, Barbara.

Barbara: Isn't science proper reading?

Doctor: What some people don't know, my dear, don't trouble them.

Barbara: In other words, it's a good thing one half of the world doesn't know how the other half lives, eh?

Doctor: Excellent—in most cases. (100)

It is possible to read Mae West's play as an attempt to show the terrible effects of ignorance, particularly the ignorance imposed on women by paternalistic men when it comes to sex. Men keep secrets and hide the truth, and the victims of these deceptions are women. Women try to compensate by sharing advice, as well as gossip (both Barbara and Marion know about Allen's interest in Clair through "common gossip"). In this case, however, Marion's strategies for husband-wife relations prove useless since Clair is "not a wife" and Rolly is "not a husband."

By now the audience is fully aware of what is wrong with Clair and Rolly's marriage, and it seems likely that Marion has solved the puzzle, too. Interestingly, Marion's next move is not to expose Rolly or extract Clair from the sham marriage. Rather, Marion twice insists that she "*must*" see Grayson, who is waiting in the library. A brief exchange between Marion and Grayson takes place offstage, and there is no way for the audience to know what Marion says to him. But immediately after this exchange, Grayson and Clair are alone onstage, and Grayson takes her in his arms, kisses her, and confesses his love for her, bringing act 2 to a thrillingly romantic conclusion. Is it possible that Marion has given Grayson encouragement, even permission, to make love to this married woman because, since her marriage is not consummated, she is not "really" married at all? Marion takes action as a benevolent matchmaker, securing love for an unhappy young woman.

The match of Clair and Grayson is, arguably, the real dramatic spine of West's play. Act 1 establishes their interest in each other, act 2 climaxes with the realization of their love, and the tension in act 3 relies on the audience's fear that their relationship will be ruined when Grayson is falsely accused of Rolly's murder. Interestingly, Grayson is the primary suspect because he refuses to "out" Rolly, even now that Rolly is dead. When asked by the Inspector why he and Rolly fought and why he refused to attend Rolly's party, Grayson declines to give the real reason, protecting Rolly's secret and making himself more suspect. West positions Grayson as the innocent hero, unjustly accused of murder—a typical melodramatic formula.

The playwright gives *The Drag* the subtitle "A Homosexual Comedy in Three Acts," but the conventions of comedy—traditionally, the unification of a couple and a community—apply not to the play's homosexual characters but to the heterosexual characters. The play ends with the straight couple (Clair and Grayson) pursuing their romantic happiness, but there is no future for any possible gay couple (Rolly and David or Rolly and Grayson). The community that is healed in the final scene is not the gay community but the upper-class straight world of heterosexual propriety, as the Doctor and the Judge save their families' reputations by covering up the scandal of Rolly's murder. Rolly is the play's "problem," and it ends with his removal, allowing for the happy ending of a straight couple and straight society. Mae West's play may have homosexual characters, but it is still a heterosexual comedy.

Murder Will Out: The Crime, Confession, and Containment of Gay Love

Nevertheless, Rolly is not murdered by a justice-seeking representative of the straight world against which he has transgressed. His murderer is his gay lover, David, and the play repeatedly links the act of murder not just with the feeling of love but with the *expression* of love. It is important to note that David might have escaped detection, relying on the heterosexist world's reluctance to acknowledge the existence of anything or anyone gay in general and its blindness to his and Rolly's relationship in particular. His life and his love are so thoroughly marginalized that he could have escaped detection and gone unpunished. But this means that David's reason for committing the murder would have gone unexposed and unexpressed, and David's very reason for committing the murder *is* exposure and expression. David's turning himself in and confessing grant him the chance to expose and express his love for Rolly openly to the straight world for the first time. It is his confession of murder that breaks down the separation between Rolly's two lives and allows gay love finally to emerge from the shadows of secrecy and into the straight world.

In a dramatically savvy move, West brings her play full circle by creating an act 3 debate between the Doctor and the Judge, which functions as an echo and coda to the act 1 debate. At the top of the play, in almost Shavian fashion, these two authorities argue over the proper treatment of the homosexual in modern society. While the Judge reasons that "a man is what he makes himself," and therefore homosexuality is a vice that must be criminalized, the Doctor argues that "a man is what he's born to be" and the born invert should be treated with charity. This theoretical debate becomes more concrete in the final scene, in which the Doctor and the Judge argue not over "the homosexual" but over the fate of a particular homosexual, David. Again, the Doctor offers sympathy and protection while the Judge threatens violence and condemnation.

Doctor: Inspector, there will be no further need for investigation. I have your man. . . . (*David enters from hall up-stage left. He is pale and nervous.*) This is the madman. The poor, depraved, unfortunate who shot our boy.
Judge: (*Struggles with detective to get at David.*) You killed my boy! You killed my boy!
David: I killed him because I loved him. (*He collapses.*)
Judge: (*Gazing at David*) A madman, a madman.
Doctor: This is the poor, abnormal creature we discussed the other day.
Judge: Take him out of my sight, before I strangle him.
David: Strangle me, strangle me! You Judge Kingsbury—the great

> supporter of justice—you would crush me, destroy me—but your son was the same as I. Yes, I killed him. I came into the garden—I heard the music, the singing, the dancing—I waited until they were all gone. Then I shot him. When you condemn me, you condemn him. A judge's son can be just the same as another man's son—yes a king's son, a fool's son—Oh! I loved him—(139)

As in his first appearance, David repeatedly talks of love, and it is no coincidence that his final words in the play are "I loved him." Throughout the play, David's gay love has been in danger of being erased. The Doctor offers to "cure" him of it, Rolly tries to push it aside, the Judge orders that it be removed from his sight, the fairies (focusing on sex rather than romance) seem generally unconcerned with it, and the rest of the straight characters don't even know that it exists. Because of his collaboration in keeping Rolly's homosexuality a secret, even David himself is initially complicit in the denial of his love for Rolly.

In itself David's murder of Rolly does not break down the barrier between the straight and gay worlds. It is only David's confession that forces everyone onstage to acknowledge the truth. David does not want to escape detection; on the contrary, he desperately wants people to acknowledge him and his love for Rolly. The revelation of the gay murderer occurs in the same breath as the revelation of the gay lover: "I killed him because I loved him." David confesses to two crimes at once, killing another man and loving another man, and the slippage between and joining of these two acts create gay love as passionate and powerful, but also sinister, horrific, and fatal. Through the violent act of murder, David overcomes the secrecy that stifled his love, but he simultaneously eliminates any chance of that love having any future. Thus West maintains a disturbing ambivalence: gay love is finally expressed with force and compassion, but it is expressed as something dark and terrible, and only fully acknowledged after it is too late to save it.

So why does David commit this murder, and what has he accomplished by it? On one level, it is easy to attribute the murder to revenge: Rolly abandons David, so David murders Rolly. Since David cannot control Rolly's actions in any positive way, he can only limit his actions in a negative way. David attempts to control the fickle nature of love, but ultimately he creates the absence of love, depriving himself of the object of his affection. Thus it is possible to see David's murder as an act of self-mutilation by a self-loathing homosexual who exacerbates his own abandonment by eliminating his chance to reclaim his lover altogether. But while David is self-loathing, he is also defiant, striking out not only at Rolly or himself but indeed at the world at large for having abandoned him. As an outcast mired in self-hatred and shadowy secrecy, David displays pent-up fury not just toward himself but toward the world, and this rage is unleashed in his destructive act. It also should be noted that David, an effeminate male who has been stripped of any esteem or power, finds power (however limited or misguided) through violence. Even while enacting the feminized role of the abandoned lover, he reclaims phallic power by firing his gun, penetrating Rolly's body with a metal bullet, asserting his control over Rolly, and tearing down the duplicitous worlds of heterosexist blindness and homosexual secrecy in the process.

The difference between David's role as homosexual and his role as murderer is thoroughly blurred at this point. When the Judge states the charge against David, it is murder: "You killed my boy!" But David focuses on the unstated but implicit other charge against him (homosexuality), which is why he defends himself by comparing himself to Rolly. Rolly's "crime" is not murder but homosexuality, and in this he and David are "the same." In pleading David's case, the Doctor also mounts a defense of homosexuality, not directly addressing the murder itself. Clearly, both the murderer and the homosexual are on trial here, but no clear difference is maintained between the two. This lack of differentiation is made all the more dramatic by the characters' reaction to David's double revelation. Their response to the murderer/homosexual is to recoil in horror from the monster, while also wondering "why or for what purpose these poor degenerates are brought into the world" (140). It is impossible to discern whether this reaction is directed at homosexuality or murder, since the two crimes are inextricably wrapped up in each other. Arguably, the play merely uses the crime of murder to magnify and make visible the horror of the "real crime" of homosexuality. Although the play seems to make a plea for compassion, it follows the models of nineteenth-century criminologists and sexologists by placing both "the murderer" and "the homosexual" as a distinct kind of person, "one of *them*," different from the rest of humanity, regarded as an aberration who ultimately must be expelled from "normal" society.

In terms of the audience's possible perception of and reaction to the murder, it is important to remember that the murderer is *not* the villain of the play. The villain of the play is the murder victim, and therefore it is possible to see David as the embodiment of justice. As an upper-class, narcissistic, hedonistic, abusive, lying, bribing, and generally deceiving scoundrel, Rolly has it coming.[27] Therefore, David's murder is, in both moral and dramatic terms, a necessary act. Rolly is the problem of the play, standing in the way of true romance between Clair and Grayson, and David unwittingly acts as the deus ex machina who "solves" the problem, allowing the heterosexual couple to find happiness and allowing straight society to heal the rupture caused by Rolly's duplicity. As much as David may be discounted as insane or criminal, he is the madman who speaks the truth that others—even attractive, sympathetic, manly heroes like Grayson—cannot speak, and he takes action that other characters, bound by propriety and morality, cannot take. In a bizarre twist, society *needs* the homicidal homosexual in order to achieve happiness and wholeness.

This homicidal homosexual can serve his function for normal society, but he must maintain his status as an outcast, and his personal success in expressing gay love and rage must be limited. The Doctor guides the final moments of the play, urging sympathy for David but insisting on the need to "fight" to keep their respectable family names "without a spot or blemish." The result is that the Judge declares his son's death a suicide, confirming for the audience that Rolly's villainy brought about his own downfall but also indicating that David will not be convicted as a murderer *and* his love for Rolly will once again be erased, consigned to secrecy and forgotten. His status as lover and murderer go hand in hand, but he does not have the power to control that status; more powerful men appropriate the meaning of his murder and use it to satisfy their goals of respectable normalcy. Thus the play raises a challenge to the status quo of heterosexual propriety, but it ends with the reestablishment of that status quo. Within the world of the play, gay love will remain a crime too terrible to be spoken, relegated to marginality and secrecy.

"Take Him Out of My Sight": Dragged off the Stage

The fate of gay love within *The Drag* mirrors the fate of the play itself: its public expression, which caused both sensation and anxiety, led to its eradication. The play began to stir controversy while it was still in rehearsal, and it attracted large crowds (as well as the police) to its tryout performances in Bridgeport, Connecticut, and Bayonne, New Jersey. Critical response varied from particular disgust with the drag scene, with one critic referring to such spectacles as "the most disgusting orgy imaginable," to sanctimonious dismissal of the play as vulgar exploitation, to admiration of a "clean" play that includes a "moral lesson."[28] But *The Drag* was not a play that would sink or swim by the opinions of the critics. As Marybeth Hamilton concisely notes, a coalition of forces was gathering to stop *The Drag* from ever reaching Broadway.

> [I]t was opposed by *everyone:* by moral reformers because it seemed sure to provoke youthful sexual experimentation, by the theatrical mainstream because it seemed sure to provoke censorship, and by modernists because of its "mindless" appeal to prurience.[29]

The campaign for censorship, led by newspaper magnate William Randolph Hearst and endorsed by many religious leaders, was gaining momentum, despite the reluctance of Mayor Jimmy Walker and Governor Al Smith. Mae West and her producer, C. William Morganstern, attempted to bring legitimacy to *The Drag* by presenting a private midnight performance of the play before selected New York City officials and physicians. According to a report in *Variety,* West hoped to win endorsements, certifying the play's seriousness and relevance.[30] In an interesting case of life imitating art, West presented a play in which a legal authority (Judge Kingsbury) and a medical authority (Doctor Richmond) decide the fate of a homosexual (David) to a group of legal and medical authorities so that they might decide the fate of a homosexual play.

This single Broadway performance of *The Drag* occurred at midnight on the stage of Daly's Theatre, where West's hit play *Sex* was running. It took place on 8 February 1927. The very next night New York City police raided three Broadway plays: a comedy of seduction called *The Virgin Man,* a serious French import about lesbian desire called *The Captive,* and Mae West's *Sex.* Most newspapers at the time connected the approach of *The Drag* to the Broadway raids,[31] and historians agree that the closing of *Sex,* a popular success in its eleventh month, was largely an attempt to stifle *The Drag.*[32] The ploy worked, since West was able to run *Sex* for six more weeks but *The Drag* was closed by the Bayonne police and never reached the Broadway stage. West was found guilty of "maintaining a public nuisance," and she was given a five-hundred-dollar fine and ten days in jail. When asked about the effects of her arrest, she replied, "I expect it will be the making of me."[33]

Indeed it was, and West emerged from jail a celebrity who would go on to become one of Hollywood's highest-grossing stars and an international sex symbol. Another product of the Broadway raid and the closing of *The Drag* was legislation known as the Wales Padlock Law, which was passed on 19 March 1927. This amendment to the penal code specifically prohibited the staging of any play "depicting or dealing with, the subject of sex degeneracy, or sex perversion." Kaier Curtin sums up the effect of this new law, which remained on the books until 1967.

> For almost half a century after *The Drag* and *The Captive* were forced to close, a penal code prohibition inhibited the emergence of lesbians and gay men in Broadway dramas. Consequently, their real-life counterparts bore the stigma of being the only citizens of the United States adjudged too loathsome and morally infectious to be seen even in fictitious characterizations in legitimate theater productions.[34]

Murder was a crime repeatedly depicted onstage, but homosexuality was a crime deemed more horrific and dangerous to represent than murder. Curtin notes that theater critics and historians also participated in enforcing this judgment by neglecting the raids in general and *The Drag* in particular. Just as David and his love are silenced within the play, so West and her play were silenced on the American stage.[35]

Yet silence is never absolute. Although David is whisked offstage and the murder that testified to his love is covered up, the fact is that his love is real and the other characters have recognized it, however their hypocrisy may lead them to deal with it. And, although *The Drag* was also whisked offstage and its gay characters legally barred from the theater, the fact is that West wrote and produced a play in 1927 that persists to this day as a subject of theater history, as a written text, and even as a live theatrical event, with readings and productions by theater artists of today.[36] The play has the potential to intrigue a modern audience because it presents various and even contradictory models of homosexuality from the era, many of which, arguably, we still wrestle with today. While West's romantic melodrama is undeniably old-fashioned, it may still have the potential to resonate with modern audiences. If David is merely an object of pity for the audience, then the play can be little more than a sentimental horror show. But if David is an object of empathy, then the play can open up to richer and deeper layers. The feeling of abandonment, both by a lover and by society, is not limited to effeminate gay men in 1927. Nor are feelings of self-loathing or powerlessness. And, while the desire to act on pent-up anger and resentment is resisted by most, there can be pleasure in seeing it enacted by a character on a stage. David, for all his weakness, is a dramatic character who takes action, realizing a dark fantasy of self-assertion and revenge. And while the price he pays is madness, the loss of love, and the solidification of his position as an "outcast," the fact remains that he gets away with murder.

CHAPTER TWO

Queer Justice

In the same decade that the homicidal homosexual appeared on the American stage in the romantic melodrama *The Drag*, newspapers told the sensational story of real life murderers Nathan Leopold and Richard Loeb. These two young men made national headlines when they went on trial for the 1924 murder of Bobby Franks, and the "unnatural" sexual relationship between Leopold and Loeb became a part of America's fascination with the case. These real murderers inspired many theatrical representations, first in the 1920s, but again in the 1950s, the 1990s, and the new millennium. Each retelling of the case is different, not because the facts changed in any significant way but because the social and ideological contexts changed radically. American culture's dominant understanding of homosexuality—and its understanding of homosexuality as criminality—went through great transformations during the twentieth century, reshaping the significance of the homicidal homosexual as a figure in the cultural imagination. An exploration of the many theatrical representations of Leopold and Loeb (as well as their cinematic adaptations) reveals major changes in how theater artists constructed the homicidal homosexual, initially encouraging audiences to condemn such characters, then to pity them, and finally to identify with and possibly even admire them.

The relationship between the events of the real world and the drama of the theatrical world is one that has intrigued our culture for centuries. Throughout history, playwrights and performers have "made history" by creating dramatic narratives based on real people and real events, from the comedies of Aristophanes and the history plays of Shakespeare to the documentary theater of Anna Deavere Smith and Moisés Kaufman today. There is, perhaps, a basic pleasure in seeing the real world re-created in the artificial world of the theater, especially when art gives form and meaning to a reality that is filled with chaos and uncertainty. But when it comes to real violence and death, the relationship between reality and art can be more complex and disturbing. This is especially true of dramatic narratives inspired by real homicidal homosexuals, since the significance of these killers is highly contested within a homophobic society. Because performances about real homicidal homosexuals are read in relation to historical reality, they open up a wide variety of possible interpretations. Examining the fictional representations of real queer killers highlights the ways in which ideologies and historical contexts, systems of theatrical production, and genre conventions fully influence the creation and reception of these representations, which change radically over time.

While the homicidal homosexual may have originated as a homophobic construction, there are, of course, actual gay and lesbian people who commit murder, and the representations of these real people raise more complex problems about queer villainy. Antigay organizations are fond of pointing to gay and lesbian murderers like Jeffrey Dahmer, Andrew Cunanan, and Aileen Wuornos as "proof" of the evil of homosexuality, which then becomes "evidence" in the argument to deny civil rights to LGBT people. For example, the antigay Family Research Institute publishes the writings of Paul Cameron, who directly links the gory details of Jeffrey Dahmer's cannibalism to a "substantial minority" of gay men and lesbians who practice "violent sex," as well as the reportedly high rate of suicide among gays and lesbians. The conclusion to be drawn from these tenuously connected assertions is that "most violence involving gays is self-induced" and therefore hate crime legislation should not be passed.[1]

The imagined link between homosexuality and murder is so strong that even when murderers are *not* known to be gay, the tabloid media sell the fantasy that they are. Soon after the 2002 capture of John Muhammad and John Lee Malvo, known as the "Beltway Snipers," the *National Enquirer* ran a picture of the two men smiling and with their arms around each other under the headline "Snipers: Their Secret Gay Life—& Why It Made Them Kill."[2] Similarly, after the 2007 massacre at Virginia Tech, the *Globe* "exposed" the killer Seung-Hui Cho's "Secret Gay Life: What REALLY Drove Him to Kill."[3] These tabloid stories are largely devoid of reliable facts about the murderer's sexuality; rather, the "evidence" is constructed to fit neatly into the ready-made template that positions homosexuality as the cause of murder and the homosexual as pathologically driven to murder. When the queer killer trope is extended to mass murderers like Adolf Hitler and Mohamed Atta, homosexuality is constructed as a threat not just to individual lives but to civilization itself.[4]

Interpretations of queer villainy are further complicated when real homicidal homosexuals become the basis for characters in fictional narratives. Although murderous queer characters in plays, movies, and novels can be—and have been—used to vilify LGBT people, all representations of queer killers should not be automatically dismissed or condemned as negative representations. Dramatic narratives about real homicidal homosexuals, often created by LGBT theater artists and presented to queer and queer-friendly audiences, have the potential to create more complex responses and interpretations, interrogating and possibly even combating the homophobia promoted by antigay ideologies and narratives. Performances can create new narratives that wrest the homicidal homosexual out of the hands of the homophobes and allow different meanings to emerge.

I would further argue that the significance of a homicidal homosexual can change radically depending on the context of its historical moment. As Eve Kosofsky Sedgwick asserted, there is no singular "homosexuality as we conceive of it today" but rather multiple, competing, and often contradictory understandings of homosexuality.[5] The supposed link, then, between homosexuality and criminality is also multivalent, and exploring how this link is created and re-created over time can shed light on the construction and deconstruction of queer villainy. In plays and films inspired by real queer killers, real criminal cases are once again brought before the public, inviting the audience to take their place in the jury box and render judgment—not just on the criminals but also on systems of justice and the homophobic ideologies that influence those systems.

Perhaps real homicidal homosexuals have inspired so many "retrials" because our society still wrestles with fears of queer villainy. To confront the stigma of criminality placed on all queers, we re-create queer killers in dramatic narratives that provide opportunities to reassess their criminality and imagine different versions of justice. Conflicting fantasies, fears, and ideologies are all evident in these retrials, nowhere more noticeably than in the many retrials of Leopold and Loeb. Over the better part of a century, they have inspired more performances than any other queer killers, and these dramatic narratives reveal as much about our changing notions about queer sexuality and criminality as they do about the facts of the case itself.

The Scene of the Crime: Leopold and Loeb on Trial

Nathan Leopold, age nineteen, and Richard Loeb, age eighteen, brutally murdered fourteen-year-old Bobby Franks in Chicago in 1924.[6] In its time, the case of Leopold and Loeb was celebrated as "the crime of the century" and "the trial of the century," and since then people have continued to find mystery and horror in the case, particularly in the motive for this seemingly motiveless murder, as well as the "strange relationship" that existed between the two teenage killers. Famed defense attorney Clarence Darrow represented Leopold and Loeb, instructing them to plead guilty and thus avoid a trial by jury. Even though he kept the public out of the jury box, Darrow could not eliminate its desire to render judgment upon Leopold and Loeb. Along with the three thousand people who fought every day to claim one of the hundred seats available in the sweltering Chicago courtroom, a media frenzy fed a constant stream of information and opinion to a national audience hungry to know, judge, and (in most cases) condemn. The theatrical retellings of the case fulfill a similar desire, encouraging the audience to take its position in the jury box, reexamine the facts of the case, and render judgment. Each performance reimagines the case according to the genre conventions and cultural concerns of its own times, resulting in new opportunities for audiences to retry the case for themselves and enjoy different fantasies of justice based on different values and desires.

First, it may be helpful to review the facts of the case. Leopold and Loeb believed that they were capable of committing the "perfect crime" and were free to do so because their superior intellects qualified them as Nietzschean supermen, above common law and morality. They typed a ransom note addressed "Dear Sir," and chose their victim at random. They happened upon Bobby Franks and offered to give him a ride home in their rented car. While Leopold drove the car, Loeb struck Franks on the head with a chisel wrapped in tape and then suffocated him. They poured acid over the face and genitals of the corpse, then buried it in a culvert. Leopold and Loeb attempted to collect a ransom, but the body was soon found. Also found at the scene of the crime was a pair of glasses, which the police were able to trace to Leopold. The teenagers' alibis didn't hold up against the facts of the investigation, and Leopold and Loeb soon made full confessions. Their parents hired Darrow, who entered a plea of guilty—thus avoiding trial by jury—and convinced Judge John R. Caverly that the state should not execute the two teenagers. The sentence was life plus ninety-nine years.

In 1936 a fellow prisoner killed Loeb, but Leopold earned a reputation as a model prisoner and was released on parole in 1958. He spent the remainder of his life in Puerto Rico, where he married, worked as an x-ray technician in a hospital, and died in 1971 at the age of sixty-six.

There are many elements that inspire our continuing fascination with the case beyond the usual narrative thrills of crime, detection, and justice. Leopold and Loeb were young, wealthy, from respectable German Jewish families, remarkably intelligent, and well educated. These factors set them apart from other murderers in the public imagination, making them extraordinary and intriguing characters. Their case also stands out in the history of jurisprudence because of the importance of psychoanalytic testimony in a legal setting, as well as the famously solid and eloquent argument Darrow made against capital punishment. But the case lends itself to drama mostly because of two elements that remain elusive and mysterious and therefore open themselves up to creative interpretation. The first is the motivation for the "motiveless" crime: not anger, not love, not revenge, not money, but pleasure—the killers did it simply for the thrill of the experience. Most people are not satisfied with this explanation, which leads to the question of what motivates such a motivation. What internal or external forces cause someone to want to murder for kicks? The second element is the relationship between the criminals: Leopold and Loeb had sex together. But what exactly was the nature of their relationship, and what connection is there between their homosexuality and their murder? As our society changes its understanding of crime and of homosexuality, and of homosexuality *as* a crime, these factors are reimagined in each retelling of the case.

Rope: *The Detective's Fantasy of Justice and the Elimination of Homosexuality*

The earliest dramatic version of the Leopold and Loeb story is also the one farthest removed from the facts of the actual case, and although it was an English play with English characters, it had a significant impact on the representation of the homicidal homosexual in America. The playwright Patrick Hamilton denied that he had heard of the infamous American murder when he wrote his three-act melodramatic thriller *Rope,* retitled *Rope's End* for its American production in 1929, just five years after the Leopold and Loeb case. Nevertheless, nearly every drama critic dismissed

Hamilton's disclaimer and interpreted the play as "inspired by" Leopold and Loeb. *Rope* takes place over the course of a single evening and is set entirely in a posh Mayfair flat shared by two Oxford undergraduates, Brandon and Granillo.[7] To prove their Nietzschean superiority and experience the sheer thrill of it, they strangle their classmate Ronald Kentley, put his body in a wooden chest, then invite Ronald's friends and family over for a party, serving food and drinks from the chest. One of the guests, however, is Rupert Cadell, the boys' former housemaster, and he grows increasingly suspicious of foul play, piecing together the clues until he confronts the killers and exposes their crime. The play is not a whodunit, since the audience knows the crime and the killers from the start. Rather, the tension of the play concerns whether the killers will get away with it or whether Rupert the amateur detective can find the truth.

It should come as no surprise that the text of Hamilton's play makes no direct reference to any sexual relationship between the two killers. The Lord Chamberlain maintained the prohibition of the depiction of homosexuality on the British stage, and in 1927 the New York legislature had introduced the Wales Padlock Law, which prohibited plays "depicting or dealing with the subject of sex degeneracy or sex perversion." The young killers' sexual relationship is an unspoken secret, one constructed only by insinuation, merely hinting at a physical intimacy between the two boys.[8] The first time we see them in full light, Brandon puts his arm around Granillo as he lights his cigarette from the other boy's match, making this postmurder cigarette seem very much like a postcoital cigarette. As Alan Sinfield has noted, Hamilton also creates the killers as a masculine/feminine couple.[9] Brandon is blond, athletic, and "paternal" and will become more assertive and threatening as the play progresses. Granillo is dark, slim, and courteous, and, in stereotypically Spanish fashion (i.e., as someone from an "intemperate" country), he will become more hysterical as the play progresses, even emitting falsetto screams when he is caught.

Like Rupert, the audience can search for clues. Isn't Granillo rather effeminate? Doesn't Brandon stand too close to him? Isn't there something they are hiding from us about their relationship? We search for clues to ascertain their guilt, but we cannot know for sure. In a world where homosexuality is criminalized and cannot be directly acknowledged onstage, the violent act of murder stands in for the sexual act, merging to become a "sex crime" made up of a sexual murder and a murderous sexuality. Both consist of two men together performing an intimate and pleasurable physical act that they must keep secret within the privacy of their home.

The conspiracy of criminals mirrors the conspiracy of secret lovers. This point was made extravagantly clear in a 1994 London revival of the stage play. The director, Keith Baxter, staged an opening tableau featuring three naked men (the murderers and their victim) sprawled by the chest. Has there been a murder or an orgy? Is there a difference? In either case, Brandon and Granillo are a couple with a secret, hoping no one will find out the criminal act they have committed together.

Interestingly, and perhaps most surprisingly to those familiar only with Alfred Hitchcock's 1948 film adaptation of *Rope,* the queerest character in the play is the starring role, the amateur detective-hero Rupert Cadell. This poet, who is also a veteran of the Great War, is, according to the playwright's character description, "foppish, affected, [and] verges on effeminacy," spouting quips in the Wildean manner and professing a complete disdain for traditional moral standards, as well as for the mawkishness of heterosexual wooing. New York critic Robert Littell praised Ernest Milton, who received top billing in the role on both sides of the Atlantic, for masterfully presenting "a warped orchid of an effeminate Oxford decadent."[10] Rupert is very much coded as queer in the mold of Oscar Wilde, the most famous "effeminate decadent" to ever come out of Britain. But what does this cynical, perfumed poet have to do with our homicidal homosexuals? In Hamilton's play, everything. Brandon and Granillo have learned their moral, ethical, and aesthetic philosophies from Rupert, and the playwright both figuratively and literally places the boys' murder at Rupert's feet. Upon discovering the corpse of Ronald, Rupert is confronted with the results of his freethinking philosophies, and, like Dr. Frankenstein, he is forced to reckon with the monstrosity that he has created.

The decadent poet, thrust into the role of criminal detective and enforcer of justice, sheds his world-weary pose to reveal a firm moral conscience. Hamilton creates a telling theatrical metaphor for this transformation when Rupert unsheathes his walking cane, previously a symbol of his effeteness and lameness, to reveal a pointed metal sword, a phallic symbol of strength and justice, with which he holds the boys at bay. In order to claim this new role, Rupert must atone and reform, and he does so by destroying his malformed progeny, renouncing his previous teachings, and reestablishing a clear moral order. Using terms like *sin* and *blasphemy,* Rupert condemns his former pupils, extols the sanctity of individual life, and places his faith in society's system of justice. As he delivers the play's final words, he predicts what society will do to the boys, sounding not unlike a judge himself, handing them their sentence: "You are going to hang,

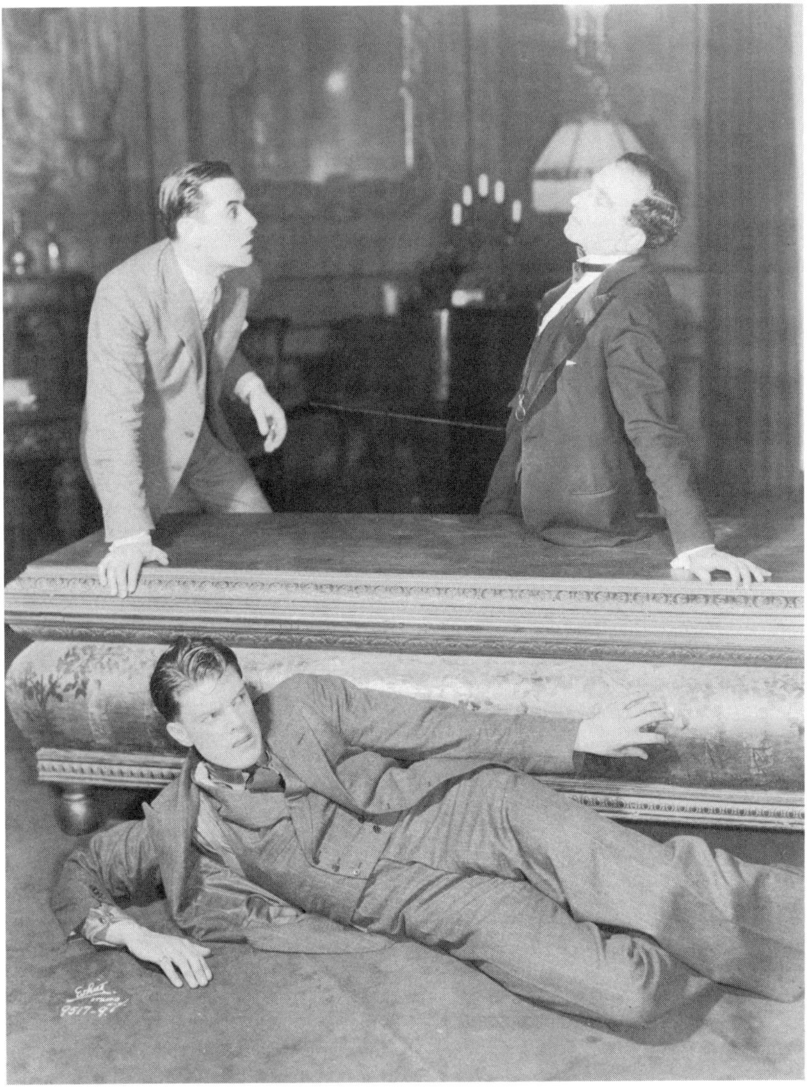

Rupert Cadell (Ernest Milton) holds Brandon (Sebastian Shaw) at bay with his walking cane, while Granillo (Ivan Brandt) cowers by the chest containing the victim's body, in the 1929 Broadway production of *Rope's End* (also known as *Rope*) by Patrick Hamilton. Photo: White Studio. Courtesy of Billy Rose Theatre Division, The New York Public Library for the Performing Arts, Astor, Lenox and Tilden Foundations.

you swine! Hang!—both of you!—hang!" (86). In Hitchcock's film version, Rupert is a dry, intellectual, American oddball rather than a flamboyant English decadent, and the role is further normalized by the star persona of Jimmy Stewart.[11] Bringing his "average guy" charm to the role, Stewart re-creates Rupert as a normative (and presumably heterosexual) hero who contains and condemns queerness in order to preserve the moral order.

Rope, then, allows its audience to enjoy the homophobic fantasy of eliminating homosexuality. Rupert renounces his decadent morality, while Brandon and Granillo are condemned to die. Thus *Rope* offers a cleaner, less complex fantasy version of the Leopold and Loeb case. Since the narrative is constructed through the conventions of detective fiction, the detective-hero's success in exposing the crime and capturing the criminals is the end of the story. The detective's fantasy of justice has no room for the lawyers' arguments or the judge's sentencing; it presumes eye-for-an-eye retribution and the removal of the criminal monsters, the moral aliens, from the society of "normal" people. This fantasy avoids the seemingly outrageous possibility that Brandon and Granillo might somehow escape the death penalty and eventually find a place in society. But justice is not as simple as this melodramatic thriller would have it, especially when it comes to condemning the homicidal homosexual. In the real world, Judge Caverly sentenced Leopold and Loeb to life in prison, and Leopold earned parole in 1958. Some historians believe that he achieved his freedom thanks in part to the novelist and playwright Meyer Levin, who argued for a different understanding of the link between homosexuality and criminality.

Compulsion: *The Social Worker's Fantasy of Justice and the Cure for Homosexuality*

In 1956, Simon & Schuster published Meyer Levin's *Compulsion,* a "documentary novel" that mixed the facts of the Leopold and Loeb case with constructed fictions to create a national best seller. Levin had been a student journalist during the Leopold and Loeb case, and in *Compulsion* he changed the names of those involved but followed many of the facts of the case very closely, even quoting entire passages of transcripts from the court case. Levin's stage adaptation had a difficult journey, as he publicly fought with his producer over control of his script. After much legal wrangling, a "producer's version" of Levin's script ran on Broadway for 140 performances in the 1957–58 season, with Roddy McDowall and Dean Stockwell as the killers.[12] Levin disowned the Broadway production but published his version of the script for use in subsequent productions, along with a lengthy essay vilifying his producer and his "writing assistant" for hijacking the play.[13] In 1959 Twentieth Century Fox released a film version, scripted by Richard Murphy and directed by Richard Fleischer.[14]

While *Rope* follows a nearly Aristotelian model of unity, Levin's script for *Compulsion* has twenty-seven scenes and at least thirty-nine roles, is three and a half hours long, and jumps around in time and location. It participates in a variety of narrative conventions: a sensational depiction of antisocial excesses; a psychological exploration of juvenile delinquency; a philosophical argument on fate and free will; a crime story with police, detectives, and journalists searching for a murderer; a tragic (heterosexual) romance; and finally a courtroom drama. In general *Compulsion* is not so much interested in the crime of Leopold and Loeb, here renamed Judd Steiner and Artie Strauss, as it is in their social deviancy and psychological neuroses. The play begins with old Judd Steiner (Leopold) in prison, up for parole, and being interviewed by the journalist who uncovered evidence against him at the time of the crime. Judd is reluctant to talk about the crime, but the journalist insists, saying, "Things like yours have been happening more and more. People are frightened, worried. If you could help them understand it, control it" (4). By "things like yours," the journalist means crimes of juvenile delinquency, an obsession of 1950s popular entertainment, most famously exemplified by the film *Rebel Without a Cause* (1955) and the Broadway musical *West Side Story* (1957). *Compulsion* offers the thrills of teenage sex and violence but with a stated agenda of social exploration, understanding, and improvement.

In attempting to locate the cause of the crime, Levin aims for complex psychological portraits of Judd and Artie, showing that they are "abnormal" in a variety of ways, especially when it comes to American ideals of masculinity. David Savran has written about the 1950s as a time of "domestic revival" that relied on "a rigorously gendered division of labor and a corresponding polarization of masculine and feminine 'sex roles.'"[15] Savran argues that "the dread of a feminine male" plays a crucial role in constructing "Cold War masculinity" in the era's plays.[16] *Compulsion* dramatizes this struggle over the meaning, cause, and proper treatment of "malformed" masculinity with Judd and Artie as subjects for examination. For starters they are very wealthy, which is positioned as a corrupting, feminizing force that leads to moral laxity and unmanly ease. They are highly educated, pompous intellectuals influenced by European philosophers, which Levin contrasts with the frumpy homespun American "commonsense" intellect of Darrow, here renamed Wilk.

The boys are also set apart by their Judaism, a factor ignored in the film version but central to the play version.[17] Levin intertwines Judd's experience as a "sissy" with his experience as a Jew—being called "dirty names" and having his trousers torn down by "normal" boys. Sander Gilman has written about how the difference of the circumcised penis figures in anti-Semitic prejudice, marking the Jewish man as not fully masculine, and Levin highlights this physical difference as a factor in Judd's humiliation.[18] In all these ways, Levin shows how Judd and Artie are not "normal" men, yet he also enters a plea of tolerance and understanding for such men. Levin seems to argue that Judd and Artie become criminals not simply because they are failed men but because they are the victims of an ignorant society that has unfairly rejected them as failed men.[19]

The failures of masculinity caused by wealth, intellectualism, and Judaism are contributing factors to what Levin constructs as the greatest failure of masculinity: homosexuality, which he presents as a pitiful yet treatable condition. While *Rope* could not directly acknowledge homosexuality, *Compulsion* hinges on its revelation as an explanation for Judd and Artie's crime. Judd, a weak intellectual, desperately wants to keep the attention and affection of Artie, a thrill-seeking scofflaw. Judd's sexual/submissive deviance directly correlates with Artie's criminal/aggressive deviance. Judd has a moral conscience and is reluctant to pursue criminal activity, but his adoration of Artie leads him to agree to a pact in which Judd will participate in crimes if Artie will participate in sex—a trade that creates an economic equivalence between murder and gay sex. The issue comes to the forefront in the climactic third-act courtroom scene, when a psychiatrist explains the pact and states that Judd was "helplessly bound by his passion," setting off a shouting match between the prosecution (Horn) and the defense (Wilk).

> *Horn:* When a man willfully engages in murder to gratify unnatural lust—you call that helpless?
> *Wilk:* When a man is invaded by typhoid germs, is that willful?
> *Horn:* If perversion is an excuse for murder, then we had better shut up our courts!
> *Wilk:* Or better, turn them into hospitals. (110–11)

The doctor goes on to explain that sex per se was not the motive in the crime—although the prosecution tries to insinuate that Judd and Artie raped their victim and the murder was part of a homosexual act. There was no evidence in the actual Leopold and Loeb trial that they had raped Bobby Franks, but the prosecution did try to suggest it.

The hysterical linking of homosexuality, pedophilia, and murder reached its high point in the 1950s,[20] and Levin is careful to address and dismiss the charge in a scene with Wilk and Judd's family, including his brother Max.

> *Wilk:* People want to hang them if only because of the homosexuality.
> *Max:* But the coroner swore it wasn't in the crime. (97)

The extent to which homosexuality is "in" the crime is renegotiated in every retelling of this case. Levin goes out of his way to avoid demonizing the homosexual as a child rapist and murderer, criticizing those who would hang someone simply for being homosexual. Yet he cannot avoid the creeping suspicion that even if homosexuality is not in the crime, it is still lurking somewhere around the scene of the crime.

Levin views homosexuality as a common teenage malady that can be cured or outgrown. To prove this point, he introduces the fictional character of Ruth Slimovitsky, a fine exemplar of Cold War femininity, a nurturing and understanding young woman who meets and befriends Judd the day after the murder, when he is wracked by guilt and shame. She insists that Judd could be "normal" if he received "a girl's affection." In this Levin echoes the philosophy put forth by one of the biggest stage hits of the 1950s, Robert Anderson's *Tea and Sympathy* (1953), which shows how the love of a strong, nurturing woman can redeem a young man who has been rejected as unmanly. As Ruth hugs and consoles Judd, defense attorney Wilk, as the authoritative voice of compassion and reason, addresses the audience.

> Between fifteen and twenty-one, the child has the burden of adolescence, of puberty and sex thrust upon him. Boys, without instruction, are left to work out the solution themselves. They may be led to excess. They may be led to perversion. Who is to blame? Some succumb to the darkest urges perhaps at the very moment when they are about to grow out of them. (44)

Levin asks his audience to appreciate the cruel irony: if Judd had met Ruth one day earlier, maybe he wouldn't have become a homicidal homosexual. He succumbed to his darkest urges, as one might succumb to an illness, a weak victim who deserves our sympathy and our help—not a hanging but a hospital.

The film version, still constrained by the last vestiges of the Production Code, which regulated the discussion and depiction of sexuality in Hollywood films, soft-pedals the exact nature of these "darkest urges," focusing on Judd's anemic intellectualism and merely connoting his homosexuality. The film alludes to homosexuality but constructs it simply as the absence of masculinity and heterosexuality. For example, Judd's older brother Max berates him for spending too much time with Artie and asks, "Don't you ever go to a baseball game or chase girls or anything?" In addition, Judd's long and longing stares at Artie leave little doubt that Judd is a homosexual waiting to happen, but the relationship is never named or dramatized.

The film version ends with the judge giving his sentence and sparing the lives of Judd and Artie, but neither of the boys seems grateful—they are unrepentant delinquents. The film asks the audience to pity Judd and Artie, but not necessarily to sympathize with them: the film's top-billed stars are not the actors playing the criminals but the actors playing Wilk (Orson Welles) and Ruth (Diane Varsi), the normative characters who show the audience the "correct" way to react to the killers. The play shows much more sympathy for the killers, particularly Judd, whom we see in old age in prison, wise and repentant, having gained self-knowledge and moral understanding. The play presents a triumphant narrative of 1950s liberal humanism in which a just society rejects the death penalty and treats and cures criminal delinquency with mercy and compassion.

Reopened Cases: The Lover's Fantasy of Justice and the Defense of Homosexuality

By the time the next retelling of the Leopold and Loeb case appeared on stage, several events had occurred that would influence and radically reshape new versions of the story. During the interim, the Supreme Court struck down stage censorship, the Stonewall Riots gave a major push to the modern gay rights movement, Leopold died, the American Psychiatric Association decided that homosexuality should no longer be classified as a mental disorder, and a few states began to repeal their sodomy laws. Furthermore, our culture "discovered" the existence of gay plays, gay films, and (most stunningly) gay audiences. All of these events created an atmosphere in which finally there could be a dramatic retelling of the Leopold and Loeb case that (1) used people's real names, (2) did not have to fear censorship, (3) could consider homosexuality as something other than a sinister crime or a pathetic mental illness, and (4) did not presume the heterosexuality of the audience. Presented early in the century as ruthless killers whom the audience is encouraged to condemn, then in midcentury as juvenile delinquents whom the audience is encouraged to pity, in recent decades Leopold and Loeb have been presented as romantic lovers with whom the audience is encouraged to identify. In these later narratives, Leopold and Loeb are the stars of their own story, with no detective, lawyer, or would-be girlfriend to direct the audience's response.

John Logan's play *Never the Sinner* went through many incarnations between its debut in Chicago in 1985 and its off-Broadway success in 1998. The play is, in Logan's own words, "a love story," and while it recounts the crime story, the court case, and the media frenzy, the main focus is the *relationship between* Leopold and Loeb.[21] *Compulsion* imagined Leopold as sexually desperate and Loeb as rather reluctant "rough trade," but *Never the Sinner* presents a romantic couple dependent on each other, perfectly represented by the closing image of act 1: the two boys waltzing together to Irving Berlin's "What'll I Do?" In act 2, as they await their sentencing, Loeb is stunned and saddened by the realization that if they go to prison they will be sent to separate prisons. He asks, "If they hang us—would they do that together? At the same time?" When Leopold replies, "Probably," Loeb decides, "Then I hope they hang us" (117). The main question of the play, then, is not so much why they killed Bobby Franks or how society should deal with them but rather what effect these events will have on their relationship. Logan insists that Leopold and Loeb are not moral aliens but that "we all could, given some unkind twists of fate and character, be them" (17). *New York Times* critic D. J. R. Bruckner recognized this intention with the title of his review: "Leopold and Loeb as Everymen."[22]

The 1992 independent film *Swoon,* written and directed by Tom Kalin, also imagines the story as a gay romance.[23] Over the title credits, we see Leopold and Loeb walking arm in arm, then going into an abandoned warehouse where they passionately kiss and then exchange rings while shafts of light slice the shadows to create a romantic atmosphere. As John Clum notes in his analysis of the film, the infamous sexual/criminal pact is presented as an exchange of wedding vows.[24]

Leopold: If I do what you want . . .
Loeb: . . . I'll do what you want.

If previous versions could be accused of distorting the truth by making the sexual relationship between Leopold and Loeb sinister and pathological, then *Never the Sinner* and *Swoon* distort the truth by making it romantic. While it is true that Leopold and Loeb could clinically be described as "homosexuals," Logan and Kalin create fantasies in which they are lovers and a "gay couple," at times bickering or abusive but mostly romantic, even comically domestic.

Swoon emphasizes that Leopold and Loeb were victims of the homophobia of both the court and the press. As doctors give testimony about their sexual relations, suddenly they are shown frolicking in their bed, which has surrealistically appeared in the middle of the courtroom: their homosexuality is on trial here. Janet Maslin argued in the *New York Times* that *Swoon* "is more successful in taking apart this particular chapter in criminal history than in reassembling it with a clear point of view."[25] But the film's postmodern anachronisms encourage the audience to create links to the queer world of 1992, with its Queer Nation/Lesbian Avenger era defiance and celebration of the sexual outlaw.[26] Leopold and Loeb become emblematic figures, enacting queer fears and anger over (but perhaps also taking pleasure in) being treated like criminals in a homophobic society. *Swoon* is the one version of the story that continues through Loeb's death in 1936 and Leopold's in 1971. Being a love story, the film begins with a marriage and follows the ups and downs of the couple, till death do they part.

In the first decade of the twenty-first century, the romantic paradigm was evident in two small, experimental productions that brought the story into new theatrical territory. In 2003 New York witnessed a fringe festival production of *Thrill Me: The Leopold and Loeb Musical,* with book, music, and lyrics by Stephen Dolginoff.[27] The show was remounted as *Thrill Me: The Leopold and Loeb Story* for an extended off-Broadway run at the York Theatre in the summer of 2005, and has since gone on to numerous productions around the United States and the world, including a long-running production in South Korea. This dark, two-character chamber musical attempts to sever the link between murderous criminality and sexuality by presenting Leopold sympathetically as a love-struck young man who enters into a Faustian bargain with the cool and sadistic Loeb: he signs the sexual-criminal contract in order to ensure his romantic fulfillment, but he loses his soul in the bargain. In other words, Leopold is the queer, but Loeb is the killer, literally an *homme fatal* who combines sexual allure with deadly menace. Indeed, the show's most seductive song is the one Loeb sings to the unseen Bobby Franks as he lures the boy into his car and to his death. The author's unique contribution to Leopold and Loeb lore, which is crucial to his project of redeeming Leopold, is that Leopold purposefully orchestrated their arrest so he could assuage his guilty conscience, as well as achieve his romantic goal of being with Loeb forever. From a realistic point of view, this motivation may seem unlikely, but it redeems Leopold as a "good boy" who had the misfortune to fall in love with a "bad boy"—a popular motif in gay male fantasy, from the novels of Genet and Mishima to the HBO prison soap opera *Oz*. Loeb is guilty of murder, Leopold is guilty of falling for a sexy sociopath, and Dolginoff's show ends with the killers/lovers singing a duet about how they'll be together for "Life Plus Ninety Nine Years."

Laural Meade and the Anodyne Ensemble turn the story into "deconstructive vaudeville" in *Leopold and Loeb: A Goddamn Laff Riot,* presented in Los Angeles in 2003.[28] The characters of Leopold and Loeb are each performed by a pair of actors—one male and one female—giving us four actors who continually alternate lines and express contradictory feelings and thoughts, truly queering the notion of singular, let alone singly gendered, identity. This multiplication can also be read as a comment on the many previous portrayals of these characters, as can the constant replaying and revising of scenes, as if identities and actions might be endlessly reproduced. Meade also creates Leopold and Loeb as a tragicomic duo not unlike Tom Stoppard's Rosencrantz and Guildenstern: the individual identity of one relies on an association with the other, one cannot exist without the other, and there is often confusion as to which one is which.

While many of the familiar facts of the case are presented, they are interspersed with dance numbers, jokes, and games. When asked in court if they plead guilty, the Leopolds and Loebs respond by putting on wedding veils and dancing to the ABBA song "I Do, I Do, I Do." The link between gay romance and murder is reiterated, but through the distortions of a funhouse mirror, making it simultaneously creepy and ridiculous. Juxtaposition allows for a variety of possible meanings, so it is hard to know exactly what to think when Loeb tells "fag" jokes as he repeatedly strikes Bobby Franks, or when the Leopolds and Loebs pull down their trousers, erotically humping and slapping each other while Darrow gives his stirring closing argument in court. *Laff Riot* invites the audience to sit in judgment, but consistently shifts truth and meaning, dismissing any normative character (like a detective, lawyer, judge, or nurturing girlfriend) who might give the audience a firm moral foothold. The significance of the story is more elusive than ever, which may be the most accurate representation of all.

It would be misleading to state that there exists some sort of "progression" in the Leopold and Loeb narratives, especially since all these plays (and even the films) continue to circulate in a variety of different circumstances before a variety of different audiences. Patrick Hamilton's *Rope* has proven remarkably enduring, with recent revivals in London (2010), Sydney (2010), and New York (2012), along with many university productions. A contemporary audience of *Rope,* then, might view the murderers as villains to be condemned, victims to be pitied, *and* lovers with whom to identify. *Never the Sinner* has also maintained its popularity, with productions around the country, two fringe revivals that ran back to back in New York in the summer of 2007, and a Chicago revival in 2009. The proliferation of Leopolds and Loebs satirized by Laural Meade shows no signs of abating. Other additions include Sky Gilbert's *Rope Enough,* in which two modern-day defendants cite Leopold and Loeb as role models, staged at Toronto's Buddies in Bad Times Theatre in 2005; *Golden Age,* by Roberto Aguirre-Sacasa, seen at New York's Kraine Theater in 2005, which imagines Nathan Leopold dating all American redhead Archie Andrews of comic book fame; Nicky Silver's metatheatrical *The Agony and the Agony,* staged at the Vineyard Theatre in 2006, which has Nathan Leopold expressing his anger over having to appear in yet another play (see chapter 6); and Los Angeles's Blank Theater Company's 2008 world premiere of *Dickie & Babe: The Truth About Leopold & Loeb,* a docudrama written and directed by Daniel Henning.

All three major film versions of the Leopold and Loeb story continue to circulate, available to contemporary audiences and also, in the case of *Rope,* influencing new artists. In 2002 Kansas City filmmaker Kendall Sinn "remade" *Rope* in a super-low-budget HDV version, using Hamilton's script with a smattering of Arthur Laurents's screenplay but updating and resetting the drama in Kansas City. (Sinn's goal was to accomplish with video what Hitchcock could not with celluloid: an entire film made from a single take, without a single edit.) But, while nearly every reference has been updated, the film's attitude toward homosexuality has not: it remains the sinister secret, never directly shown or named but folded within the murderous crime. Barbet Schroeder's film *Murder by Numbers* (2002) dramatizes but never names the affections of a murderous young man for his partner in crime, making the sexual attraction all the more sinister. Michael Haneke's *Funny Games* (1997, remade in English in 2007) ironically names homosexuality as one of many psychological "reasons" for a murderous duo's evil, only to then deny it, chastising the audience for its willingness to accept the facile and clichéd explanation.

Reid Farrington combines film and theater in his performance piece *Gin & "It"* (2010), in which Hitchcock's *Rope* is projected in various fragments, while technicians and grips perform the "offscreen" duties that make Hitchcock's seamless vision possible.[29] But among the team of men, one performer, who frequently fails in his job, is singled out, gay baited, and finally bundled into a sack, which is hung suspended above the stage. As in Hitchcock's film, homosexuality is a problem and hindrance that must be silenced and erased, and Farrington's piece enacts the homophobia offscreen that is implicit onscreen. The position of the homosexual, then, shifts from perpetrator to victim, and although others have attempted to erase him, he still hovers over the proceedings.

Queer Verdicts: The Audience as Jury

The proliferation of homicidal homosexual narratives, along with the proliferation of different attitudes about homosexuality in our society, allows for a wider variety of possible reactions to the representation of real queer killer cases than ever before. While the tabloid media often flatten controversial and complex cases into easily digestible and melodramatic narratives, theater artists can bring another perspective, becoming a valuable part of our social discourse by "queering" the stories and offering audiences alternative ways to see and understand. In the case of Leopold and Loeb, for example, Hamilton leads his audience to righteous condemnation with the belief that homosexuality is evil, Levin leads his audience to righteous mercy with the belief that homosexuality is a sickness, and a handful of more recent narratives lead the audience to romanticize and identify with the criminalized homosexual.

But just as a jury might resist the arguments of a persuasive lawyer, so audiences can come up with resistant readings of these texts, coming to various and often contradictory conclusions of their own. Different narrative elements may inspire different reactions, depending on whether the narrative foregrounds "positive" qualities (e.g., romantic longing) or "negative" qualities (e.g., horrific violence). Audiences can also choose to focus more on the positive or negative, creating their own understanding about the guilt or innocence of the characters. An audience member's verdict may also depend on how he or she interprets "the crime," which functions not just literally but also emblematically. Leopold and Loeb murdered Bobby Franks—but they are on trial for much more than that.

As a gay man involved in queer studies, I have had a variety of different responses to plays and films about Leopold and Loeb. I do not wish to essentialize my own response as a universal "gay response," nor do I imagine that such responses are limited only to audience members who identify as gay or queer. Rather, I hope to show how an audience member who is not homophobic and does not dismiss these narratives out of hand as "negative representations" can have a rich and complex response to these plays and films. Sitting in the metaphorical jury box of the retrials, such an audience member may come to a variety of "verdicts" in some sequence or combination.

The "Guilty as Sin" Verdict. No matter how out and proud I am, it's hard to escape all of the stigma and shame still associated with being queer. Stories about Leopold and Loeb present a magnified version of my own internalized sense of criminality. These plays and movies give me a chance to explore, even to indulge, my own feelings of criminal guilt in a "safe" way. I identify with these criminals, and even find some satisfaction in their punishment, because part of me feels that I, too, deserve to be punished.

The "Scapegoat" Verdict. Leopold and Loeb were truly evil, and I'm both ashamed and angry that they have been identified as part of the queer community. Therefore, it is satisfying to watch them be caught, condemned, and expunged from our society. The experience is cleansing, especially since Leopold and Loeb represent the stigma of "evil" still attributed to queer people. I can enjoy the fantasy of getting rid of the "bad gays," which enacts my desire to get rid of the stigmatized part of myself.

The "Guilty Past" Verdict. These plays and films show how homophobic social forces and ideologies of the past twisted Leopold and Loeb, turning them into monsters. I can watch their comeuppance with some sadness because they are victims of homophobia, but also with pleasure because I'm happy to be rid of the warped, "abnormal" queers produced by previous generations. I can reflect on how society has changed and that we are not like that anymore.

The "Guilt by Disassociation" Verdict. These plays and films show how those qualities that I do not share—rather than the quality of homosexuality, which I do share—are really the crucial factors in creating a murderer. For example, being upper-class intellectuals is what twisted Leopold and Loeb's morality, not their homosexuality. And even if it were, the sexual relationship between Leopold and Loeb was rather strange, warped by the closet, and not at all like my sexual relationships.

The "Guilty of Love" Verdict. I'm comforted by the fact that Loeb was the real killer of Bobby Franks, while Leopold was simply a love-struck gay kid who acted as a reluctant accomplice. (When I was young and foolish, I certainly did things I'm now ashamed of in order to keep the affections of an unworthy and ill-chosen beloved.) Loeb is a sociopath who is guilty of murder, but Leopold is guilty only of being in love. It's a relief to be able to separate the queer from the killer.

The "Extreme Case" Verdict. Leopold and Loeb represent the most villainous homosexuals in our culture. If a play or movie can show that even these monstrous killers are human beings who deserve understanding and sympathy, then surely queer people like me (who are *not* committing murder) can find a place in our society. Their extreme case helps to normalize my own position.

The "Gay Martyr" Verdict. Homophobes think that queer people are as evil as murderers and treat them like criminals. The depiction of the legal prosecution of Leopold and Loeb mirrors my own sense of persecution, allowing me to feel sadness and anger over the mistreatment of these queer characters. They are victims just as we are victims.

The "Gay Criminal" Verdict. Society treats queer people like criminals, and we're glad to be outlaws because the laws are unfair. Leopold and Loeb are not bound by common morality and homophobic repression. There is strength and power in their criminality, and I admire their arrogance, daring, and rebelliousness. I hate feeling like a victim, and so the role of the aggressor fulfills an empowering fantasy.

The "Fair Trial" Verdict. These plays and films show that Leopold and Loeb were tried and convicted not just for murder but also for homosexuality and gender nonconformity. Neither the legal system nor public opinion ever treats them fairly because of bigotry and prejudice. These plays and films allow me to finally give these queer men a fair trial. My verdict: guilty of murder but innocent on all other counts.

The *"Gay Avenger" Verdict.* In reality I know that Bobby Franks was an innocent victim, but in the realm of fiction he represents reproductive heterosexuality and the family, the symbols of innocence and goodness used to oppress the supposedly wicked and "antifamily" homosexual. In these dramatic fantasies, Leopold and Loeb strike a blow against the oppressive and repressive homophobic ideologies that torment them. There is righteousness in their rage, and therefore I can root for them, since these homophobic ideologies also torment me.

The "Good Drama" Verdict. Murder makes for good drama. Oedipus, Medea, Richard III, Macbeth, and even Hamlet—they're all killers. The dramatic depiction of murderers is thrilling because they enact extreme and violent passions in a way that I will never experience. As a queer person, I enjoy seeing queer characters who have this magnitude and stature within the story, and there are now enough "good" gay characters in our culture that I don't have to feel guilty about enjoying the "bad" ones once in a while. Of course murder is wrong, but the depiction of it is thrilling because it helps us explore the full depth of our humanity.

Narratives that retry real homicidal homosexuals allow the audience to reexamine and reconsider murder cases that have the power to raise troubling issues about the relationship between homosexuality and criminality—a relationship that, despite great changes between 1924 and today, is still being negotiated in our legal system and our daily lives. Although it is possible to dismiss plays and films about real life queer killers as inherently homophobic because they depict "negative representations," I believe that these narratives benefit from being read as performances that actively wrestle with fears and fantasies about social stigma and criminality. Especially since antigay ideologues and the tabloid press often assume a simple pathological link between the sexual deviant and the murderous criminal, these plays and films offer alternative narratives—or at least more complex ones—that ask audience members to interrogate their assumptions, fears, and fantasies about homicidal homosexuals.

Artists involved in creating theater and film inevitably wrestle with cultural legacies that include heroes and villains, as well as everything those heroes and villains represent. The retrials of Leopold and Loeb and other real queer killers are the results of artists' and audiences' need to create new meanings out of these particularly fascinating, mysterious, and troubling parts of our cultural legacy. As long as audiences sense that queers do not always achieve justice in our society, both in courts of law and in public discourse, then plays and films that rewrite criminal cases and imagine alternative "queer" versions of justice will play an important role, showing that the case is always open for reexamination and the final sentence can always be rewritten.

CHAPTER THREE

The Closet Is a Deathtrap

The previous chapter encompassed a broad range of time, showing the changes in the dominant understanding of the homicidal homosexual in three different eras. The next two chapters explore in greater depth the "gay liberation era," from the rise of gay political activism and culture in the late 1960s through the emergence of the AIDS crisis in the 1980s.[1] This era witnessed great changes in the position of LGBT people within American culture, and changes in the representation of homosexuality onstage were evident in two very different realms of theatrical production, both of which featured many instances of the homicidal homosexual. In this chapter, I focus on thrillers produced mostly by straight playwrights for Broadway in the 1970s and 1980s, but concurrent with these productions there was a "queer theater" produced mostly by gay men and lesbians in alternative theater venues, which I'll discuss in the following chapter.

Since this chapter examines the construction and deconstruction of the homicidal homosexual within popular thrillers, I am compelled to include a spoiler alert. *WARNING: This chapter candidly discusses many of the secrets and surprises contained in a number of thrillers. Readers who do not wish to have these works "spoiled" are encouraged to read and/or view the relevant plays, films, and novels and then return to this chapter.*

The 1969 Stonewall Riots have taken on symbolic significance in gay culture and politics in part because that queer uprising against police harassment functioned so successfully as public performance.[2] Marginalized minorities are more easily intimidated as long as they are stigmatized, ashamed, and afraid of public exposure—in other words, in the closet. Stonewall was an instance of public resistance when queers stormed "out of the closet and into the street," declaring public identities in a public space. The rebellion resulted in the unprecedented public exposure of queer people, first through media coverage of the riots themselves and subsequently through the annual marches and parades that commemorated the event. All this exposure was part of "coming out," one of the key principles of the gay rights movement. Eve Kosofsky Sedgwick argues in *The Epistemology of the Closet* that in the nineteenth century homosexuality was "distinctively constituted *as* secrecy," most famously named "the love that dare not speak its name," and that "the closet is the defining structure for gay oppression in [the twentieth] century." [3] The gay liberation movement viewed coming out as a crucial strategy not just in personal liberation from the closet but also in fighting social perceptions of queer villainy. If members of society could realize that gay people were their family members, neighbors, teachers, movie stars, and so on, then they would not fear or hate gay people as immoral monsters who threaten civilization.

Theatrical performance also played a role in opening the closet door, especially since the theater was often a more hospitable site for gay representation than were other cultural venues during the gay liberation era. The 1970s saw the flourishing of a queer theater movement that included openly queer theater artists such as Charles Ludlam (discussed in chapter 4), queer theater companies such as Theatre Rhinoceros and TOSOS (The Other Side of Silence), and scores of queer characters ranging from the ordinary to the outrageous. However, this community-based movement did not beget the most popular play with queer characters in the post-Stonewall/pre-AIDS era. *Deathtrap* (1978), by straight playwright Ira Levin, is a Broadway thriller about two men who must remain in the closet with two secrets: they are lovers, and they are murderers. Sidney and Clifford collaborate on the murder of Sidney's wife in act 1 and then murder each other in act 2. With 1,809 performances on Broadway, hundreds of professional and amateur productions around the world, a Hollywood film version, and revivals continuing in the twenty-first century, *Deathtrap* is one of the most commercially successful plays ever written about same-sex lovers.[4] Despite its immense popularity, however, few studies of gay drama include *Deathtrap:* John M. Clum's *Still Acting Gay* makes a passing reference to the film version, and Alan Sinfield's *Out on Stage* neglects it altogether.

The murderous lovers in *Deathtrap* raise the familiar specter of queer villainy, but a close reading can highlight the queerness of Levin's play and its potential to subvert the homophobic formula that conflates sexual deviance with murder. Instead of locating evil within a particular person, thus essentializing the sinister queer, this thriller identifies the closet, a space of entrapment for queer people, as an unsafe space where people die—a deathtrap. *Deathtrap* enacts anxieties and fantasies about the dangers of the closet in the post-Stonewall era, thus offering a productive and provocative site for exploring our perceptions of queerness—and especially closeted queerness—as both exciting and dangerous, both dramatic and terrifying.

Setting the Trap: The Construction of the Closet in the Postmodern Thriller

The traditional thriller might be read as resolutely "straight": a normative detective discovers the truth, thereby restoring the moral order temporarily upset by the transgressive act of murder. Marvin Carlson, in *Deathtraps: The Postmodern Comedy Thriller,* suggests that during the 1970s and 1980s the genre took a more postmodern form, embracing "self-reflexivity, epistemological incertitude, and subversion of traditional codes."[5] Elements identified by Carlson as typical of the postmodern comedy thriller (all of which operate in *Deathtrap*) include a mixture of witty repartee and shocking gore, a false death that leads to a "resurrection," a blurring of the distinction between reality and contrived theatricality, and a playful destabilization of genre conventions. It is little wonder, then, that many of these thrillers have a queer bent. One of the most enduring narrative conventions is heterosexuality, and the postmodern comedy thriller often surprises spectators by playing into and then subverting their heterosexist expectations.

The "epistemological incertitude" of the postmodern thriller makes it an ideal genre for the representation of anxieties about the closet, which Sedgwick describes as "the relations of the known and the unknown, the explicit and the inexplicit around homo/heterosexual definition."[6] Alisa Solomon, in *The Queerest Art,* highlights the theatricality inherent in this understanding of the closet.

> Gay men and lesbians may have long found some pleasure and solace in theater as a place where the acting they employed in everyday life to hide their sexuality enjoyed more productive expression.[7]

In other words, the closet of everyday life is a theatricalized space, one that demands a performance of the self. The closeted queer enacts a heterosexual identity in order to survive in a homophobic society, and thus, supposedly, he or she develops a more profound understanding and appreciation of the art of theater. Furthermore, Solomon suggests that dramatic art inherently utilizes and celebrates such epistemological incertitude.

> Theatre, by *its* nature, reveals and revels in the very angst the antitheatricalists were frantically trying to quell: the notion of identities as contingent and malleable and the suggestion that categories can be playfully transgressed—*queered.*[8]

Solomon supports this point by focusing on the Elizabethan boy-actress, arguing that the goal of his performance was not to deceive audiences into believing that they were watching a woman but to enjoy the boundary-defying pleasure of the performer's "both-at-once status," boy *and* woman, thus calling into question the absolute or insoluble nature of either category.

Both of Solomon's observations point to duplicity—that is, contradictory doubleness—as a trope of queerness and theatricality. Duplicity, however, is generally regarded as a negative quality since it implies deception and dishonesty. The sinister threat of the traditional thriller is based on the duplicity of the killer, who deceptively tries to conceal his or her identity, thereby creating a crisis of identity (e.g., "Any one of us might be the killer!"). It is up to the detective to distinguish between truth and lie, expose actual identities, and facilitate the return to moral certainty. It is not coincidental, then, that theater people (especially playwrights and actors) and closeted queer people often feature in postmodern thrillers. Both are skilled in the techniques of deception, making the queer theatrical a doubly dangerous person.

The exploitation of queer duplicity has a long and well-documented history in the theatrical thriller. The genre has a predominantly English pedigree, and two of the most successful English thrillers, both of which have exerted great influence on the American thriller, contain direct and indirect allusions to queer sexuality. Agatha Christie's *The Mousetrap*, which has been in performance in London's West End since 1952 and is the longest-running play in the world, features two queer suspects in a murder mystery set in a remote guesthouse.[9] Miss Casewell is a strident young woman who walks and talks in a "manly" fashion, while Christopher Wren is a sensitive young man with an appreciation for attractive policemen and chintz. As Alan Sinfield points out, neither of these characters turns out to be the murderer, but their sexual difference marks them as potentially psychopathic and therefore "plausible red herrings."[10]

Another landmark thriller, Anthony Shaffer's *Sleuth* (1970), does not have blatantly queer characters but still invokes a creepy homoeroticism. *Sleuth* involves two male rivals matching wits and playing intricate games, supposedly in order to win a wife and a mistress, but the play ends with the older man (Andrew) begging the younger man (Milo) to forget the women and come live with him so they can continue playing games together. Milo, in a knowing parody of the legal language surrounding homosexuality, mocks and belittles Andrew when he scornfully asks, "Is it legal in private between two consenting games-players?"[11] He knows that there is something perverse, even perverted, about two adult men involved in role-playing. Rather than let Milo leave, Andrew shoots him dead. Queerness, even when it seems contained in the world of theatrical parlor games, proves deadly.

In *Deathtrap* Levin takes the sinister queerness that lurks in Christie and Shaffer and combines it with a plot motif that runs through many of his previous works: the innocent wife threatened by a duplicitous husband. Levin, of course, was not the first to use this version of the woman-in-jeopardy formula, which appeared perhaps most famously in Patrick Hamilton's *Gaslight* (1938), known on the American stage as *Angel Street* (1941).[12] In it a criminal marries a young woman and then deliberately tries to drive her insane so he can gain control over her home and a hidden fortune. The duplicitous husband is the villain in two of Ira Levin's best-selling novels, which were both adapted into popular films, *Rosemary's Baby* and *The Stepford Wives.*[13] Levin creates women who are simultaneously innocent victims and detectives, piecing together the clues that lead them back to their own homes, where their deceptive husbands have put them in mortal danger. In both works, the husband has secret allegiances that the wife must discover. In *Rosemary's Baby,* Rosemary's husband has joined a cabal of Satanists who will use her womb to spawn the antichrist, and in *The Stepford Wives,* Joanna's husband is part of the Men's Association, which kills women and replaces them with servile robots. Even in Levin's previous stage play, *Veronica's Room* (1973), a young woman is "sold out" by her boyfriend, who is in cahoots with an old couple who murder the young woman as part of a cathartic ritual.[14] In each case, the duplicitous man succeeds, while the woman, who often turns to the duplicitous man for help, is doomed.

In *Deathtrap* the husband's secret association is not with a satanic cabal or robot-making conspirators but a same-sex lover. The murderous triangle of husband, wife, and same-sex lover also has some precedent within the genre. Henri-Georges Clouzot's 1955 film *Les Diaboliques* was based on the novel *The Woman Who Was No More (Celle qui n'était plus)* by Pierre Boileau and Thomas Narcejac, in which a man and his mistress conspire to kill the man's wife.[15] But once the deed is done, the wife returns from the dead, literally scaring the man to death. The wife and the mistress are revealed as lesbian lovers who planned and staged all the events in order to get rid of the husband, whose weak heart made him susceptible to their deadly theatrics. (Clouzot's film alters the allegiances within the triangle so that there is no explicit lesbian relationship, although some viewers may see these man-killing women, who also form a butch-femme duo, as coded lesbians.)[16]

Closer to the time of *Deathtrap*'s creation, another Broadway play combined the elements of the duplicitous queer and the spouse in jeopardy within a theatrical milieu. Bob Barry's *Murder among Friends* ran for a mere seventeen performances during the winter of 1975–76.[17] This flop serves as an interesting precursor to *Deathtrap,* however, because it concerns a vain actor and his wealthy wife, both of whom are having a secret affair with the same man—a handsome young agent—and both of whom are collaborating with the agent to murder their spouse. The question raised in the first act is who will succeed in murdering whom, and this question is directly tied to the question of which partner—and thus which gender—the bisexual young man will choose. Will he side with the husband and kill the wife, or will he side with the wife and kill the husband?

Christopher James has noted that *bisexuality* is a term frequently applied disapprovingly as a "misfit third category of sexual identity" to "indiscriminate lovers, fence sitters, or closet cases."[18] This (mis)understanding of the bisexual is central to *Murder among Friends,* which perpetuates the notion that bisexuals are people who simply have not made a choice between heterosexuality and homosexuality. Critics referred to the young man at the apex of this triangle as a "dastardly double agent" and an "AC/DC sneak,"[19] disparaging bisexuality as inherently duplicitous because being attracted to men *and* women supposedly precludes faithful monogamy. If the bisexual man is faithful to a woman, then he is no longer considered bisexual and becomes "straight," just as he becomes "gay" if he is faithful to a man. The faithful bisexual would seem to be an oxymoron, making him a perfect character for a play about deception and switching allegiances. As it happens, the bisexual agent is released from the necessity of choosing a homosexual or heterosexual identity because at the end of the first act he turns out to be the murder victim, double-crossed by the husband. In act 2, we learn that the husband plans to frame his wife for the murder, but she outsmarts him, sends him to jail, and wins a handsome new lover before the final curtain. With the queer husband going to jail and the bisexual lover in the morgue, heterosexuality wins the game.

Intriguingly, the sinister threat in *Murder among Friends, Deathtrap,* and other postmodern thrillers is not closeted homosexuality but closeted bisexuality. By the mid-1970s, bisexuality was enjoying a certain vogue, with celebrities such as Joan Baez, David Bowie, and Elton John publicly announcing their bisexuality. Both *Time* and *Newsweek* ran cover stories in May 1974 titled "The New Bisexuals" and "Bisexual Chic."[20] The bisexuality of central characters was important to the plots of plays such as *Butley* (1972), *Gemini* (1976), and *The Shadow Box* (1976), as well as films like *Sunday Bloody Sunday* (1971) and *Dog Day Afternoon* (1975).[21] Despite all this exposure, critics of bisexuality still viewed it as even more destabilizing and sinister than homosexuality. Fritz Klein elaborated on the nefarious reputation of the bisexual in his book *The Bisexual Option* (1978).

> The bisexual resembles the spy in that he or she moves psychosexually free among men, among women. As well, the bisexual resembles the traitor in that he or she is in a position to know the secrets of both camps, and to play one against the other. The bisexual, in short, is seen as a dangerous person not to be trusted, because his or her vision of party loyalty, so to speak, is nonexistent.[22]

Often mistrusted as the most duplicitous of deviant sexualities, bisexuality denies the heterosexual/homosexual binary. The bisexual visits both "camps" but has "loyalty" to neither.

The supposed threat of bisexuality has survived the 1970s and is part of current discourse, from popular advice columnist Dan Savage warning of the emotional dangers that threaten gay men and lesbians who date bisexuals,[23] to fear-inducing reports of African American men "on the down low," secretly having unsafe sex with other men and carrying HIV back to trusting wives and girlfriends.[24] The bisexual is constructed as a threat in these thrillers (as in real life) because he or she brings the menace of homosexuality into the domestic sphere of heterosexuality. Homosexuality may be threatening, but as long as it is something separate and distinct from heterosexuality, heterosexuals can recognize it and safeguard themselves. The bisexual spouse who blurs these distinctions brings homosexuality into the home, posing a danger to the innocent and unsuspecting partner and destabilizing the binaries that structure heteronormative ideologies: hetero/homo, safe/dangerous, clean/diseased, and us/them.[25]

Deathtrap, which premiered in 1978, performs the generic tropes and the cultural biases of its era; but Levin's postmodern thriller "plays" with these tropes and biases, particularly with respect to his characters' sexual orientation. As a result, the play is open to both normative and subversive interpretations. *Deathtrap* presents queer villainy but complicates this homophobic convention by locating the source of the villainy not in the queer characters' sexual orientation but in the closet that confines them. Even while Levin uses the closet to generate the shocks and thrills necessary to the genre, he creates a smart, nuanced depiction of how the closet actually functions. A close reading of *Deathtrap* reveals that this enormously popular play, sometimes dismissed, as many popular works are, as "mere entertainment," contains a surprisingly strong critique of the closet as a dark and deadly place.

Springing the Trap: Queer Killers Caught in the Closet

A pair of piercing blue eyes, topped with masculine black eyebrows and a black wave of hair, stares out from the poster and program art (designed by Frank "Fraver" Verlizzo) for the original production of *Deathtrap.* But where there should be a nose and mouth we see instead bold capital letters created by a typewriter spelling out "DEATHTRAP," with the final four letters in bright red. The letters function as a partial mask, such as a bandit might wear, obscuring the man's identity. The covered mouth also signifies secrecy, since this man is unable to speak, and perhaps even suffocation, since he is unable to breathe. We must then stare deeper into his eyes to search for any expression of the secret. Are the eyes seductive, inviting attraction and desire, or are they sinister, showing the predatory glare of the hunter staring down his prey? This man with an unspeakable secret is both seductive and threatening.

Deathtrap takes place entirely in the Connecticut home of Sidney Bruhl, a middle-aged playwright who has not had a hit in years.[26] The stage

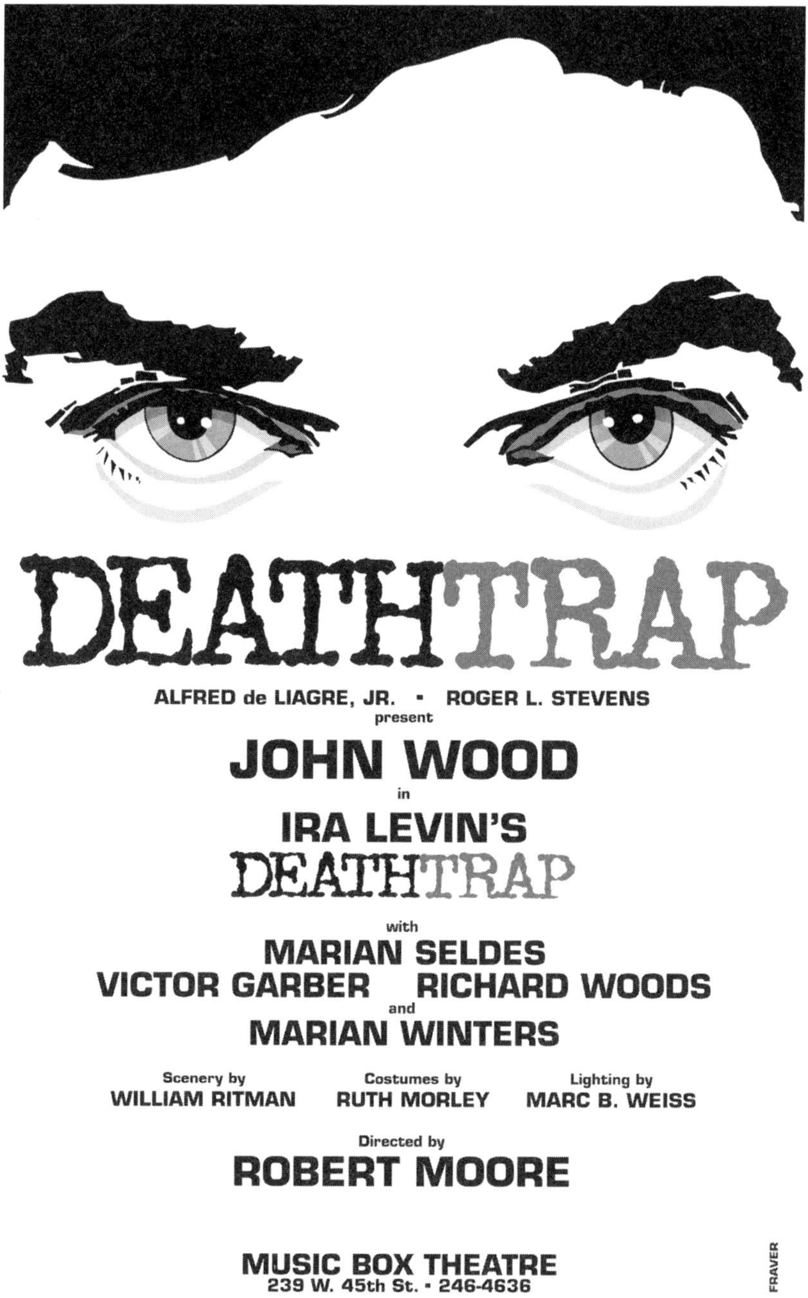

Window card featuring the artwork of Frank "Fraver" Verlizzo for the 1978 Broadway production of *Deathtrap* by Ira Levin. ©FRAVER

props that decorate his writing studio are evidence of his life's work as the creator of thrillers: guns, handcuffs, maces, broadswords, and battle-axes. As the curtain rises, Sidney tells his wife Myra that he has received a manuscript from a former student, one Clifford Anderson, who has written a play called *Deathtrap,* a "one-set five-character moneymaker." Sidney half jokingly says that he would consider killing his former student in order to pass the play off as his own, but the perpetually worried and highly strung Myra convinces him that it would be more prudent to collaborate with the young man. That evening at the Bruhl home, Clifford is impressed and flattered by Sidney's offer to collaborate, but he politely declines, convinced that *Deathtrap* is fine as it is. As Sidney gives Clifford a demonstration of some of his props, particularly Houdini's trick handcuffs, he suddenly grabs a garrote off the wall and strangles his guest to death. Myra is horrified, and as soon as Sidney has finished burying Clifford in the vegetable patch, she requests a divorce. They are interrupted by the arrival of Helga ten Dorp, a Dutch psychic who is renting the house up the road. She comes because she senses great pain in the Bruhl household, and she warns Sidney that a young man in boots will attack him. Soon after Helga leaves, Clifford, covered in mud and blood (and wearing boots), bursts into the house and clubs Sidney over the head with a piece of firewood. As he advances on the terrified Myra, she drops dead from a heart attack. Sidney gets up, and the truth is revealed: Sidney and Clifford are lovers who staged a fake murder in order to cause Myra's fatal heart attack.

In act 2, Sidney discovers that Clifford, who is now living with him as his "secretary," is secretly writing a play called *Deathtrap,* dramatizing everything that has happened so far: the ruse of a surefire playscript, the fake murder of a young playwright, the wife's fear-induced heart attack, and so on. Clifford tries to convince Sidney that in the current culture of scandal, the play's similarity to real life will only make it more successful. Sidney, however, is flabbergasted and refuses to let Clifford write the play.

> No. Absolutely, definitely *no.* I have a name and a reputation—tattered, perhaps, but still valid for dinner invitations, house seats, and the conducting of summer seminars. I want to live out my years as "author of *The Murder Game,*" not "fag who knocked off his wife." (52)

Clifford threatens to leave and write the play elsewhere, which drives Sidney to deceit: he pretends to relent and agrees to collaborate on writing the play. Under the pretext of "working out" some stage combat scenes for act 2, Sidney and Clifford confront each other with a variety of weapons. Soon, however, they begin to fight in earnest: supposedly harmless stage props become lethal weapons, and the struggle between the men culminates when Sidney shoots Clifford in the chest with a crossbow, and Clifford uses the same bolt to stab Sidney to death. A week later Helga ten Dorp and Sidney's lawyer, Porter Milgrim, piece together the events that led to Sidney's and Clifford's deaths and decide that it would make a great plot for a thriller. But they begin to argue over who has the right to write the play, and they threaten to kill each other as the curtain descends.

After successful tryouts in Boston and previews in New York, *Deathtrap* opened on Broadway at the Music Box Theatre on 26 February 1978. Directed by Robert Moore,[27] the cast included John Wood as Sidney Bruhl, Marian Seldes as his wife Myra, Victor Garber as his student Clifford, Marian Winters as the psychic Helga ten Dorp, and Richard Woods as the lawyer Porter Milgrim. *Deathtrap* opened to mixed reviews, with an especially bad notice from the *New York Times* critic Richard Eder. In the Sunday edition of the *Times,* however, Walter Kerr gave *Deathtrap* a rave review, as did other critics, who praised the play's clever plotting and mixture of witty comedy, thrilling suspense, and knowing satire of the theater world. In general critics who liked the play usually kept its secrets, making little or no mention of the queer "surprise." Critics who did not like the play, however, felt less obliged to be discreet. Eder led the pack by boldly stating, "Mr. Wood and the student are revealed to be homosexual lovers."[28] Erika Munk in the *Village Voice* made the same revelation, adding that "the use of homosexuality as a plot device is pure exploitation."[29]

While these critics should not, perhaps, have let the queer cat out of the bag, they did not ruin *Deathtrap* for audiences, since homosexuality is not just a shocking surprise at the end of act 1. Rather, the entire play can be read as a dark exploration of the sinister yet exciting duplicity involved in constructing and maintaining the queer closet. *Deathtrap* is remarkable because the characters, particularly Sidney as the masterful writer of thrillers, are amazingly skillful and clever (and therefore entertaining to watch) as they manipulate the truth and each other to achieve their goals. For Sidney the big deception, the one that masks the darkest truth and the one worth killing for, is the pretense of heterosexuality. By killing Myra, he avoids a messy divorce, which could expose his homosexual affair. By killing Clifford, he prevents the younger man from writing a play about their relationship. Sidney is motivated by the desire for wealth, fame, artistic success, and romantic happiness, but all these can be sacrificed if the appearance of heterosexuality is in danger. The closet must be maintained at all costs, even murder.

Sidney spends much of act 1 constructing his closet. One of the key techniques he uses is to accuse other people of queerness. Sometimes the comments are offhanded and comical, such as when Myra reprimands him for not knowing about their new neighbor, Helga ten Dorp.

> *Myra:* Sidney, what were you smoking Friday night when the rest of us were smoking grass? She's taken the McBain cottage for six months. Paul Wyman is doing a book with her. He was impersonating her for fifteen minutes.
>
> *Sidney:* Oh. I thought he was finally coming out of the closet. (10)

Sidney's gratuitous and bitchy comment is for the benefit of Myra *and* the audience. In the very first scene, Sidney has commented derisively on someone else's closet, thereby deflecting any suspicion about his own. The first scene also establishes Sidney as a habitual liar on matters both large and small, causing Myra (and the audience) to second-guess his motives and intentions. When friends call to invite them out, Sidney conceals their reason for staying home: to meet with a young playwright. Worried that Sidney is seriously planning a murder, Myra asks him why he lied, to which he responds, "Is it their business? *I* don't know why I lied; I'm just a liar" (13).

In act 2, after Clifford has moved in with Sidney and is even sharing a symbolically laden partners' desk with him, Sidney goes out of his way to maintain his closet. To divert any suspicions that his friend and lawyer Porter Milgrim may entertain about his relationship with Clifford, Sidney uses the technique of preemptive accusation against his lover. Sidney exposes and then defuses the issue by asking Porter if he thinks Clifford is gay. Sidney says:

> I have a sneaking suspicion he might be. . . . But, as long as he does his job well I suppose it's none of my business, is it? [. . .] Besides, people would talk if I took in a female secretary, wouldn't they? (43–44)

Through savvy manipulation, Sidney convinces Porter (who represents Sidney's privileged access to legal, financial, and social networks) that the very fact of hiring a handsome, young, male secretary, even one who "might be" gay, is proof of his own heterosexuality. For the audience, however, which already knows that Sidney and Clifford are lovers, this exchange is loaded with dramatic irony. Sidney must continue to hide his relationship with Clifford because that relationship is based on two crimes: murder and queer sexuality. If either one of those crimes is exposed, the other one will be exposed with it. The other important element of Sidney's exchange with Porter is the revelation of his readiness to betray his lover in the interests of preserving his own closet.

Sidney's wife Myra, the first victim of his duplicity, becomes another entry in Levin's collection of doomed wives. At the beginning of the play, Sidney's announcement that he has received a "perfect play" from a former student clues the audience in to Myra's impending demise.

> *Myra:* I should think you'd be proud that one of your students has written a salable play.
>
> *Sidney:* For the first time in eleven years of marriage, darling—drop dead. (8)

Dropping dead is precisely what Myra will do at the end of the first act. In contrast to the heroines of *Rosemary's Baby* and *The Stepford Wives,* however, Myra is not a wholly sympathetic victim. As a character, she can be unpleasant, both agitated and agitating with her fears and demands. Her ethics are also not unblemished. After Clifford's murder, she does not turn her husband over to the police and admits, "Part of me—was hoping you would do it" (35).

Genre conventions, however, dictate that Myra will not be an accessory but a victim. For a brief moment after Clifford's staged murder, Myra has a glimmer of insight into Sidney's duplicity. Telling him that his murderous actions are incomprehensible, she says:

> You're—alien to me, Sidney, and it can't be only since five o' clock this afternoon. You must always have been very different from the person I thought you were. (30)

Myra seems to be tapping into the core of the duplicitous-spouse drama: other people, even our most intimate and trusted companions, are ultimately unknowable and potentially dangerous. Even though Myra is reacting to Sidney and Clifford's fabricated scenario, she hits upon a crucial truth: her husband is capable of murder. She simply has not realized that he is capable of *her* murder. Sidney wants to keep Myra's wealth, but he does not want to keep her. More important, he wants—perhaps needs—to maintain his silence about his reasons for rejecting Myra, a secret better contained through murder than divorce. Myra is not the victim of Sidney's queer sexuality but of his need to conceal his queer sexuality.

The representation of queerness is oddly coded in *Deathtrap.* Both Sidney and Clifford exhibit attributes that might be read as stereotypically gay: Sidney "prowl[s] the antique shops" (17), and Clifford "work[s] out with weights every morning" (18). Even their mutual love of thrillers sounds vaguely like an old-fashioned notion about homosexuality. They were exposed to and got "hooked" on thrillers as adolescents, and Myra comments, "It sounds like a disease, being passed from generation to generation" (16). Furthermore, when Clifford sends the manuscript of *Deathtrap* to Sidney, the attached note says, "I couldn't stand the thought of waiting a few days to send my firstborn child off to its spiritual father" (8). Thrillers are both the carriers of a disease between men *and* the product of male-male intercourse.

A full revelation of queer sexuality comes at the end of act 1, shortly after Sidney and Clifford are revealed as accomplices in Myra's murder. Avoiding a sensational, shocking revelation of queerness, Levin instead lets it creep out through an exchange of smiles between the two men, with Sidney suggestively instructing Clifford to "get into bed and stay there" (39). Queerness becomes more explicit in act 2 as Sidney and Clifford live and work—and fight—together as a couple. When Clifford threatens to move out because he suspects that Sidney might harm him, Sidney makes a protestation of love.

> *Sidney:* Don't be silly. I—I love you; I wouldn't think of—trying to harm you. Besides, you'd break my neck.
> *Clifford:* Goddamn right I would. (53)

This moment, the most forthrightly "gay" in the play, is couched in threats and fears of physical violence, which is consistent with the representation of same-sex desire throughout the play. Sidney and Clifford speak to each other without the usual endearments, and physical contact happens only in moments of violent physical attack. Since the play does not depict homoerotic sexuality, homoerotic violence stands in its place. The play's only other moment of affection occurs as Sidney prepares to kill Clifford. He points the gun at the young man and sighs, "Oh God, I shall miss you very much" (62). Not, however, enough to stay his hand.

Ultimately, the real conflict between Sidney and Clifford, the one that leads to the second murder, is sparked by the closet. Sidney is terrified of being known as the "fag who knocked off his wife." His concern about being exposed as queer equals his concern about being exposed as a killer, especially since the two crimes are intertwined and collaboratively accomplished with the same man. That man, however, does not share Sidney's concerns about "public humiliation." Trying to convince Sidney to collaborate on *Deathtrap,* Clifford argues, "Everybody's opening up about everything these days, aren't they?" and accuses Sidney of being old-fashioned and uptight (52–53). It is hard to understand someone being "old-fashioned and uptight" about being accused, tried, and convicted of murder. Clifford's argument makes sense only insofar as it applies to coming out of the closet. In this Clifford displays something of a gay liberation era freedom from shame, while the older Sidney is still firmly rooted in embarrassment, secrecy, and lies. As Clifford notes, "Sidney uses three kinds of deodorant and four kinds of mouthwash; not for him the whiff of scandal" (62). But if Clifford "comes out" by writing *Deathtrap,* he will drag Sidney out of the closet with him. Therefore, to stop Clifford from betraying the mutual secrecy that binds collaborators, conspirators, and secret lovers, Sidney chooses to eliminate him. The closet must be maintained.

The murky depths of Sidney's closet are further indicated by his inability—and the play's refusal—to name his sexuality. When Sidney states, "I want to live out my years as 'author of *The Murder Game,*' not 'fag who knocked off his wife,'" it is the only time Sidney *names himself* as queer—while also saying he does *not* want to be named as queer. In a brilliant act of performative duplicity, Sidney simultaneously tells the audience that he *is* and *is not* a fag, both coming out and firmly shutting the closet door. Furthermore, a fag (indicating that one is homosexual rather than bisexual) is not something he calls himself but something he fears other people will call him. He cannily avoids labeling himself with any fixed sexual identity. The audience may understand Sidney as genuinely bisexual or as a gay man who was in a sham marriage. Similarly, audiences might interpret Clifford as gay or as a manipulative hustler who is simply using sexuality to gain privilege, wealth, and success from the older man. The lack of self-labeling, combined with their persistent habits of deceit, makes it impossible to fully know the true desires of either man. Thus the play deliberately (and, I would argue, queerly) avoids essentialized notions of sexual identity in depicting this same-sex relationship.

Many critics consider the coda to *Deathtrap* odd and unnecessary, but it presents yet another view of the closet and the desire to kill. With the three main characters dead by the final scene, the psychic Helga ten Dorp is left to explain to the lawyer Porter Milgrim exactly what has happened. They both have the same idea: the events would make a surefire hit play. But they begin to argue over the rights to this theatrical gold mine. If Porter will not grant Helga half the profits, she threatens to expose his dirty secret: he makes obscene phone calls to his friends. In retaliation, Porter hurls accusations at Helga—"Bitch! Whore! Foreign slut. Dutch pervert!" (68)—as Helga advances threateningly on him with a dagger. Although both characters are motivated primarily by greed in this comic scene, it is no coincidence that Levin raises the specter of "perversion" once more before the final curtain descends. Everyone, it seems, has some sexual secret, some closet, or some queerness that can be exposed or exploited, and the desire to prevent exposure leads inevitably to violence.

The performance and perception of queerness in *Deathtrap* is not fixed, and slippage was especially evident in the long run of the original Broadway production. As the play hit various landmark performances, New York critics took the opportunity to comment on some of the changes various lead actors had brought to the play. Five very different actors played Sidney Bruhl: (1) John Wood, a classical British actor best known for appearing in Tom Stoppard's intellectually sharp plays; (2) Stacy Keach, a handsome leading man onstage and in television; (3) John Cullum, who won Tony Awards for his work in musical comedies; (4) Robert Reed, best known to audiences as the suburban dad on the sitcom *The Brady Bunch;* and (5) Farley Granger, a boyish leading man in Hollywood in the 1940s and 1950s, known for his films with Alfred Hitchcock (including coded queer characters in *Rope* and *Strangers on a Train*). Although their sexuality was not publicly known at the time, both Reed and Granger would later become widely known as queer. Tabloid newspapers discussed Reed's "secret gay life" after his death in 1992, and Granger wrote about his bisexuality in his 2008 memoir *Include Me Out.*[30] Giving a quick overview of the various Sidneys, William Henry III of the *New York Sunday News* wrote:

> The central characters are two male playwrights. Sometimes there has been sexual tension between them, especially in what Levin reportedly considers the best version, the national tour with Brian Bedford and Kevin Conroy.
>
> By contrast, Cullum and Keach were stolidly macho as the older playwright. Wood was flamboyant but almost asexual. Reed was, in

> producer [Alfred] DeLiagre's words, "flitty"—but uninterested in the younger man.[31]

Henry's comments suggest that Levin's representation of the relationship between Sidney and Clifford is more connotative than denotative, leaving space for actors to perform (and audiences to perceive) varying degrees of queerness onstage.

The 1982 film version of *Deathtrap,* directed by Sidney Lumet from a screenplay by Jay Presson Allen, is more explicit and emphatic in its depiction of same-sex desire.[32] The film includes a kiss between Michael Caine and Christopher Reeve, which occurs immediately after Myra's murder and reveals Sidney and Clifford as conspirators and lovers. The kiss was immediately controversial. Talking to film scholar Vito Russo, Reeve commented:

> I heard that a preview audience in Denver booed the kiss, and that was reported in *Time* magazine, thus ruining the plot for millions of people. We later referred to it as "the ten million dollar kiss" as an estimate of lost ticket revenue.[33]

The kiss, of course, is meant to surprise and shock at this point in the narrative, but the kiss is also shocking because of the identity of the kissers: two major Hollywood stars, one identified with Superman, an icon of American masculinity.[34] At this time, Hollywood was experiencing an unprecedented flowering of mainstream films with queer subjects—*Making Love, Personal Best,* and *Victor/Victoria* were all released in 1982—but audiences generally knew what to expect from these films, thereby containing the threat of the queer. In *Deathtrap* same-sex desire was sprung on an unsuspecting audience, and many were not pleased.

Screenwriter Allen did more than just insert a shocking kiss. Unlike their theatrical predecessors, the men in the film address each other with terms of affection such as "dear," "baby," and "luv"—making the sexual relationship between Sidney and Clifford much more explicit in the second half of the film. Allen also added an exchange between Sidney and Clifford that tacitly plays into the homophobic notion that same-sex relationships are inherently immoral. As they argue about outing themselves by writing *Deathtrap,* Sidney accuses Clifford of being a sociopath, using Clifford's troubled youth as evidence.

Sidney: Clinically it means, as I'm sure you know, it means one who has no sense of moral obligation whatsoever. Now if, and I repeat if, I decide to kick over the traces and actually write *Deathtrap*—

Clifford: With me.

Sidney: Oh yes, of course, with you . . . If I decided to enter into such a risky and exciting collaboration, I wonder if . . .

Clifford: If what?

Sidney: If it would be, well, just a trifle starry eyed of me to contemplate a partnership where I could count on no sense of moral obligation whatsoever.

Sidney speaks of collaboration, of which there are at least three: the writing of *Deathtrap,* Myra's murder, and a queer relationship. The same-sex love affair is a "risky and exciting" partnership because it does not require any "moral obligation." Heterosexuality, often imagined in its idealized form as marriage, carries a whole host of moral obligations determined by religious, legal, and social structures; the same-sex relationship, however, exists in its own closet, removed from normative social institutions. The film states explicitly what is implicit in the play: a secret, illicit relationship may be thrilling, but it is also dangerous.

Escaping the Trap: The Afterlife of the Queer Thriller?

Theatrical and social landscapes have changed considerably in the years since *Deathtrap* premiered on Broadway. In the wake of its success, at least two other notable thrillers featured queer theatrical characters. In *Corpse!* (1984), by Gerald Moon, a queer actor plots to murder and take the place of his wealthy, straight twin brother.[35] The actor's skill in duplicity is crucial to the plot: although avowedly queer, he boasts that he can impersonate his womanizing brother because he is "versatile," raising once again the specter of the bisexual. *Accomplice* (1990), by Rupert Holmes, employs the metatheatricality of a play within a play within a play, as not one but two pairs of secret same-sex lovers use theatrical artifice in order to murder their spouses.[36] Both plays had modest runs in New York, which perhaps discouraged producers of the genre; since 1990 new thrillers on Broadway have become increasingly rare. Even in London, where

Christie's *The Mousetrap* continues to draw audiences, critics have noted that the thriller, as a genre, is "in the theatrical morgue."[37]

The decline of the thriller coincided with the expansion of the LGBT rights movement, which helped to change the position and increase the visibility of queer people in American society. Activists, scholars, pop culture bloggers, and organizations like GLAAD (founded in 1985) have opposed gay stereotypes—particularly the villainous ones—and championed representations of "normal" and even exemplary queer characters. And, for theatergoers who have experienced numerous plays with queer characters, queer sexuality is no longer surprising or taboo. Might today's audiences, so eager to see open, well-adjusted, and normalized queers, find the closeted queer killers of the thriller reprehensible, unpleasant, or as quaint as the electric typewriters and carbon copies that figure so prominently in the logistics of *Deathtrap?*

Social and cultural change seems to discourage revivals of Levin's play. In 1996 a touring production directed by John Tillinger and starring Elliott Gould received bad reviews and failed to come to New York. Chris Jones, the critic for *Variety,* complained that Gould "affects an inappropriately camp sensibility that suggests his sexual relationship with Clifford long before the audience is supposed to have figured that out."[38] In 2000 Leonard Foglia directed a revival starring Jonathan Hadary at the Paper Mill Playhouse in New Jersey. Alvin Klein of the *New York Times,* who found much of the play "dead" and "tired," also observed "a distinctly audible reaction, not to the thunder or the gunshots, but to Sidney kissing Clifford."[39] Despite the changes in the queer political landscape, it seems that the dramatic power of the closet remains strong, and an audience can still be surprised by a same-sex kiss that reveals a secret relationship and a secret motive for murder.

The most successful revival of *Deathtrap* opened in London's West End, directed by Matthew Warchus, in September 2010. While some critics decried the play's genre as terminally unfashionable, others praised the production's dark wit, declared it a hit, and predicted a Broadway transfer. This revival also highlighted how the closet no longer exerts as much force on people who make their living in the theater, since two openly gay actors played Sidney and Clifford: Simon Russell Beale, one of England's most acclaimed actors in classical and contemporary plays, and Jonathan Groff, a young American actor best known for his roles in the musical *Spring Awakening* and the television series *Glee.* If real life queer theatricals like Beale and Groff can thrive outside of the closet nowadays, then Sidney's desperate need to remain closeted may not seem as credible to a contemporary audience. Yet within the world of the play, a secretive same-sex relationship remains dramatically potent because it is inextricably linked to a murder. Even if most audiences no longer consider queer sexuality a dark secret, Levin's play makes it so by combining it with the act of murder.

Deathtrap cannot, however, be dismissed simply as a homophobic narrative that equates sexual deviance with murder in the interests of shocking audiences with the spectacle of queerness. Indeed, this thriller can function as a site of queer pleasure, especially for audiences who appreciate the queerly inverted world of the postmodern thriller. In this genre, duplicity is not a moral failing but an asset in a strategic, high-stakes game in which survival requires deception. Normative social behavior and even law are abandoned here, as the audience secretly hopes that the murderers will "get away with it"—and that the lovers will "get away with it" too. Sidney and Clifford share their secret desires with the audience, thereby making them part of their erotic game. Although the play lacks any explicit physical displays of those desires, *Deathtrap* has the potential to crackle with erotic energy as Sidney and Clifford, usually played by handsome and charismatic actors, enact violent scenarios that cause them to sweat, cry, gasp, grunt, and bleed. The final dramatic scenario of two men stabbing each other with a phallic arrow might be experienced as a dark but erotic fantasy of same-sex desire.

Fantasy narratives often allow audience members to enjoy anarchic pleasures before returning them to reality and the status quo, and *Deathtrap* concludes with the genuine fear of the deadliness of the closet. The play dramatizes the difficulty of keeping a terrible secret and the anxiety around the threat of exposure. Even within the artifice of the thriller genre, queer spectators may see a fantastic reflection of their own real experiences of the closet. The play enacts the fear that love cannot exist inside a closet since there can be no trust between lovers who are bound by guilt and shame. Sidney must ultimately destroy his lover in order to keep his secret. The closet is the deathtrap, and maintaining the closet quite literally is murder.

Audiences can still find queer pleasures in *Deathtrap* because it demonstrates the insidious functioning of the closet—not just in the heady post-Stonewall days of gay liberation but in contemporary queer culture as well. Rarely fully open or fully closed, the individual's closet door is often ajar, swinging back and forth in a constant negotiation of silence and disclosure, threatening to trap the individual who hovers on the threshold. In order to function successfully as a thriller, *Deathtrap* must trade on ambiguity: characters cannot be fully closeted or fully exposed but must exist instead on a threshold of possibility. Levin's thriller exploits the ambiguities of its cultural moment, when the relatively new concept of gay pride wrestled with the dominant discourse of queer villainy and shame, creating a broad cultural fascination with peeking inside closet doors, even while most social systems worked to keep the closet firmly in place. Sidney and Clifford are simultaneously in and out, protagonists and villains, murderers and victims. The ambiguity of their identities may not challenge the homophobic spectator to reconsider his or her preconceptions, but it does create a more intriguing plot and the possibility for progressive interpretation; rather than condemning queer characters as inherently sinister, the play shows the closet itself as the sinister force—the "deathtrap" that causes shame, duplicity, and violence.

Even with the advances in LGBT rights in recent years, our culture still vacillates between acceptance and rejection of queer people, leaving the closet door swinging on its hinges with varying degrees of openness and concealment. Individually and collectively, queer people may be out in the open, but they are still stigmatized and vilified. This is why the repression and the anxieties of the closet still matter—and as long as they do, a thriller about negotiating the closet will have the power to intrigue, provoke, and entertain. Indeed, an audience that fully understands the vicissitudes of the closet will perhaps find more value and meaning in such a play.

Not all closets are the same, and it would be a mistake to universalize the experience of the closet as it is depicted in *Deathtrap*. Scholars of African American sexuality such as Roderick A. Ferguson and Marlon B. Ross have argued that race, class, and other social differences affect the construction of sexual identities and that the closet is not the appropriate paradigm for all queer subjects.[40] Indeed, *Deathtrap*'s closet may be particular to its era and the milieu of its affluent white male characters. But if the play can still draw an audience, its appeal may rest on the enduring dramatic potency of secrecy, revelation, shame, and guilt. While these experiences and feelings may be heightened for some queer people, they are hardly unique to queer people. The duplicitous queer characters of the postmodern thriller tap into a variety of experiences and conflicted emotions around the closet, creating a world of ambiguity where homophobia and homoerotic fantasy merge, the sexuality of the villainous protagonist simultaneously threatens and thrills, and the audience finds pleasure in both the enactment and the containment of murderous desire.

CHAPTER FOUR

Rage and Revelry

At the same time that postmodern comedy thrillers were successful in the commercial mainstream theater, a very different brand of queer theatricality was flourishing in very different venues. Previously, straight playwrights, with varying degrees of homophobia, had created homicidal homosexuals in plays produced at mainstream theaters that presumed straight audiences.[1] But the growth of off- and off-off-Broadway in the 1950s and 1960s created alternative venues and radical changes in the representation of queer characters. Many factors contributed to this striking shift. Free of the commercial demand for hit plays that appeal to the widest possible audience, smaller, alternative theaters could be more daring, in both the style and the content of their plays. The decline of stage censorship laws, which had barred the representation of gay and lesbian characters, also allowed for greater freedom of expression. Mart Crowley's hit off-Broadway play *The Boys in the Band* (1968), featuring an ensemble of gay characters, broke new ground, and the Stonewall Riots of 1969 helped spark the gay liberation movement. In the wake of these events, the culture saw an increasing number of plays by queer theater artists who were creating performances for predominantly queer audiences and exploring what queer characters—including homicidal homosexuals—could be, do, and mean onstage.

The late 1960s and 1970s witnessed the flowering of what has been called *queer theater*, offering not pleasant depictions of "normal" gay life but a performance aesthetic that is transgressive in both form and content, queering the normal rather than normalizing the queer. The thrillers of the previous chapter might be considered the Swiss watches of contemporary theater: carefully constructed, finely tuned, functioning with precision, and expensive. Queer theater, on the other hand, is more like a

Rube Goldberg contraption: stringing together cheap materials and found objects, quirky, inventive, and somehow still capable of accomplishing its goal. Since queer theaters exist on the margins of mainstream culture, they often have a certain freedom to be theatrically daring and indulge a wider range of expression, bursting with an emotional, physical, and imaginative outrageousness that would be deemed "excessive" in mainstream theaters. The result is a theater that acts out against the repression and restriction of the closet, featuring queer characters who engage in both sexual and violent behavior, bringing the homicidal homosexual into yet another theatrical realm.

The aesthetic at the heart of this style of performance is often categorized as *camp,* a term that has been much debated by scholars and practitioners. Camp became one of the first subjects of critical inquiry into a specifically queer style of theatricality, explored by Susan Sontag in her 1964 essay "Notes on Camp" and then by Stefan Brecht in his 1978 book *Queer Theater.*[2] Brecht described and analyzed the overarching style and attitude he observed in the works of Jack Smith, Ronald Tavel, John Vaccaro, Charles Ludlam, and others from the mid-1960s to the mid-1970s in New York. He finds this style of theater

> portraying mankind as low (lecherous and depraved), evil (malevolent and vicious) and ridiculous (preposterously pretentious, foolish and devoid of dignity and stature), and love as the supreme lie, but upholding the aesthetic ideal . . . the beauty of the low, the evil and the ridiculous.[3]

Camp describes a performance style that mixes highbrow and lowbrow genres, the sublime and the vulgar, and an ironic sensibility that simultaneously satirizes and celebrates the artificiality of the theater, with cross-dressing as a common convention. Furthermore, Brecht points to the artists' anger and rage as part of the exuberance of their art, and later critics have also noted the political function of camp, using outrageous humor as a weapon against the repression of the closet and subverting the values of the dominant culture.[4] Queer theater, then, is a theater that is sometimes cruel in the Artaudian sense but more often burlesque and carnivalesque, not just mixing highbrow and lowbrow art forms but mixing the expression of "noble" emotions and ideals with orgiastic sexuality, gluttonous appetite, and gory violence.

The early queer theater described by Brecht existed outside mainstream commercial theaters, functioning on the fringe and usually without much financial profit. For the most part, these performances did not play to large audiences over extended runs but to small audiences for brief engagements; critics often ignored them, and their texts (if texts existed) were left unpublished. Although some audience members may have been slumming with the desire to experience a queer "freak show," the queer theater often fulfilled W. E. B. DuBois's criteria for a community-based theater: for us, by us, about us, and near us. Indeed, most of the queer theater in New York occurred nowhere near Broadway but in off- and off-off-Broadway theaters, clubs, and downtown lofts, particularly in Greenwich Village and the Lower East Side, neighborhoods known for their queer and bohemian inhabitants. In other cities, such as London, Toronto, Chicago, and San Francisco, queer theaters existed under similar conditions: removed from the mainstream and located in the "gay ghettos" that became more prominent during the gay liberation era. But certain works from the queer theater found a modicum of success, breaking out of the queer cultural ghetto, reaching wider audiences, and even entering the "mainstream." The most critically acclaimed practitioner was Charles Ludlam, who led his own company, the Ridiculous Theatrical Company, from 1967 until his death in 1987, writing, directing, and starring in twenty-nine plays.[5]

Excessive and Outrageous: Queer Killers in the Realm of the Ridiculous

Ludlam was a native of Long Island and a graduate of Hofstra College who joined John Vaccaro's Play-House of the Ridiculous in 1966 before forming his own troupe.[6] His early plays were epic in scope: grand pageants with large casts, often borrowing classical, mythological, or Elizabethan plots and themes, filled with spectacles of sex and violence, and employing cross-gender casting. His first production with his own company was *Conquest of the Universe, or When Queens Collide* (1967), which retells the story of Tamberlaine with wanton violence and exuberant pansexuality. The interplanetary warrior Tamberlaine turns the kings and queens of the worlds he conquers into sexual slaves, and he develops a particular fondness for Bajazeth, the King of Mars. Tamberlaine is a comic grotesque, descended as much from Alfred Jarry as from Christopher Marlowe. His uncontrolled sexual desires are matched by his uncontrolled murderous rage: near the end of the play, he brutally murders his wife and their nine infant children. The sexual monster and murderous monster are one and the same, but they are presented in a style that subverts the impulse to pathologize or moralize with an appeal to id-driven fantasy and revelry.

Ludlam achieved his first major critical success with a play featuring another queer monster, *Bluebeard* (1970), which combines science fiction and Victorian woman-in-jeopardy narratives, liberally sprinkled with dialogue from a variety of sources, including *Richard III, Doctor Faustus,* and *All About Eve.* Ludlam's hero-villain is a mad scientist who surgically mutilates men and women in his quest to create a "third gender," turning them into genitally deformed "freaks," who cannot return to normal society. He is satanic, cavorting with Hecate, using children's body parts for his surgery (135), and standing against all "good" values, including marriage, motherhood, and Christianity. And like the bisexual murderers of the commercial thrillers, Bluebeard is particularly dangerous because he marries women under false pretenses and then destroys them. Also as in the thrillers, Bluebeard is a man of the theater: an amateur playwright who thinks of his experiments—his endeavors to create new characters, as it were—as works of art, even if others deride his work as "queer quackery" (129). Ludlam's fevered theatrical imagination makes Bluebeard more than a mere "bisexual," however; he is perversely pansexual, his desires encompassing men, women, and uncategorizable creatures of his own devising. Traditional notions of gender and sexuality are further ruptured when considering the play in performance, where heterosexuality is performed by gay men and lesbians, as in an infamously over-the-top sex scene between Ludlam's Bluebeard and Lola Pashalinski's Miss Cubbidge, or by gay men in drag, with Mario Montez's Leopard Woman and Gary Tucker's Mrs. Maggot placing themselves in "heterosexual" relationships with other men. The result is a play that mocks conventional heterosexuality and also gleefully indulges in, and even encourages the audience to root for, queer villainy.

Conquest of the Universe, Bluebeard, and many other plays of the Ridiculous Theatrical Company were not quite in step with the gay liberation politics of their day. In an interview given late in his career, Ludlam looked back and commented on the disapproval that sometimes met his plays.

> People wanted gay theatre to be a political theatre that catered to gay people's needs for group reinforcement and self-respect, dignifying the gay image. My theatre is terrible for dignifying anybody's image.

> The people who wanted to show the respectable gay image—La Coste shorts and pleats—were horrified that in my plays they were always disreputable drag queens, and that monstrosities were being committed. In my plays, people exhibit terrible behavior because it's showing the ridiculous side of life.[7]

For Ludlam, neither theater nor homosexuality should be about normalcy. He argues, "Gay people should be more *queer.* We shouldn't give up our difference." Ludlam is opposed to theater that attempts to show that gay people can be "just as straight as straight people."[8] He notes that "dangerous characters [are] more interesting" and that his theater is inherently not "straight": "This theatre is weird, it is odd, it's peculiar, it's eccentric, it's different."[9]

Ludlam's queer killers, then, can serve a variety of functions in the theater. He appropriates magnificent monsters like Tamberlaine and Bluebeard and incorporates deviant sexuality into their personas. Because the characters are "ridiculous," they exaggerate and satirize common notions of gay villainy, but they also invite the audience to indulge in the fantasy of gay villainy. Ludlam's outrageous queer killers stand in direct opposition to notion that gay people should conform to standards of middle-class propriety in order to "earn" their rights in American society. If the increased visibility of gay people during this era resulted in greater pressure to "keep up appearances" for the sake of social acceptance, then Ludlam's theater offered a fantastic escape into a theatrically excessive world in which sexuality and murderous rage defied the tyranny of "good taste" and allowed audiences to revel in the odd, the eccentric, and the dangerous.

Of course, Ludlam did not create this sensibility on his own, and many theater artists operated in the same atmosphere during the late 1960s and 1970s, influencing and inspiring each other to varying degrees. The performances created by Jack Smith, Ronald Tavel, and John Vaccaro, as well as the collective collaborations of troupes like the Cockettes and Hot Peaches, often explored the boundaries of queer impropriety, finding the theatricality of overlapping queer sexuality with violence and murder. The aesthetics and techniques of these queer theaters found their greatest mainstream success when they were appropriated for a British musical that became a cultural phenomenon in the United States. *The Rocky Horror Show* (1973), which shares certain plot elements with Ludlam's *Bluebeard,* is a camp rock and roll musical by Richard O'Brien that was not initially successful on the American stage when it premiered in 1975, but after being turned into what is arguably the most successful cult movie in history, *Rocky Horror* was successfully revived on Broadway in 2000 and has become a cult industry, with countless productions by amateur and student groups throughout America.[10]

Reimagining classic horror films through the glam rock bisexuality of the 1970s, *Rocky Horror* centers on a transvestite mad scientist from "Transsexual Transylvania," Dr. Frank-N-Furter, who is trying to construct the perfect male lover, along the way seducing both men and women and killing off his "failed" experiments. In one particularly ghoulish sequence, the mad doctor chases one of his creations with a pickax, kills him, and then serves the remains to his dinner guests. Frank-N-Furter is stereotypically "queeny," originally played by Tim Curry on both stage and screen as a cross between Mick Jagger and Joan Crawford. Dressed like a vampire-dominatrix, Frank-N-Furter is a pansexual menace who must be (and is) stopped, but he is also a prophet of sexual liberation, urging the audience "don't dream it, be it"—a call that was taken up by a generation of fans who repeatedly came to screenings of the film version dressed as their favorite characters, performing floor shows and interacting with the characters onscreen, merging cinema with live performance and making the audience's theatrical outrageousness part of their sexual liberation. When the mad doctor is defeated, it is a sentimental moment that begs the audience's sympathy, and while the "good" characters may return to reality, we know that they will never return to "normalcy." The murderous, sexually omnivorous queen is both the hero and the scapegoat, an erotic Prometheus who shares the secret of sexual knowledge but must ultimately be punished for it.

Some critics would argue that camp is not a quality that resides in the work of art but rather is a transgressive perspective or "way of seeing" that artists and audiences can share. The camp dynamic of Ludlam's *Bluebeard*, originally performed by gay and lesbian theater artists in a gay community, may not be the same as that of *The Rocky Horror Show*, a commercial commodity that potentially contains the queer as a spectacle for nonqueer audiences. It is important to acknowledge the circumstances of production to appreciate the wide range of possible interpretations of the camp queer killer. O'Brien's Dr. Frank-N-Furter is a hero-villain who might be admired and emulated by audiences, but he can also be mocked and demeaned by fans interacting with the film or play, often in homophobic terms. He can also be almost completely normalized and packaged for mass consumption. In 2010 the popular television series *Glee* depicted a group of high school students performing *The Rocky Horror Show* onstage, but Frank-N-Furter was played by a female character, the word *transsexual* was eradicated from the song "Sweet Transvestite," and Frank-N-Furter's murderous rampage was not depicted. The sinister alignment of queer sexuality and murder was eliminated from the narrative, leaving a representation that was perhaps mildly "naughty" and "weird" but sadly lacking in any camp transgression, particularly for a queer audience.

Less seductive but more transgressive than Frank-N-Furter was the other evil queen of the midnight movie circuit, Divine (aka Glen Milstead), a three-hundred-pound cross-dressing performer most famous for starring in the low-budget, independent films of John Waters. She also starred in the off-off-Broadway plays of Tom Eyen and performed onstage with the San Francisco–based hippie-drag troupe the Cockettes. In Waters's *Pink Flamingos* (1972), Divine created her most infamous role, Babs Johnson, who performs all sorts of "filthy" acts—from incest to murder to shit eating—to beat her rivals for the title of "Filthiest Person Alive."[11] The point of her murders and other disgusting acts is to prove her superiority to the world: she is the best at being the worst, thus turning her queer abjection into triumphant queer supremacy. In nearly all her roles during the 1970s, from the homicidal good girl gone bad in Waters's *Female Trouble* (1974) to the sadistic bull-dyke prison matron in Eyen's *Women Behind Bars* (1976) and the murderous burlesque performer in Eyen's *The Neon Woman* (1978), Divine played women who were vicious in both senses of the word: morally depraved and dangerously aggressive.[12] Divine's characters are also poor or lower middle class (i.e., "white trash") and distinctly without Ludlam's classical erudition or Curry's rock and roll glamour. Stefan Brecht described Divine's roles as embodying the bad taste and artlessness of "proletariat vulgarity,"[13] but the homicidal tendencies of all her roles point to more than a lack of social and theatrical graces. In a culture that criminalizes both the poor and the queer, and positions (female) ugliness and fatness as moral flaws, Divine's filthiness and violence can be read as revenge against a world that has either done her wrong or not given her her due. In doing so, she champions and encourages her audience to root for those who are despised and disposed of by "normal" society—a celebration of trash as a style of performance and a countercultural way of life.[14]

Crossing Over: Charles Busch's Multiple Personality Disorder

The influence of the queer theaters of the gay liberation era is evident in the work of Charles Busch, who became one of the most successful practitioners of queer theater in the 1980s and 1990s. As a prolific playwright, drag performer, and guiding spirit of his own company, Theater in Limbo, Busch has often been compared to Charles Ludlam.[15] In many of his plays, he takes the role of a murderous woman, although she tends to earn the audience's sympathy and ultimately exist in a moral (i.e., not a "ridiculous") universe. While presenting early works in fringe venues like the Limbo Lounge in New York's East Village, Busch earned mainstream success with *Vampire Lesbians of Sodom* (1985), which transferred to the Provincetown Playhouse and ran for five years. In it Busch (in drag) and Meghan Robinson played rival vampires, traveling from biblical Sodom to 1920s Hollywood to modern-day Las Vegas.[16] Although no one is actually murdered onstage, the audience hears many stories about the young virgins these two evil women have destroyed, and the 1920s segment presents a parody of the seduction of an innocent fiancée by an older sophisticated woman from Edouard Bourdet's 1927 lesbian drama *The Captive*. But these monsters are also eternal outsiders, having to keep their secret identities (read the closet), hounded by crucifix-wielding vampire hunters (read religious homophobes), and never finding peace, security, or love. It is no coincidence that they are also "show people": stars of stage and screen whose lust for virginal blood is matched only by their lust for fame and top billing.[17] These lesbian vampires are dueling divas, trading bitchy barbs and clever insults, until at the end they realize that as eternal enemies they only have each other to depend on and they desperately need each other. Busch knows that it's fun to play the villainess, but even monsters have feelings, so he makes his vampire lesbians endearing to the audience and gives everyone a happy ending based on queer solidarity.

Busch's other major hit of the 1980s is *Psycho Beach Party*, a campy parody of teenage surfer flicks of the early 1960s. Teenage Chicklet (read Gidget) has a multiple-personality disorder, and one of her personas is Ann Bowman, a sexual dominatrix with plans to take over the universe. Again mixing violent aggression with show biz ambition, Busch reveals that Ann "wants to set up concentration camps for her enemies and public executions and her own NBC variety series."[18] Ann Bowman also demands sex from the surfer boys—something the virginal "good girl"

Leading lady Madeleine Astarté (Charles Busch) prepares to bite into the neck of innocent ingénue Renee Vain (Theresa Marlowe) in the 1985 off-Broadway production of *Vampire Lesbians of Sodom* by Charles Busch. Photo: Adam Newman.

Chicklet would never do. Chicklet's murderous persona is the same as her sexual persona, and it is not difficult to read her multiple personalities as a metaphor for the closet, which separates the secret "monstrous" sexual self from the cheerfully presentable nonsexual self. The multiple personalities also serve as a metaphor for drag performance, in which the performer's body becomes "home" to a slew of outrageous personalities. It is only after being "healed" through psychotherapeutic ritual that Chicklet can emerge as a mature woman capable of heterosexual happiness—which happens to look a lot like homosexual happiness, since Chicklet is played by Busch.

In the film version of *Psycho Beach Party* (2000), Busch adds a serial killer to his screenplay and turns the role of Chicklet over to a female performer, Lauren Ambrose.[19] The audience is led to suspect Chicklet of the murders, but the real culprit is Larry, a sociopath who kills people because they have physical imperfections. This twist creates a parable in defense of queerness: people suspect the abnormal Chicklet of murder, but the real threat is from the seemingly supernormal Larry, who despises abnormalities in others. Even when a woman plays Chicklet, however, the multiple-personality disorder of the character can function as a metaphor for the sexual closet. Indeed, it creates an even stronger comparison between the supposed monstrousness of male homosexuality and that of *any kind* of female sexuality, which has, historically, been "closeted" and considered both evil and shameful. *Village Voice* critic Laurie Stone argued in her review of the play version that Busch is, in fact, a feminist, different from earlier, "traditional" drag queens, who depicted femininity as "a debased state" and a part of themselves that they despised. "He not only enjoys the femme part of himself," she wrote, but "he sees it as admirable: theatrical, emotionally expressive, receptive, and seductive."[20]

While Busch's earlier works often reflect the carnivalesque sensibilities of Ludlam, his later works are more direct parodies of Golden Age Hollywood melodramas, although they still contain sexual and violent excess. In plays like *Die! Mommie! Die!* and *Shanghai Moon* (both 1999), Busch's murderous heroines exist in a moral universe, so even though they are sympathetic, they are not allowed to get away with their crimes. In *Die! Mommie! Die!*, set in the 1960s, Busch is Angela Arden, an aging pop singer who murders her abusive husband (with a poisoned suppository) so she can be with her younger lover. Near the play's end, we learn that Angela is actually Barbara Arden, the less talented, down-on-her-luck twin of Angela who murdered her sister and assumed her identity. She makes a full confession, and with great dignity she turns herself over to the police.

Shanghai Moon parodies the "yellow peril" narratives of the early twentieth century, which imagined white women sexually enslaved by Asian men.[21] Set in China in the 1930s, the play follows the glamorous Lady Sylvia Allington (played by Busch) as she falls prey to General Gong Fei (played off-Broadway by B. D. Wong). She finally escapes her cruel lover by murdering him, but then she must face a trial in which her secrets are revealed. We learn that Lady Sylvia was formerly a tough-talking poor girl from Chicago who "raised [her]self from the gutter by way of the carnival midway" as a "novelty hula dancer." She stole money to travel to England, where she "passed [her]self off as an American debutante."[22] In both *Die! Mommie! Die!* and *Shanghai Moon,* Busch presents a murderous heroine with show biz in her blood, a secret criminal identity in her past, and a strong sexual appetite. The queerness and rage of these characters are made explicit in a heartfelt speech that Sylvia makes in her defense before a packed courtroom.

> I will speak the truth if you can take it. Can you take it? All of you sitting there squarely in your seats judging me, secure in your picture of me as a woman of ill repute, smug in your own morality. Could you face the truth about yourselves?[23]

In this moment, the audience of *Shanghai Moon* is cast in the role of the audience at Sylvia's trial. Sylvia/Busch stands up as a woman/queer of "ill repute," a tawdry performer masquerading as a grand lady, and guilty of murder, which metaphorically stands in for sexual crimes: in Sylvia's case, adulterous affairs and miscegenation; in Busch's case, homosexuality and cross-dressing. Sylvia/Busch angrily defies "smug" and hypocritical moralizing, refusing to be a scapegoat for other people's hidden truths.

In the end, both Angela and Sylvia earn forgiveness for their crimes, Angela from her children and Sylvia from the court. But neither woman can escape her guilt, and in keeping with Hollywood codes of decency and morality, Angela goes off to prison and Sylvia deliberately sniffs a poisoned chrysanthemum and dies. Busch follows this pattern again in *Judith of Bethulia* (2012), in which he plays a biblical heroine who, in order to save her people, beheads the despotic Holofernes and then sacrifices herself. When playing these murderous heroines, Busch succeeds in having it both ways: he simultaneously plays these melodramas for their genuine sentimentality and mocks them for their ludicrous constructions of gender, romance, and morality. He takes delight in transgression, yet his heroines must pay the penalty for their crimes. In the process he redeems the murderous heroine—and the queer performer—not only with sympathy but also with dignity.

In his early analysis of queer theater, Stefan Brecht recognized that rage was an intrinsic part of the camp sensibility, and one can certainly see the anger expressed in Ludlam's and Busch's murderous characters. Within the culture at large, gay rage became even more vocal in the 1980s and 1990s as gay and lesbian activists fought against political and social policies that positioned homosexuality as a threat to "family values." The Reagan administration's seeming indifference to the loss of gay lives during the early years of the AIDS crisis further devastated the gay community. Across the country, LGBT people organized chapters of radical groups such as the AIDS Coalition to Unleash Power (ACT UP), Queer Nation, and the Lesbian Avengers. Emblematic of the times was the clarion call made in a leaflet, distributed by Queer Nation during the Gay Pride parade in New York in 1990, entitled "Queers Read This: I Hate Straights."

> They've taught us that good queers don't get mad. They've taught us so well that we not only hide our anger from them, we hide it from each other. WE EVEN HIDE IT FROM OURSELVES. We hide it with substance abuse and suicide and overachieving in the hope of proving our worth. They bash us and stab us and shoot us and bomb us in ever increasing numbers and still we freak out when angry queers carry banners or signs that say BASH BACK. . . . LET YOURSELF BE ANGRY.[24]

In the queer theater of the 1980s and 1990s, this rage achieved greater expression than ever before, with the queer killer functioning as an avatar of anger. Unlike more mainstream systems of theatrical production, this milieu also fostered a vibrant lesbian theater culture, and women's theater collectives channeled their rage into powerful queer killer characters of their own.

The Lesbian Killer: Shameless Orgies and the Death of the Good Girl

While the majority of this book's subjects are murderous gay male characters, it would be negligent to write about the queer theaters of the 1980s and 1990s without also discussing the key examples of lesbian killers that emerge from this milieu. Lesbian theater is often distinct from gay male theater, with its own systems of production, political contexts, aesthetics, and codes of interpretation. As scholar David Savran has noted, gay men in the theater still benefit from male privilege and "have achieved levels of visibility and power in theater that are routinely denied women, whether straight or lesbian."[25] While women were frequently collaborators in queer theaters like Ludlam's Ridiculous and Busch's Limbo, women also founded their own theater spaces, creating work that was for, by, and about women.

Lesbian killers are not simply the "female versions" of the more prevalent gay male murderers; as female characters in a sexist society, they occupy their own unique cultural position. Yet both gay male and lesbian characters are queer subjects in a homophobic society and therefore may find common ground in the theater, just as they do in politics. Furthermore, distinctions of gender and sexual identity may become blurred in the theater, particularly in queer performances that destabilize these categories. How, exactly, does an audience read a straight sex scene when the actors involved are a gay man and a lesbian, as in Ludlam's *Bluebeard?* What if two lesbian actors, with one of them in male drag, enact a straight romance, as in *The Secretaries* by the Five Lesbian Brothers? What happens when a butch woman and a gay man in drag play out a lesbian seduction, as in Busch's *Vampire Lesbians of Sodom?* Such queer performances open themselves up to a variety of different interpretations, perhaps depending on the fantasies (or fears) of the individual audience member.

With the rise of the feminist movement, women's theaters and lesbian performance groups developed around the country during the 1960s and 1970s.[26] One of the most lasting and influential began as an international festival in 1980 and eventually found a home in New York's East Village under the name WOW, or the Women's One World Café. Much has been written about the WOW Café, and the performances produced there have served as the basis for much of the theoretical and critical writing about feminist performance and lesbian representation in the 1980s and 1990s.[27] Since its beginning as a festival organized by Pamela Camhe, Jordy Mark, Peggy Shaw, and Lois Weaver in 1980, WOW has presented numerous works and more than a few "crossover" successes, including plays by Holly Hughes, Split Britches (the collective of Shaw, Weaver, and Deb Margolin), and the Five Lesbian Brothers.

In *Lady Dicks and Lesbian Brothers,* Kate Davy writes that the WOW Café was unique because "lesbianism was assumed on stage and in the audience," allowing for performances that created different kinds of representations and significations. Davy acknowledges that "gay male culture has been an obvious and important influence on WOW's development, but it is neither the only influence nor the primary one." So while it was very much a part of the same East Village club scene that produced Charles Busch, "WOW remained on the margins of this marginalized scene" and developed an aesthetic separate from the drag-queen-dominated performances of that sphere.[28]

Holly Hughes was instrumental in creating one of the house styles of the WOW Café, which C. Carr described as "dyke noir."[29] Her 1983 cult hit *The Well of Horniness* was an over-the-top all-female burlesque that was part parody of the classic lesbian novel *The Well of Loneliness* (1929) by Radclyffe Hall, part trashy lesbian pulp novel, and part radio soap opera, complete with vocal sound effects, organ stabs, and commercial breaks.[30] In the play, Vicki is engaged to marry Rod, but her secret past as a member of a "sapphic sorority" is in danger of being exposed when she meets Rod's lesbian sister, Georgette. When Georgette is shot dead in a lesbian lounge, Vicki is suspected, and private detective ("lady dick") Garnet McClit is on the case. Garnet falls in love with Vicki and reveals that the real killer is Babs, the tough-talking hatcheck girl who was Georgette's previous lover. Babs (who is greeted with hisses each time she enters) tries to frame Vicki and is about to kill Rod, but suddenly the scene shifts—and we realize that everything we've seen was Vicki's dream.

Babs the killer lesbian was, in fact, imagined by Vicki, a closet case who fantasizes about "killing off" her own lesbianism so she can be "the best little wifeypoo a man could ever want."[31] Yet Vicki is perhaps also expressing a fear and desire when she fantasizes that Babs will kill Rod, thus relieving Vicki of the need to be a wifeypoo and allowing her to continue her affair with the lady dick. Even while the play revels in campy presentations of the villainous dyke, Hughes exposes the actual murderous rage (and lesbian passions) in the dream life of Vicki, the femme who has "defected" from the sisterhood and is trying to pass as straight. Repressive heteronormativity becomes the real villain of the play. Of course, the heteronormativity in *The Well of Horniness* is presented queerly, since a woman plays Vicki's future husband Rod, and the playwright herself originally played Vicki. Kate Davy has argued that Hughes's work "liberated lesbian and feminist theater from the 'good-girl syndrome,'" freeing it from the need to beg for acceptance and allowing it to be "sexy and dangerous."[32] Hughes's play about the expression and repression of erotic and violent passions set the stage for similar works that would find a home at the WOW Café.

Dark fantasies fueled by stifling realities are also central to Split Britches' *Lesbians Who Kill* (1992), which had two main sources of inspiration: news stories about serial killer Aileen Wuornos and Margolin, Shaw, and Weaver's rage over and frustration with rampant sexism. The play is, in part, an expression of what Sue-Ellen Case has called "gender anger."[33] *Lesbians Who Kill* is set entirely in and around an automobile, where a couple named May (Weaver) and June (Shaw) wait out a thunderstorm and listen to radio reports about two killer lesbians on the loose. The claustrophobic confines of the car are contrasted with the expansive actions and emotions of the women's violent fantasies, which take a variety of forms: they reenact a Hollywood melodrama (*Deception*) in which Bette Davis (May) shoots Claude Raines (June), they fantasize about murdering men who are strangers to them, they fantasize about murdering Frank Sinatra and Ed McMahon, they sing about stopping the men who are empowered by a patriarchy of violence, they threaten to kill each other, and they threaten the audience.

Even though May and June don't kill anyone, they feel and express a murderous rage, and, as Lynda Hart points out, they feel they must be guilty of murder because, like the women demonized on the car radio, they are also lesbians.[34] Interestingly, it is often May (the "femme" Weaver) who pulls the trigger or is the aggressor in these fantasies, but it is June (the "butch" Shaw) who is disappointed that May is not actually a murderer and ends the play by confessing to the audience, "I'd love to watch her *really* kill somebody."[35] In acknowledging the difference between these fantasies of murder and "real" murder, the members of Split Britches acknowledge the gap between themselves as theater artists and Aileen Wuornos as an actual murderer, yet it also creates a sort of bridge. Although Split Britches' violence is not "real" (i.e., it is theatrical), it expresses very real rage over very real sexism and homophobia, which are silencing, demoralizing, and threatening to very real women.

Perhaps the most acclaimed lesbian killer play to come out of WOW is *The Secretaries* (1993) by the Five Lesbian Brothers, known individually as Maureen Angelos, Babs Davy, Dominique Dibbell, Peg Healey, and Lisa Kron. Writing and performing their plays collectively, the Brothers found a home at WOW, where their first play, *Voyage to Lesbos* (1990), told the story of Bonnie leaving behind her lesbian lovers in order to marry Brad—

although just before she does, the maid of honor appears at the wedding covered in blood, apparently having just killed Brad. Like Hughes's *Well of Horniness,* this early play is structured around the anxiety created by one of a group of women "leaving the fold." *The Secretaries,* however, is about a woman entering the fold.[36] Up in the wooded mountains of Big Bone, Oregon, the secretaries of a lumber mill welcome Patty into their all-female circle, initiating her into a cult with its own secret language, strict rules regarding diet and sexual activity, and monthly rituals of murder and mayhem. Under a full moon, the secretaries hold a wild party in the woods, a savage bacchanal in which they eat junk food, swig alcohol, blare heavy metal music, wear sexy lingerie, and cut a lumberjack to bits with a chain saw. The play follows Patty's resistance and eventual submission to the group, as she finally abandons her position as the overachieving "good girl" and joins the other secretaries in acts of murder.

It is not a coincidence that the Brothers are a collaborative collective, and *The Secretaries* is very much about the power and violence of which a *group* of women is capable, as well as the de facto lesbianism of such a group in the popular imagination. While the single murderous woman has a proud lineage in drama (Medea, Clytemnestra), there is also ancient precedent for dramatizing a group of women as a murderous and sexually deviant cabal. Throughout *The Bacchae* of Euripides, Dionysus insists that the women who participate in his rites are "chaste."[37] But the young king Pentheus is obsessed with what he believes to be the women's "obscene disorder," "filthy mysteries," and "shameless orgies." He is eager to be a spectator—that is, an audience member—at the performance of the sexual secrets he imagines the women share with each other. His curiosity and blasphemy result in his brutal murder at the hands of the band of frenzied women, including his own mother.

This notion of "Bacchic violence"—the frenzied physical power that exists among women when they join forces, uncontrolled by men—occurs in modern drama, both as a celebration of feminist collective power and as an eroticization of patriarchal fears of women's power, often read as "man hating," which carries the assumption of "lesbian." As Lynda Hart makes clear, "If desire always verifies masculinity, whatever the subject's sex, so does crime."[38] Since lesbian desire is seen as active rather than passive, the lesbian is seen as a masculine woman, thus taking the place of (and erasing the need for) men. Aggression and violence are also constructed as masculine, so the violent woman is considered an unwomanly woman. Gender deviance, sexual deviance, and criminal deviance are intertwined, and thus the female murderer is always a lesbian, and the lesbian is always a murderer.

The Secretaries, however, troubles this "killer dykes" formula because the women's motivation for murder is *not* revenge against the political, social, or sexual crimes of men. Indeed, the Brothers have complained that the murdered men in *Voyage to Lesbos* and *The Secretaries* were given more prominence in the reviews of male critics than they had in the plays themselves.[39] When Patty questions why the women want to kill Buzz Benikee, her gentle boyfriend who "never hurt anyone," Susan, the "cult leader" of the secretaries, explains, "We don't kill them because they're bad. We kill them because we're bad" (180). *The Secretaries* is, at least in part, about the impossibility of being good all the time, especially within the narrow confines of how *good* is defined for women in our society, not just by men but by women themselves. Patty works hard at being "good" and "pretty," but this is just a facade that masks her darker feelings. Susan tries to win Patty over by forcing her to realize that only the other secretaries understand and appreciate her true, complex self.

> I love you. Peaches, Ashley, Dawn—we love you. Buzz doesn't love you. He loves an idea of you. I even love the killer in you. Now that's love. (180)

What Patty comes to learn from Susan is that she cannot maintain the charade of being perfectly good and pretty and that she has "dirty" and "ugly" feelings, including the desire for sex with another woman and enough rage to commit murder.

Patty "crosses over" and joins the secretaries because they alone understand and give her the space in which to express this side of herself. For most of the play, the women keep very tight control over their bodies—their clothes, hair, food, sexuality, and even menstruation are all regulated, often by physical force—but on "kill night" they can indulge their physical appetites and desires in a carnivalesque ritual that involves "stuffing their faces with pizza and cake, chugging Jagermeister, and screaming drunkenly," as well as "wearing wacky, slutty lingerie" and otherwise "going off the deep end" (184). During the murder itself, the victim is only a screaming voice offstage. The play deliberately focuses on the perpetrators—their feelings, their desires, their expression of the physical self.[40]

The Secretaries is first and foremost a comedy, and nonrealistic theatricality allows it to combine laughter with blood and parody with pointed

After the slaughter, Peaches (Lisa Kron), Ashley (Babs Davy), Patty (Dominique Dibbell), Dawn (Maureen Angelos), and Susan (Peg Healey) confront the audience in New York Theatre Workshop's 1994 production of *The Secretaries* by the Five Lesbian Brothers. Photo: Joan Marcus. Courtesy of Theatre Communications Group.

criticism. The characters break the fourth wall and directly address the audience, they participate in choral chants ("We are secretaries and we do things secretarial / And once a month we kill a guy and cut him up for burial"), and they sometimes communicate with each other in an invented "clicking and giggling" language. The play also features Maureen Angelos playing Buzz (in drag) and the "out" lesbian Dawn, both of whom have sexual relations with the play's main character. One possible result of this double casting is breaking down the strict division between hetero and homo, since regardless of whether Patty is having sex with Buzz or Dawn she is having sex with characters played by the same actress. Other comic exaggerations exist throughout the play, including the "hallucination" that Patty experiences during the adrenaline rush of clubbing a wombat to death (173).

Interestingly, the combination of nonrealistic theatricality, feminist critique, dark humor, queer anger, bloody violence, and explicit lesbian sexuality worked together to create the Brothers' most popular and acclaimed work. After its start at the WOW Café, *The Secretaries* was presented at major queer performance venues in San Francisco, Los Angeles, Seattle, and Houston before coming to a "mainstream" off-Broadway theater, New York Theatre Workshop, in 1994. The play won an Obie Award and was eventually published in a trade paperback anthology of the Brothers' plays.[41] The Brothers succeeded in bringing their funny and vicious bacchanalia to a mainstream audience, and while some audience members may have walked out (as Dibbell notes in the published edition) and some critics seemed to miss the point, other audience members were thrilled and turned this play about a murderous cult into a cult hit.

Hell Is for Children: The Next Generation of Bloodbags and Beauty

Many of the queer artists who dramatized queer killers in the 1990s found inspiration in elements of popular music and youth subculture. The anarchic and confrontational aesthetic of punk, with its celebration of violence, and the dark and macabre aesthetic of goth, with its eroticization of death, influenced a particular subset of queer culture. The aesthetics of the queer-punk subculture were evident in the New Queer Cinema of the 1990s, particularly in films by Gregg Araki and Bruce La Bruce, as well as in novels by Dennis Cooper. In at least one notable instance, theater artists combined these aesthetic influences with the traditions inherited from Ludlam and others to create wildly theatrical spectacles of glitter and gore. Blacklips Performance Cult performed at the Pyramid Club in the East Village beginning in October 1992 and presented different performances nearly every Monday night through March 1995.[42] The group consisted of fifteen core members of both sexes and various sexualities, some known only by their first names (Antony, Lulu, Hattie) and others with stage names like Sissy Fitt and Psychotic Eve. Blacklips' members were decidedly queer, with both men and women in drag, and they performed at a queer venue for a largely queer audience. They called themselves a "performance cult" in order to sound "dangerous," according to troupe member Kabuki Starshine,[43] and they were distinguished by an excessive use of gore.

Although the scripts varied in style and tone depending on which member had scripted that week's event, certain genres dominated, particularly twisted parodies of classic gothic stories (*Frankenstein*, *Dracula*), fairy tales (*Sleeping Beauty*, *Hansel and Gretel*), gory history (*Jack the Ripper*, *The Swiss Family Donner Party*), or tabloid headlines (*The Amy Fisher Story*). No matter what the story, nearly every performance featured murders, blood, and body parts spilled onstage and sometimes flung at the audience. The performances were gleeful horror shows that, despite or perhaps because of their often childlike frivolity, could occasionally stun an audience with the appearance of genuine anger or anxiety about death. Blacklips never won mainstream attention, and there is not much evidence left of its performances. But for a brief period it was the highly prolific creator of a queer-drag-punk-goth subculture that found unique expression in "bloodbags and beauty."[44]

The links between queer culture and horror were also evident in Theatre Couture's 2006 adaptation of Stephen King's first novel, *Carrie*.[45] *Carrie* tells the story of a teenage misfit with telekinetic powers who avenges herself on her cruel classmates by turning prom night into a deadly inferno. Sissy Spacek won acclaim playing the title role in Brian DePalma's popular 1976 film adaptation, while theater aficionados remember the disastrous 1988 stage musical version as one of the most notorious flops in Broadway history.[46] The persistent fascination with Carrie, in all her various incarnations, is perhaps rooted in America's interest in the tension between individuality and conformity, queerness and normalcy. Therefore Theater Couture's queer reinterpretation of *Carrie,* with drag performer Sherry Vine (aka Keith Levy) playing the title role, uses camp comedy not simply to send-up *Carrie* but to highlight the themes of gender and sexual difference inherent in the original story. The result is a playful revenge fantasy for anyone who ever felt awkward, lonely, or "queer" in high school.

Set in 1979, the play follows the Cinderella story of Carrie White, a painfully shy girl who is taunted and bullied by all her classmates, never more so than when she has her first period in the gym shower. She finds little comfort at home with her Bible-thumping mother, who tells her that menstruation is the result of sinful desires and then locks her in a closet to force her to pray to Jesus for forgiveness. But Carrie begins to notice that at times of great stress or anger she can move things with her mind: teacups break, and light bulbs burst.

One classmate with a conscience, Sue Snell, decides to help Carrie, so she persuades her own boyfriend, Tommy, to take Carrie to the prom. At first Carrie assumes that the invitation is a prank intended to humiliate her, but once she is convinced of Tommy's sincerity, she allows herself to believe that she has found her Prince Charming. Defying her mother, she goes to the prom and is elected queen, only to have her moment of triumph ruined when a cabal of students dumps a bucket of pig's blood on her. Stunned and enraged, her mental powers unleash hell, trapping everyone in the school and burning them alive in a horrific blaze. She returns home and crucifies her mother with kitchen knives before burying herself under an imploding house.

Following the tradition of Charles Ludlam's *Camille,* writer Erik Jackson and director Josh Rosenzweig take a female character—a social outsider and victim who finds a reservoir of strength but is ultimately doomed—and reinterpret her as a drag diva, adding material that underlines the character's queerness. When she is bullied into the prayer closet by her mother, Sherry Vine's Carrie whines, "But Momma, I don't wanna go in the closet!" and then gives the audience a knowing look. Later Carrie's mother begs her not to go to the prom, crying, "You're leaving me for a man, just like your father," pausing just long enough to allow the audience to consider the similarities between the daughter's coming of age and the father's pursuit of a gay relationship. Watching an actor in drag perform Carrie with a mixture of pathos, irony, and wicked glee, it is easy to interpret *Carrie* as the story of a queer boy who is rejected by heteronormative high school society and is further oppressed by his hyperreligious and virulently antisex parent. When his innocent dreams of fitting in and finding love with a handsome jock are cruelly dashed, he destroys both high school and home, empowered by a murderous rage.

The play's framing device is Sue Snell, the sole survivor of the horror, recounting events before an investigatory commission. In her final speech to the authorities, Sue sympathizes with Carrie and warns that society should not mistreat its outcasts and "freaks" or we can expect more such bloodbaths in the future. She warns that Carrie was not unique and there are more victims of abuse out there, just waiting to explode. Carrie, rising from the dead, appears behind Sue, looks out to the audience, and utters the play's final warning—"We are everywhere"—which some might recognize as one of the rallying cries for recognition during the gay liberation era. By creating a queer Carrie, Couture gave its audience a camp travesty of a well-known horror film, but it also tapped into queer feelings of alienation and oppression and queer fantasies of empowerment and revenge.

The figure of the genderqueer victim-perpetrator was also placed center stage in Kate Bornstein's *Strangers in Paradox,* a Grand Guignol comedy that premiered at San Francisco's Theatre Rhinoceros in 2003. As the creator of plays, performances, and theoretical texts about transgender identity, Bornstein functions quite differently from drag performers like Charles Busch or Sherry Vine, who "cross genders" for the sake of theatrical performance. Bornstein and other transgender activists question the gender binary itself, often using gender-neutral pronouns such as ze (instead of he or she) and hir (instead of him or her). In hir plays, ze has created characters who transition from one gender to another, and in some cases elude the gender binary altogether. [47] In doing so, Bornstein has also shed light on the way all gender is constructed through performance. Ze is also one of the few theater artists to create a specifically transgender queer killer in the American theater.

In *Strangers in Paradox,* a transsexual lesbian named Casey and hir partner in crime (known as "The Kidd") meet at a goth club, become lovers, and go on a murder spree. They practice "consensual murder," since all their victims are tired of their empty bourgeois lives and agree to be killed. Meanwhile, imprisoned in an insane asylum is a woman named Angel who knows all the details of Casey's crimes, but Angel's body bears the wounds of all forty-two murder victims too. Angel seems to embody the guilty psyche of the murderous lesbian killers (and she may, in fact, be the grown-up version of The Kidd), so she identifies both with the criminals and with the victims. Just as Bornstein's performances frequently collapse the supposed dichotomy of "opposite" genders, here ze finds a theatrical method for erasing the clear distinction between murderer and murder victim, as well as between the queerness of the outlaw and the normativity the murderer destroys.

In one particularly provocative moment, Casey presents hirself as a male actor and confronts a gay male playwright. The playwright believes theater should present only good role models and ennobling representations of gay people. Casey insists that artists must be free to explore the bad and the dark in everyone. The playwright ultimately admits that his plays are awful, conceding the argument and his life to Casey. Thus Casey both argues for and enacts the role of the "bad" queer—even while the play expresses anxiety about the violence, madness, and guilt that trail the figure of the queer killer. *Strangers in Paradox* uses the figure of the transgender lesbian killer to explore the ambivalence and ambiguity surrounding gender, normativity, and theatrical representation itself.[48]

While the many queer theaters that have presented queer killers do not form a single movement or even participate in a single aesthetic, they do share some common traits. They tend to combine an Artaudian sense of visceral theater with a carnivalesque focus on the corporeal. This combination sets the stage for performances that explore the sexual and violent capabilities of the human body, often "ridiculously" with imagination and exaggeration that defy realism, but are still tied to social and political realities. Rather than displacing sexual crime though the metaphorical use of murderous crime onstage, queer theaters dramatize *both* crimes, placing them side by side in a world that invites audience members to enjoy their own status as sexual outlaws but also to express their rage over being labeled sexual outlaws by a homophobic society. Since society views queer gender and sexuality as "monstrous" and tries to contain the monster by keeping it in the closet, queer theaters offer a space in which the monster can run free. Perhaps the monster wreaks more havoc than necessary in these theaters, but one can hardly blame the monster for wanting to get a few things out of its system since it has been caged for so long. Besides, we know the monster can do no real damage as long as it is kept inside the walls of the theater. Yet theater walls can be more porous than we realize. The queer killers of the queer theater can play a crucial role in breaking down the closet: with "excessive" theatricality, they break the silence, brazenly mock the shame, and allow audience members to engage in visceral expressions of both sexuality and murderous rage.

CHAPTER FIVE

Arias of Love and Death

At the same time that theater artists like Charles Busch and the Five Lesbian Brothers were creating queer killers on the cultural fringes, some gay male playwrights found artistic homes at mainstream theaters. As dramas began to appear less frequently in the commercial theaters of Broadway, more new American plays emerged from not-for-profit off-Broadway and regional theaters. In these venues, certain gay playwrights created homicidal homosexuals quite different from those found in queer theaters. Rather than staging the "ridiculous" aspects of rage and revelry, these playwrights worked to ennoble the homicidal homosexual, and to do so they returned to the original prototype: the gay man who kills his abandoning lover. It is unlikely that Terrence McNally and Chay Yew, writing in the 1980s and early 1990s, were familiar with *The Drag,* since it was largely neglected in theater history and the text was not widely available until 1997. Nevertheless, the homicidal homosexuals discussed in this chapter are theatrical descendants of Mae West's David Caldwell, created out of similar theatrical conventions but responding to decidedly modern circumstances.

Produced in mainstream theaters for predominantly straight audiences, these plays participate in a serious attempt to endow gay love with the urgency, passion, and importance usually attributed to heterosexual romance. At the same time, though, they also express the fear that gay love cannot be realized in a society wracked with homophobia, racism, and other forms of oppression. Both *The Lisbon Traviata* (1985) by Terrence McNally and *Porcelain* (1992) by Chay Yew use operas as intertextual referents, reworking and reimagining operatic formulas and themes to explore modern gay relationships, ennobling same-sex desire by appropriating the cultural prestige and emotional depth associated with this highbrow form.

McNally's domestic realism and Yew's abstract lyricism operate in widely dissimilar theatrical styles. Yet both plays feature an abandoned gay lover who turns to excessive violence in order to make others take his romantic feelings seriously. Persuading predominantly straight audiences—and critics—to invest in gay passions, however, sometimes proved difficult, and this chapter focuses on the cultural fault lines made evident by the troubled production histories and mixed critical responses faced by these homicidal homosexuals.

Divas, Opera Queens, and Sublime Death: The Operatic Scene in Gay Male Culture

Maria Callas:	Is there anything you would kill for, Sharon?
Second Soprano:	I don't think so.
Maria Callas:	A man, a career.
Second Soprano:	Not off the top of my head.
Maria Callas:	You have to listen to something in yourself to sing this difficult music.

Terrence McNally, *Master Class*[1]

Most scholars trace the beginnings of opera to the Italian Renaissance of the late sixteenth and early seventeenth centuries, when early operas were presented as court entertainments by writers and composers who believed they were re-creating the drama of ancient Greece with words set to music to enact tragic stories.[2] Following the opening of the first public opera house in Venice in 1637, opera became a popular art form throughout Europe by the eighteenth century. During the nineteenth and early twentieth centuries, opera librettists continued to find inspiration in a variety of sources, including ancient myths, the Bible, and Shakespeare. Frequently librettists turned to popular melodramas for source material, thus borrowing character types, plot machinations, and social values from the era's dramas. Stage melodramas served as the basis for at least three operas that figure prominently in this chapter: Giuseppe Verdi's *La Traviata* (1853), based on *La Dame aux Camélias* by Alexandre Dumas fils; Giacomo Puccini's *Tosca* (1900), based on the play by Victorien Sardou; and Puccini's *Madama Butterfly* (1904), based on the play by David Belasco.[3] All these operas feature women who suffer for love, then die before the final curtain.

The melodramatic use of the suffering woman, she who dies for love or must be punished for an improper love, is explored by Catherine Clément in her ground-breaking feminist analysis *Opera: The Undoing of Women* (1979). She notes that those women who fall outside the bounds of the bourgeois family, such as courtesans and Gypsies, are made into "temporary queens" of the opera, but ultimately they must be sacrificed in order to maintain patriarchal authority. [4] Like the characters she portrays, the opera singer—the diva—is also a pawn in men's game of social power and relationships, and Clément chastises men who refuse to understand the woman and instead idolize the image. Nowhere is this idolatry more evident than in the cult surrounding Maria Callas, the Greek American soprano famous for her emotive portrayals and tragic personal life. In a biting passage, Clément vents her anger: "Come on, men, shut up. You are living off her. Leave this woman alone, whose job it was to wear gracefully your repressed homosexual fantasies."[5]

Although Clément may be taunting straight male opera fans with intimations of *psychically* repressed homosexuality, she has also hit (inadvertently?) on an explanation for the phenomenon of gay male opera fans, colloquially known as "opera queens." The opera diva enacts fantasies of which the gay fan is psychically conscious but which are *socially* repressed and barred from representation on the stage. The opera queen is quite aware of his fantasy of same-sex romance, but since he cannot enact that story within a heterosexist culture, the diva is sent in his place, and through her he vicariously enjoys the passions of the operatic heroine. Clément interprets this identification as inherently misogynistic, but a male audience member's identification with a female character is not necessarily an act of erasure or displacement. Indeed, Clément herself points out that masculine and feminine roles cannot be essentialized when she notes that it is not just women but *the feminine*—including "the weak sons, the lame, the hunchbacks, the blacks, the foreigners, and the old men—those who are like women"—that must be defeated by the opera's end in order to maintain patriarchal hierarchies.[6]

Wayne Koestenbaum in *The Queen's Throat: Opera, Homosexuality, and the Mystery of Desire* (1993) explores the notion that opera can counteract (or at least serve as a temporary escape from) homophobic repression and oppression. Koestenbaum positions opera as an excessive art form in which emotions, actions, and appearances transcend the ordinary, and therefore serves a crucial function for queer people who suffer the effects of the closet.

> Opera has the power to warn you that you have wasted your life. You haven't acted on your desires. You've suffered a stunted, vicarious existence. You've silenced your passions. The volume, height, depth, lushness, and excess of operatic utterance reveal, by contrast, how small your gestures have been until now, how impoverished your physicality; you have only used a fraction of your bodily endowment, and your throat is closed. This rushing intimation of vacuity and loss . . . isn't a solely gay or lesbian experience, but unsaid thoughts and unseen vistas particularly shaped gay and lesbian identities in the closeted years of the nineteenth and twentieth centuries, the dark ages, when the shadow world of the opera queen flourished.[7]

This explanation also applies to contemporary plays that borrow the "excessive" themes and techniques of opera. Rather than interpreting opera as queer fantasy, *The Lisbon Traviata* and *Porcelain* co-opt the operatic milieu and put it in the service of queer drama. As Koestenbaum notes, "A queer person may occasionally want his or her emotions to be public and statuesque as heterosexuality."[8] McNally and Yew appropriate the operatic as a means toward achieving this expression, giving their queer characters the heightened emotions and actions of the operatic.

Murder, He (Re)Wrote: Inconstancy and Inconsistency in The Lisbon Traviata

> *Paul:* It sounds like a murder mystery. *The Lisbon Traviata.*
> *Stephen:* You think so?
> *Paul:* Well, a mystery anyway. Something with criminals. *The Lisbon Traviata. The Maltese Falcon. The. . .*
> *Stephen:* You have a vivid imagination.[9]

The first act of *The Lisbon Traviata* is set in the plush and cozy Greenwich Village apartment of Mendy, a middle-aged, flamboyant opera queen who becomes frantically obsessed with obtaining a rare pirated recording of Maria Callas's performance of *La Traviata* in Lisbon in 1958. Stephen, his friend and dinner guest this evening, engages him in scathingly witty banter about opera divas and gay tricks, but he won't go home to fetch his copy of the record. We learn that Stephen can't go back to his apartment because his live-in lover of eight years, Mike, has invited a younger man over for a date. The frustration of both men—Mendy who can't find love, Stephen who is scared of losing love—is poured into their mutual obsession with opera. The second act takes place the next morning in Stephen and Mike's steel and chrome high-rise apartment. Mike and his new boyfriend Paul have spent the night together, much to Stephen's dismay. Becoming increasingly desperate and vindictive, he attempts to intimidate Paul and humiliate Mike, showing Paul some sexually explicit photos taken of him and Mike early in their relationship. Stephen also uses opera as a weapon, loudly blaring music from the stereo until Mike retaliates by punching him in the face, causing him to bleed. Horrified by the violence, Paul leaves. As another step toward ending their relationship, Mike cuts up the photos with a pair of scissors. When Mike attempts to leave the apartment to start a new relationship with Paul, Stephen takes the scissors and stabs him. While Stephen plays *La Traviata* and then *Madama Butterfly* on the stereo, Mike bleeds to death in his arms.

The Lisbon Traviata took a somewhat difficult and twisted path on its way to becoming an off-Broadway and regional theater hit, and the controversy focused largely on the murder at the end of act 2. The playwright, Terrence McNally, had had his share of hit comedies, including *Next* (1969), *Bad Habits* (1974), and *The Ritz* (1975), but after the failure of *Broadway, Broadway* (1978), he began to write for television rather than the theater.[10] His association with director John Tillinger helped facilitate his return to the theater in the mid-1980s, although Tillinger recalls that it was not an easy return: "I mean people were just not putting on his plays. We did readings of *Lisbon Traviata* at the Playwrights Horizons and the Public Theatre, nobody wanted to do it."[11] The play was produced as a showcase by Theatre Off Park in 1985 and went on to subsequent productions at Manhattan Theatre Club (MTC) in 1989, with a commercial extension at the Promenade Theatre, and then in San Francisco and Los Angeles in 1990—and in each case McNally changed the script, omitting the murder in the Promenade version and reinserting it for the West Coast production.

On 4 June 1985, *The Lisbon Traviata* opened at Theatre Off Park in New York's Greenwich Village, the very neighborhood in which the play takes place. Most of the New York critics praised the performances and direction, and many applauded the comedy in act 1 (although they felt it necessary to classify it as "bitchy humor"), but they criticized the murder at the end of the play as "melodramatic," "sadistic," and "excessive."[12] Often in homophobic terms, some critics insisted that they were unable to identify or sympathize with the characters: John Simon wrote in *New York* magazine that the play offered "a glimpse into an abyss that is deadly but uncathartic,"[13] while Clive Barnes in the *New York Post* insinuated that you could identify with the murderous Stephen only "if you are a homosexual playwright with a writer's block and a disillusioned, faithless lover." Furthermore, he chose to read the play as an indictment of an entire group: "If this is the gay life, give me straight misery."[14]

Along with the climactic murder, the other point of controversy surrounding the 1985 production was the play's frank presentation of sexuality between men. Barnes's opening sentence refers to the play as "vigorously uncensored," Gussow closes with a warning that it has "a frankness that may offend some theatregoers," and Simon reports that "homosexual sex is graphically evoked, shocking at least two of my colleagues audibly." The review in the industry-oriented *Variety* concludes, "*Lisbon* is too indigenously gay and sexually explicit for mainstream popular appeal."[15] In each case, the critic, presumably too sophisticated to be unnerved by sexual frankness, displaces his discomfort unto others, including other critics and the "general public," meaning straight people. Not coincidentally, these critics' responses reflect the reluctance to discuss sexuality and the insistence on seeing gay people as separate from the "general population" that led to government inaction during the early years of the AIDS crisis. *The Lisbon Traviata* premiered during the same season as Larry Kramer's *The Normal Heart* and William Hoffman's *As Is,* and like those plays it encourages audience identification with gay characters who are explicitly sexual. Clearly, not all critics were willing to make that identification in 1985. Homosexual acts, which are not actually performed onstage, are more shocking than murder, which is performed onstage.

The professional standing of Terrence McNally, John Tillinger, and *The Lisbon Traviata* changed dramatically between 1985 and 1989. The playwright and director created a critical and popular success at MTC, a mainstream, off-Broadway, subscription-based theater, with *It's Only A Play* (1986), a rewritten version of *Broadway, Broadway* starring James Coco (who had won acclaim in McNally's early hit *Next*). Tillinger cemented his relationship with MTC with successful revivals of Joe Orton's *Loot* (1986) and *What the Butler Saw* (1989), and McNally created a major hit with *Frankie & Johnny in the Clair de Lune* (1987). With MTC as their artistic home, Tillinger and McNally had a producer that was willing to take a chance on reviving *The Lisbon Traviata,* and the play opened at City Center Stage I on 2 June 1989.[16] It was a minor hit, due in part to the casting of Nathan Lane, an actor who would go on to be one of McNally's regular collaborators and one of the most successful stage actors of his generation.

McNally made many changes in the script for the MTC production, including a shift away from hints of autobiography: Stephen is now a fiction editor at Knopf rather than a playwright. Also Mike has become a doctor, making him and his new partner, Paul the social worker, a couple that works in practical fields that aim to help and heal humanity, in marked contrast to the aesthetically obsessed older opera queens. McNally has developed Mike's character more thoroughly, even giving him an appearance in act 1, in which he stops by Mendy's apartment to drop off the record of the Lisbon *Traviata* (although it turns out he mistakenly brings the London *Traviata,* much to Mendy's dismay), giving the audience a glimpse of the awkward tension and sadness that exists between Mike and Stephen. The confrontation in act 2 between Stephen and Mike has also been extended, giving their relationship greater depth and weight. Another major change concerns a heightened awareness of AIDS, which, as *Village Voice* critic Michael Feingold noted, was now "an ominous factor in the promiscuity-vs.-fidelity debate."[17] As in the previous version, Paul leaves before the final confrontation, but whereas in the earlier version "*we should get the feeling that Paul and Mike will never see each other again,*"[18] now Paul calls Mike shortly after he leaves, arranging a meeting so the two can talk, which indicates that there is still hope for their relationship.

Most critics continued to voice two major complaints: the radical difference in tone between the comic first act and tragic second (they "have basically nothing to do with one another"),[19] and the melodramatic violence of the murder at the end of the play ("not convincing in this domestic drama").[20] The disparity between the two acts seems to have been exacerbated by the universally praised comic performance of Nathan Lane as Mendy ("one of the great theatrical turns"),[21] with some critics feeling that he should be the play's main character and condemning his absence in the second half of the evening ("it is Mendy we really care about after all, not the constipated Stephen").[22] Only Mimi Kramer in the *New Yorker* argues for the organic link between the acts of this "almost perfect play," noting that comic Mendy and tragic Stephen both "have really been singing the same aria in different keys" as they become petulant over elusive objects of desire.[23]

Still, nearly all hailed the play's script as much improved, and, in perhaps the most remarkable turnaround, found the play accessible, moving, and "universal." Clive Barnes called it "extremely entertaining and even

Stephen (Anthony Heald) and Mendy (Nathan Lane) in the first act of Manhattan Theatre Club's 1989 production of *The Lisbon Traviata* by Terrence McNally. Photo: Gerry Goodstein. Courtesy of Billy Rose Theatre Division, The New York Public Library for the Performing Arts, Astor, Lenox and Tilden Foundations.

moving," and, even when contemplating the play's more unpleasant aspects, John Simon found that there were "moments of lurid but genuine illumination; horror is infiltrated by compassion." John Horvath in *Show Business* insisted, "McNally has successfully dramatized some very universal truths and feelings about failing relationships, needs, and possessiveness, truths which are guaranteed to speak to any audience, anywhere."[24]

In another shift from 1985, only the *New Yorker*'s Kramer makes any mention of the play's sexual frankness, and she refers to it merely as "a lapse in taste." The most hostile review, however, came from a critic writing for a gay newspaper. Whereas the critic for the *New York Native* in 1985 found the play disturbing but honest in its presentation of "hatred (self- and general),"[25] in 1989 John Hammond has no doubts that *The Lisbon Traviata* is homophobic, writing that it

> treats us to one act of generally funny and enjoyable farce and a second act that is embarrassing in its portrayal of gay men as fragile, shallow, fickle, self-centered, and mentally dangerously unstable, incapable of relating to, or communicating with each other except at the moment of their own self-inflicted destruction.[26]

Hammond condemns these failings as stereotypical and fears that they are "stroking and soothing the prejudices of audiences." This heightened awareness of the homophobic stereotype and its potential interpretation by straight audiences is also a product of the intervening four years. The Gay and Lesbian Alliance Against Defamation (GLAAD) was founded in 1985, and queer scholarship critiquing representation, most notably the revised edition of Vito Russo's *The Celluloid Closet* (1987), reached a wider audience during the late 1980s. Considered in light of the rage that, for example, led to the formation of ACT UP in 1987, Hammond's expression of anger over McNally's play may be understandable, but it also reduces this complex play to a matter of "positive" or "negative" representation.

Despite controversies about sex and violence, *The Lisbon Traviata* was a success, and MTC made plans to extend the play's limited engagement into a commercial run at the Promenade Theatre, an off-Broadway house on West 76th Street. But clearly McNally felt some pressure to reconsider his play's violent ending, and during the last week of the run at City Center, he decided to rewrite the end of it. As Anthony Heald, the actor playing Stephen, related the story to John Pereira in his history of MTC:

> We had been blasted by critics and theatre people alike, some theatre people, for the murder. . . . A lot of people—Arthur Miller, Mike Nichols—a lot of people were giving us feedback that the murder didn't work. . . . And Terrence came back—this was on a Sunday—he came to see the last show of the week, and he said "I want to take out the murder."[27]

Writing about the change in *Playbill* magazine, Louis Botto explains that the final murder scene "was so brutal that many in the audience could not watch it, and there were some walkouts" during the City Center performances. Botto then quotes McNally at length.

> I had to go to London to do my play *Frankie and Johnny in the Clair de Lune* and when I came back, I stopped in to see *The Lisbon Traviata*. Looking at it after having been away, I found myself thinking that there could be another ending to my play. I called John Tillinger, who directed it beautifully, and the actors, and I told them that before the play closed—we only had one more week at City Center—I would like to try a new ending. They said fine, and we tried it on a Tuesday night. It was difficult for me to decide how I felt about it the first time I saw it. But we did it again the next night, and I knew that it was definitely the right ending for my play. I found the play much more moving with the new climax, and I must say that the audience seemed to like the new ending much better than the old one, which, to some, was too painful to watch. In the last minutes of a play, you certainly don't want to lose your audience.[28]

McNally places emphasis on audience response rather than critical response, and he positions the flaw as one of excess ("too painful") rather than deficiency (unearned). He also insists on his ownership of the play ("*my* play"), counteracting any potential accusation that he was bending his artistic integrity to the dictates of critics or other theater artists.

The revised ending, which appears in the Dramatists Play Service acting edition of the script published in 1990, contains the brutal fight between Mike and Stephen, but Stephen does not commit murder. He threatens Mike with the scissors but does not stab him. Instead, Mike leaves the apartment to go to Paul, and Stephen is left alone.

> *Stephen slowly sits on the edge of the coffee table. Callas is spinning an elaborate web of coloratura. Stephen is drawn into it. He throws his head back with her as she reaches for a climactic high note but no sound comes out. The lights are fading. Stephen's mouth is open, his head is back, his eyes are closed. Callas is all we can hear. Blackout.*[29]

Even with this bloodless ending, it is worth noting the difference between there being no murder and there being a murder that does not occur. McNally still builds dramatic tension by threatening to commit a murder, and since the precedent in various operas (as well as that in previous versions of his own play) leads the audience to anticipate a murder, this uncommitted murder becomes highly significant. As Anthony Heald's account of the change attests, it is not easy to create an uncommitted murder on stage. McNally told Heald that he wanted to take out the murder.

> And I said (*hyperventilating*), "What?! You mean Hamlet survives?"
> Anyway, I sort of surrendered myself to it, I said, "Go ahead, Terrence, it's your play, and do whatever you want to do."
> So he said, "Yeah, you want to stab him—and, instead, he leaves."
> So I said, "Well, what do *I* do?"
> He said, "Well, you're just left in the apartment."
> And I said, "And—and—and then what happens?"
> "And then the lights go out."
> So we got together on Tuesday to sort of work this out . . . anyway we staged it . . . and that's the way we did it for the entire New York run.[30]

The absence of the murder creates a dramatic space that is not easy to fill, raising the question of what actually *happens* onstage. McNally seems aware of this problem in his stage directions, insisting that there is "*a terrible, tremendous moment*" between Stephen and Mike but not giving any indication of how the actors should physically create that moment.

Yet the final image of Stephen alone onstage, his mouth wide open in a silent cry, with Callas singing the pain that he is unable to express, was one that critics and audiences applauded. Mel Gussow in the *New York Times* wrote a review titled "A New, Nonviolent Ending for *Lisbon Traviata*," with the subtitle "A Lesson Learned: Life Isn't Opera." This subtitle may sound like praise, but it is also somewhat patronizing, since it refers not to a character but to the playwright himself.

> With his new, nonviolent ending to *The Lisbon Traviata,* Terrence McNally recognizes that life is not grand opera. In the final scene, Anthony Heald is called on to internalize his anguish over his lover's departure rather than to melodramatize it as he did in the earlier version of the play. In the end, he is alone, without life support, a victim of self-abandonment. As a result, the denouement—and the play itself—has become more moving.[31]

In other words, McNally has learned the lesson that Gussow, who reviewed the play a total of three times, has been trying to "teach" him. Similarly, Linda Winer in *Newsday* hailed the play as a triumph of the play development process, with the new ending "more realistic—and infinitely more moving."[32] Howard Kissel in the *Daily News* was one of a number of critics who happily proclaimed, "McNally has lessened the disparity in tone between the two acts and thankfully removed the gratuitous closing violence."[33]

Scholar and critic Wayne Koestenbaum metaphorically links the inability to sing, the "closed throat," with an inability to express romantic and sexual passion. Therefore he finds great significance in McNally's final stage picture.

> By lip-synching to Callas, the opera queen is not brought closer to the magical realm of the vocal, the articulate, the expressive, or the openhearted. In fact, the tableau convinces us that a passion for Callas has closed the queen's throat, has taken away his power to love. . . . In the era of Silence = Death, the opera queen's silence is freighted with fatality. The silent opera queen, drowned out by Callas, is an image of gay helplessness, the persistence of the closet, and a tragic inability to awaken the body politic.[34]

It is not hard to understand why a politically progressive gay person might take exception to McNally's original murder: it is a dark and bloody vision of gay rage. But if silence does indeed equal death, then McNally's new ending is, in fact, more acceptable to a homophobic audience because it is already more familiar: the gay suicide. The hostile queen turns his rage and self-loathing inward rather than outward, becoming impotent and silent, unloved, dying as surely as Violetta, the courtesan-heroine of *La Traviata,* must die for living outside the bounds of bourgeois heteronormativity. There is no fighting back, just acquiescence to his fate. The gay victim is more palatable than the gay perpetrator.

Ironically, a few New York critics who originally complained about the murder did not praise McNally for rewriting the end of his play. While still admiring the play in general, Clive Barnes admitted, "I think I preferred the old ending to the new. Although purplishly overwritten, it still gave a dramatic irony and purpose to what had gone before."[35] While maintaining that the murderous ending was "terrible," John Simon conceded that "the earlier versions had the courage of their conviction" and "said something that was reasonably original." In contrast to Linda Winer, Simon is dismissive of McNally's attempts to rewrite his play, wryly noting, "By now, there may be as many *Lisbon Traviatas* by McNally as there are Callas *Traviatas.*"[36] Little did he know that there would be still one more.

In the West Coast production of *The Lisbon Traviata,* which was staged at San Francisco's Marines Memorial Theatre and then Los Angeles's Mark Taper Forum in 1990, actor Richard Thomas, known to television fans as John Boy on *The Waltons* (1972–77), took over the role of Stephen. Again John Tillinger directed, Nathan Lane repeated his Drama Desk Award–winning performance as Mendy, and Dan Butler reprised his role as Mike. During the nine months between the closing of the Promenade production and the opening in San Francisco, McNally decided that his play needed to end with a murder after all, and so Stephen killed Mike in California, and he continues to do so in all subsequent productions. The "reinstatement" of the murder was apparently a sensitive subject for the playwright. In a publicity article published before the play's opening, *San Francisco Chronicle* reporter Steven Winn wrote:

> McNally is circumspect, almost defensive about the changes in the play. They aren't so much changes, he contends, as "a process" that happens in the course of any play's development. None of it, he insists, is a capitulation to the press or to anyone else.[37]

Although McNally is right to point out that all new plays go through a process of development, usually that process does not occur in full view of audiences and critics in a series of public performances in America's theater capital. Similarly, it is highly unusual for a play to go through such changes after its New York production, which is usually considered "definitive." But McNally rightly recognized that his play would continue to have a long life outside New York, and the restored murder has appeared in subsequent productions and in the 1992 version of the script still in print with Dramatists Play Service.

Certainly the artistic team involved in the West Coast production felt that the murder made for a better play—although these are the same artists who a year earlier had publicly stated that the murder-free ending was the "right choice." In a 1991 interview, McNally said

> The production of *Lisbon Traviata* that we opened on the West Coast in San Francisco and L.A. was far superior to the New York one because it took me that long to get the text really where I wanted it to be.[38]

Nathan Lane told Ray Loynd of the *Los Angeles Times*, "It's a much stronger play now,"[39] and even Anthony Heald (who was not involved in the West Coast production) acknowledged the improvements achieved in California.

> I always felt, personally, that the character was marginally easier to play without the murder, but that the murder was a more satisfying end. I never really felt in the way we were doing the murder that it worked—and I think some of that had to do with the staging of it and with the dialogue that surrounded it. And Terrence solved that problem in Los Angeles.[40]

Theater critics on the West Coast had some of the same complaints as their East Coast counterparts, but the play was generally praised and was highly successful with audiences, particularly in Los Angeles.[41]

Acts of Violence: Performing Murder in The Lisbon Traviata

McNally's controversial murder scene merits close textual analysis. The final version of the murder is an amalgam of the original scene and the MTC revision. This murder is not merely "melodramatic," and an analysis of its motivations and results canprovide a better understanding of McNally's play, including its stylistic strategy of mirroring art and life and its themes of love and loss. Therefore, it is worth quoting the murder scene at length. Note that during this whole scene, Maria Callas's version of "Sempre Libera" from the Lisbon *Traviata* plays very loudly.

Mike: Let me go.
Stephen: You love him, don't you?
Mike: I said, let me go.
Stephen: You're not getting past me.
Mike: Come on, Stephen, put those down. I'm not staying here with you. (*He takes a step forward. Stephen forces him back with the scissors.*)
Stephen: You're going to him. You do love him.
Mike: Yes. I love him.
Stephen: Then you don't love me anymore? Then you don't love me anymore?
Mike: No, I don't love you anymore.
Stephen: But I love you. I adore you.
Mike: What's the point of this? I have to go. (*Again he tries to move past Stephen who again forces him back with a violent lunge with the scissors.*)
Stephen: Am I to lose my life's salvation so that you can run to someone else and laugh at me? You're not going. You're staying here with me.
Mike: Give way, Stephen.
Stephen: I'm not going to warn you again.
Mike: All right, do it! Do it or let me by.
Stephen: (*raising the scissors above his head*) For the last time, will you stay here?
Mike: You gave me this ring. (*He pulls it off.*) I don't want it anymore. (*He throws it down.*) Now will you let me by? (*Mike walks directly past Stephen who still stands with the scissors raised. Just as Mike passes him, Stephen grabs him from behind with a cry and pulls Mike towards him. Stephen stabs Mike.*) Jesus! (*Mike begins to fall. Stephen drops the scissors and helps him to the floor. Stephen leans Mike back against him.*) Jesus, Stephen, Jesus!
Stephen: This part. Listen. No one does it like Maria.
Mike: I'm hurt. I'm really hurt.
Stephen: Listen to that. Brava, la Davina, brava.

Mike: This is real, Stephen!
Stephen: I know.
Mike: Stephen, please, you've got to call somebody. We can't handle this. You killed me.
Stephen: We killed each other. People don't just die from this. They die from what you were doing to me. They die from loss.[42]

At this point, the phone rings, and we hear Mendy's voice over the answering machine, cheerfully prattling on about opera. Mike and Stephen have no more dialogue, and after Mendy hangs up, the last words go to Maria Callas, who continues to sing "Sempre Libera," to which Stephen lip-synchs while holding Mike.

McNally borrows directly from Georges Bizet's *Carmen,* and even audience members unfamiliar with the 1875 opera and Carmen's famous rejection of Don José's ring will recognize that McNally suddenly has his characters speak less realistically and more in the purple style of nineteenth-century melodrama, with Stephen's talk of "my life's salvation" and Mike's orders to "give way."[43] The line between reality and art is blurred, inviting audience members to wonder if they are witnessing, in almost expressionist fashion, Stephen's unique, opera-riddled perception of the scene. It is also important to note that, from Stephen's point of view, he and Mike have killed *each other,* that they are both murderers. In Stephen's mind, Mike's abandonment of him and their past is just as lethal as driving a pair of scissors into someone. Indeed, the same weapon is used: Mike cuts up the photos, the documents of their shared passion, with the same pair of scissors that Stephen uses to puncture Mike's body. But if Mike's "murder" of the relationship is tearing the romantic couple apart, then Stephen's murder of Mike is what keeps them together. Because of Stephen's murder, Mike does not walk off the stage, and the final image of the play is the two men together, embracing in a moment of great physical intimacy—stabbing being the most phallic and sexualized of murders, with a climactic thrust emitting blood and a postcoital stillness descending as heated passion dissipates from the limp body.

This murderous ending dramatizes the rage that can be tied to feelings of love and the fear of the loss of love. Contrary to most critical assessments, however, this rage is *not* incongruous with the rest of the play. A close reading of McNally's play reveals that murder is a recurring motif throughout it, and all three of its main characters express rage through acts of violence. Rather than pathologizing these characters because of their acts of violence, I wish to show how the play gives dramatic expression to feelings found in the experience of unrequited or abandoned love, as well as the specific dilemmas faced by some gay men in their quest for love in a world wracked by homophobia and AIDS.

Just as much as the dramatically serious second act, the highly camp and comic first act is filled with references to and enactments of murder—and in both acts, unrequited love is at the heart of the violence. Mendy alludes to murder and death throughout the first act,[44] but the theme emerges most clearly when he recounts the night on which Stephen first met Mike at a party thrown by Mendy, leaving his own romantic feelings for Stephen unfulfilled.

Mendy: I was so in love with you.
Stephen: You just thought you were in love with me.
Mendy: That's not true. When you two left together—I remember I was right over there listening to Bobby Staub hold forth about his dinner with Susan Sontag (thank God they never made a movie out of that)—and when I saw that door close on you two, I wanted to die. I knew you'd be making love within the hour.
Stephen: It was more like ten minutes. I kissed him in your hallway . . .
Mendy: And here I was on the other side of the door feeling like a combination of the Marschallin—all gentle resignation, *ja, ja, ja* age deferring to beauty and all that shit—and the second act of *Tosca*—stab the son of a bitch in the heart. (*Mendy seizes a knife from a fruit bowl, and raises it dramatically.*)
Stephen: Careful, Mendy.
Mendy: *Questo e il baccio di Tosca!* (*He "stabs" Stephen who reacts melodramatically.*) (20–21)

On the surface, this little play of murder between Mendy and Stephen is meant to be comical, but it contains deeper and darker meanings. Throughout the act, Mendy expresses real pain and even anger over Stephen's refusal to love him. The "murder" is revenge for that abandonment but also a displaced enactment of romantic and sexual union: Mendy penetrates Stephen with his knife (taken from a fruit bowl, no less), and they are united in operatic song. Moments later a discussion of Bizet's *Carmen* inspires yet another "play murder," and this time Stephen pretends to stab Mendy, who dramatically goes into "death convulsions" (26). It is the same scene that Stephen and Mike will enact at the very end of the play: first it is played for comedy; later it is played for tragedy. In both cases, Stephen takes the role of Don José, and in the latter case, Mike's death convulsions will be real. Readers of Georges Bataille will recognize that these death convulsions are symbolic referents for orgasmic convulsions, and these stabbing murders stand in for the sexual acts that Mendy has never had with Stephen and Mike no longer has with Stephen. Murder both represents and takes the place of sex. Mendy keeps his romantic feelings in check in order to preserve his friendship with Stephen, but he expresses his desires through the two "murders" that he playacts with Stephen, made safe because they are performed under the guise of "camp" or comedy, but performed nevertheless.

Throughout the play, McNally's characters compare themselves to abandoned lovers, murderers, and murder victims in operas. When discussing old affairs, they try to decide who was Butterfly and who was Pinkerton. In Stephen's current relationship with Mike, who is Carmen and who is Don José? Even Mendy the opera queen points out that operatic characters do not always make good role models, and David Román has written that *The Lisbon Traviata* shows "the pitfalls of compulsory heterosexual identification."[45] I would argue that this slippage between masculine and feminine roles is part of the mystery and suspense of McNally's play: we know that the woman (usually the foreign or illicit woman) dies at the end of the opera, but which one of these men will take the woman's role? Will Stephen die à la Butterfly or will Mike die à la Carmen? When dramatizing the relationship of a same-sex couple, the roles are not as obviously prescribed.

If murder is sometimes a "performance" of desire, it is also frequently a threat against those who would interfere with desire. When Mendy interrupts Mike's date by phoning in the middle of dinner, Stephen warns, "Mike is going to kill you for this" (28). This offhand remark appears more threatening when Mendy interrupts Stephen's phone call with a potential trick, a young waiter named Hal. Mendy loudly camps and tries to insert himself into the romantic drama, only to have Stephen violently put him in his place.

Mendy: He's standing you up? How dare he? Let me speak to that hussy—!

> *Stephen:* (*Covers phone.*) If you don't shut up, I am going to break your face open! (43)

It's a shockingly violent threat considering Stephen's long-standing friendship with Mendy and the relative insignificance of his liaison with the waiter. It may also be the first time in the play that we see how violent Stephen can become when someone interferes with his desires. Not coincidentally, this scene is also repeated in the second act: Stephen tries to interfere with Mike and Paul's relationship by blaring opera on the stereo, so Mike—literally—breaks Stephen's face open, punching him twice until he is on the floor, bleeding. The impulse toward violence, up to and including murder, exists in Mendy, Stephen, and Mike, all of them feeling and expressing rage over the lack of, loss of, and interference with desire.

The Lisbon Traviata also has a killer who never appears onstage but still informs much of the play's action. David Román notes that "AIDS informs the reality of its protagonists as a shadow that threatens to intercede at any moment."[46] The disease takes on concrete form in that Mike is a doctor who cares for people with AIDS, and tomorrow he is going to deliver the eulogy at the funeral of a friend. Stephen, however, proposes an alternate eulogy.

> Say, instead, aren't you sick and tired of these people depressing us just because they were unable to maintain a stable relationship? How many tears are we supposed to shed? Don't you wish they'd just get it over with? Wouldn't you rather be at a nice restaurant than sitting here moping over someone who probably, if truth could be faced up to, even just a little bit, got what was coming to him? (77)

This speech is, perhaps, Stephen's most monstrous. But his bitterness is actually founded in self-loathing: *he* is the one who cannot maintain a "stable relationship," and he fears that Mike's departure will necessitate the search for a new lover, which will make him susceptible to AIDS. In Stephen's mind, disease is not a medical fact but a moral judgment against those who do not maintain monogamy. Catherine Clément points out the operatic precedent for this point of view when discussing the fate of the courtesan Violetta in *La Traviata:* "It is no great leap from syphilis to consumption: two bodily corruptions inherited by those who are not part of the family."[47] Likewise, there is no great leap from consumption to AIDS, a leap famously taken by Jonathan Larsen in his transformation of *La Bohème* into *Rent.* According to Stephen, Mike kills him not only by destroying their relationship but also by destroying Stephen's safe haven from a fatal disease. In the age of AIDS, the end of a relationship is, in Stephen's mind, murder.

When Stephen tries to explain his love of opera to the uninitiated Paul, he says, "Opera is about us, our life and death passions—we all love, we're all going to die" (59). In *The Lisbon Traviata,* McNally imagines a theatrical world in which the lives and loves of gay men have as much dramatic magnitude as those of the operatic (heterosexual) heroes and heroines. The play cannot work, however, unless the audience accepts Stephen's claim that the operatic is actually about *all* of us. As Clément astutely states, "Opera is grotesque when one takes the slightest distance on it and sublime when one goes along with identification."[48] The same is true of *The Lisbon Traviata.* If one chooses to pathologize the characters as immature queens whose obsessions serve as escapes from reality, then the play is indeed grotesque. But if one can read the play as a drama about the desire for love, the fear of the loss of love, and the rage of the abandoned lover, then it becomes a compelling drama about the depth and passion of gay love—a bold statement in 1985, and arguably still today.

Despite some of the misgivings of the play's initial critics, *The Lisbon Traviata* was highly successful in both New York and Los Angeles, which led to productions at numerous professional and amateur theaters around the country. Interestingly, the play has had many revivals in the twenty-first century, including productions in San Francisco (2000), Chicago (2002), Boston (2002), London (2003), Los Angeles (2006), and Washington, DC (2010). I believe the play remains popular not only because it is funny, sexy, and relatively inexpensive to produce but because it dramatizes queer desire and rage in an "open-throated" manner, giving voice to emotions that all too often are still silenced in a homophobic society. By linking the homicidal homosexual and the operatic diva, McNally aligns the love and loss experienced by his modern gay characters with the grand passions of opera. Thus *The Lisbon Traviata* ennobles gay love, not despite a murderous character but because of him.

Teenage Crush: Abandonment, Alienation, and Revenge in Porcelain

Opera also informs the emotions and desires of the characters in *Porcelain,* a play that dramatizes a lonely teenager's murder of his abandoning lover in a public toilet in London. Asian American playwright Chay Yew initially wrote *Porcelain* for his graduate thesis in film at Boston University in 1991, but he set the script aside after actors consistently refused to take part in the project. (Yew was no stranger to rejection: a few years earlier, the government in his native Singapore had banned *As If He Hears,* his play about a man with AIDS.) He took up *Porcelain* the following year, rewriting it under commission for the Mu-Lan Theatre Company, England's first Asian British company, "founded for the purpose of raising the cultural profile of the Chinese and Oriental communities and artists in Britain." It premiered on the fringe at the Etcetera Theatre Club in London in May 1992, and in August the production was picked up by the English Stage Company for another run at the Royal Court Theatre Upstairs, one of England's most prestigious venues for new and experimental plays.

As a young writer, Yew's career in America gained a significant boost from the prestige of having a play performed at the Royal Court in London, and *Porcelain* earned attention from the mainstream press, as well as the London Fringe Award for Best Play in 1992.[49] The play received its American premiere at the Burbage Theatre in Los Angeles in 1993, with subsequent productions around the United States, including at theaters in Dallas; San Francisco; Washington, DC; Chicago; San Diego; Boston; Seattle; and Columbus, Ohio. As part of Yew's *Whitelands Trilogy,* the East West Players of Los Angeles mounted a major production of *Porcelain* in 1996 starring Alec Mapa. This gritty yet elegant drama places a gay man of color at the center of a scandalous murder case, and while it also uses opera as an intertextual referent, it works in a theatrical style and cultural milieu that are very different from those of *The Lisbon Traviata.* Most homicidal homosexuals in the theater tend to be middle-class, white gay men, but *Porcelain* uniquely focuses on a young, gay, working-class Asian immigrant, exploring the intersections of gender, sexuality, class, race, and nationality.

Porcelain is "a play for voices" presented on a bare stage in thirty fragmented scenes that shift in time, place, and perspective.[50] Four white male actors dressed in black are "Voices" who act as a protean chorus, creating sound effects, painting stage pictures with poetic phrases, and playing a variety of incidental roles and a few supporting characters. The fifth member of the cast is an Asian actor dressed in white playing John Lee, a London teenager who is under arrest for murder after being discovered in a public restroom crying over the dead body of his lover, Will. John's story unfolds through conversations with his court-appointed criminal psychologist, various interviews conducted by a television reporter, and flashback sequences of John and Will's relationship, with the chorus occasionally giving voice to John's inner thoughts. The story unfolds: feeling rejected and ignored by the dominant gay culture, Chinese-born John looks for sexual companionship with men in public lavatories—a practice that the English quaintly refer to as "cottaging." He believes he may have found love with his latest pickup, William Hope, a builder who happens to have a penchant for Puccini. But Will does not think of himself as "queer," so when he feels the relationship is going "too far," he abandons John. John tracks Will down, finding him in the restroom where they first met, and—while the chorus describes Don José's murder of Carmen—he shoots Will six times. The driving question of the play is *why:* why did John shoot his lover, and why would anyone look for sex, let alone love, in a toilet? If these questions seem initially to pathologize John, the play's answers to them ultimately work to humanize him.

One of the London critics complained that *Porcelain* occasionally suffers from "symbolic overloading."[51] The title alone has at least three symbolic meanings, each of them spelled out over the course of the play: (1) porcelain is the Chinese art of using clay to create a fine, translucent ceramic that seems fragile but is actually quite hard, (2) urinals and toilets are made of porcelain, and (3) John says that the skin of his English lover is as smooth and white as porcelain. Along with *Madama Butterfly* and *Carmen* serving as intertextual referents, the chorus intermittently relates a fable about a crow who wishes to join the sparrows, only to find himself rejected by both groups. The bird imagery is taken yet another step as John spends much of the play folding red origami cranes, hoping in the Japanese tradition that a thousand cranes can grant a wish. While some critics found fault with all this symbolism, still others fretted that the play's subject matter (toilet sex) and story (a crime-of-passion murder) were too tawdry or melodramatic—some of the same complaints leveled against McNally's play.

The Lisbon Traviata operates within the tradition of American linear realism, with actors "becoming" their characters in realistic settings and enacting a story in chronological sequence in a style that mimics observable reality. *Porcelain,* on the other hand, fractures unities of time, place, character, and perspective, shifting sequence, location, identity, and narrative focus in thirty different scenes. But even more important is the fact that the play is not "staged" in the traditional sense. The actors sit in chairs, rarely looking at each other when conversing and even more rarely touching each other. For example, in scene 24, John finally refuses the drunken advances of the lover who has taken him for granted, but Will forces himself on John and rapes him. This scene of great physical and emotional violence occurs in a complete blackout, undercutting sensationalism and encouraging the audience's imagination and identification with the characters. John's murder of Will—which is announced early in the play as a given circumstance, not withheld as a melodramatic revelation—is "staged" only through the words and sounds created by the actors. Even the color palette of the design is limited to black, white, and red. Such a minimalist theatrical style conveys both restraint and dignity, and, as the title of the play indicates, the goal is to make something beautiful out of coarse materials. This is what John attempts to do with his toilet encounters, and it is what the play attempts to do with its own subject matter. The result is a postmodern lyrical play that may present melodramatic action but also encourages the audience to focus on the expressions of emotion and thought and the play's own theatrical artistry.

The different theatrical styles in McNally's and Yew's plays affect the ways the audience might interpret each play's murder. Essentially, Yew frees himself from the burden of strict psychological realism, which demands that characters act just as they would "in real life." Many of McNally's critics complained that operatic passions simply cannot exist believably in a domestic drama. Yew avoids this potential trap by setting his operatic passions loose in an abstracted theatricalized world. Where Puccini and Bizet used music to express "excessive" emotions, Yew's characters give voice to their larger-than-life emotions through a chorus of poetic language. But there are other notable differences between the plays that might influence an audience's reception of the murders. McNally's murderer is white, affluent, middle-aged, and abandoned after eight years of domestic coupling. John is a Chinese working-class teenager who is abandoned after briefly dating a man he met in a toilet. Even though both characters are gay, issues of race, nationality, class, and maturity further separate John from the norm of his society. While Yew reinforces John's "otherness" throughout the play, he also invites the audience to understand and perhaps even identify with him.

Yew announces the "homo toilet sex murder" at the beginning of the play, and as *Porcelain* progresses he reveals the circumstances and events that led to the murder. First, there is John's fundamental alienation: he is alone onstage folding paper cranes as the audience enters, he is the only Asian man on stage, the only character dressed in white, and he does not speak until the fifth scene of the play. The other characters rarely look

John Lee (Steven Eng) in his cell surrounded by origami cranes in the 1993 Dallas Theatre Center production of *Porcelain* by Chay Yew. Courtesy of Richard Hamburger and the Dallas Theatre Center.

directly at John and almost never touch him, adding to his imprisonment. Ironically, the character assigned to "understand" John expresses the least understanding of him. In an unethical interview given before the court case begins, the criminal psychologist tells a television interviewer:

> I think—personally, between you and me, I think this whole case is—sick. Public sex is an offense. Murder is an offense. Well, let me put it in simple words—a queer Chink who indulges in public sex kills a white man. Where would your fucking sympathies lie? Quite open and shut isn't it? . . . It's just that I have nothing in common with those types, you know. (27–28)

John is separated by race, sexuality, and criminality, and the psychologist's speech demonstrates how all three can overlap and combine in the racist, homophobic imagination to create a "moral alien" separate from "normal" people.

John reveals that he experienced the pain of racism at a young age, having been beat up at school and denied a role in that most English of plays, *The Importance of Being Earnest,* because he "didn't look the part" (22). Later, as a gay teen, he feels ignored at gay clubs and pubs, propositioned only by older white men looking to "relive the old colonial days" (57). John's alienation is furthered by his own withdrawal from his family and his Chinese heritage. He refuses to work in his father's Chinese restaurant and criticizes the "Chinese way of life," even rejecting his original name, Lone, in favor of the more English John. After the murder, in one of the play's most touching scenes, John's embarrassed and ashamed father speaks to a reporter, rejecting his son completely.

> My son no commit crime. No commit murder. My son no homo. No homo! He cannot be—I—I have no son. Son is dead. Dead to me. Dead. Perhaps better he change his name to English. Be someone else. (85)

Note the father's confusion regarding his son's crime: is the offense murder or is it homosexuality? Both cause great shame and a rupture in the family, necessitating the rejection of the son. This rejection can be particularly detrimental for a member of an immigrant community, in which the family would normally serve as a safe haven from the potentially hostile dominant society.

Even more devastating to John than familial rejection is romantic and sexual abandonment by his lover, Will. They first encounter each other in a public toilet in Bethnal Green, where John performs oral sex on Will. Even though their sexual encounter seems to suggest mutual interest and acceptance, Will's version of the encounter is riddled with distance and separation: he refers to John as a "Chink," explains that "they're not my type, generally," and insists "I'm not a queer or anything" (51–53). George Chauncey, writing about gay culture in New York before World War II, describes how some men

> sought sexual encounters in spaces, such as public washrooms, that seemed to minimize the implications of the experiences by making them easy to isolate from the rest of their lives and identities. The association with tearooms [public restrooms] with the most primal of bodily functions reinforced men's sense that the sexual experiences they had there were simply another form of release, a bodily function

that implied nothing more about a man's character than those normally associated with the setting.[52]

Will seems to fit into this category of "trade," yet John and Will build a tentative relationship outside of the toilet, even though Will doesn't want to be seen in public with John and treats him like a sex object, with John always on the receiving end of oral and anal intercourse. Finally, Will doesn't return John's calls, and it is clear that this working-class white man who happens to love Puccini's *Madama Butterfly* is fulfilling his role as Pinkerton to John's Butterfly.

Except that John refuses to play that role. David Eng has written about the ways in which Asian men are feminized in western culture, cast as the submissive bottom to the westerner's aggressive top.[53] Eng's analysis of David Henry Hwang's hit play, *M. Butterfly* (1988), also applies to *Porcelain:* the white man who makes assumptions about the passive femininity of the Asian is destined for a fall. With his father's gun hidden in his pocket, John refuses to accept what Eng calls "racial castration," demanding that Will acknowledge him. Will not only ends the relationship ("We should stop seeing each other" [94]) but completely alienates John ("I'm not queer, Johnny! I'm not one of your kind" [96]) and denies that their relationship had any significance ("This whole thing was all in your head" [96]). At this point, John gives up the suffering feminine role of Butterfly to take on the aggressive masculine role of Don José. In an overlapping cacophony of voices, building in rhythm and dramatic tension, Yew leads up to John's act of murder: Voice One tells the story of Carmen, Voice Two and Voice Three express John's thoughts and describe the scene, and John both enacts (present tense) and relates (past tense) the events to the psychologist.

Voice Two: Will continued to go.
Voice Three: Stay.
Voice Two: What else can I do?
Voice Three: You're not walking out.
Voice One: Don José raises the knife to his blood-red eyes.
John: Will?
Voice Two: The gun trembled.
Voice One: The matador thrusts his sword into the bull.
Voice Three: Don't go.
Voice Two: The gun swayed.

Voice Three: You're not going anywhere.
Voice One: The bull collapses.
Voice Two: Under his sweaty fingers.
Voice Three: Stay!
Voice One: The bullring is swimming in a sea of blood.
Voice Two: Wrapping around the trigger.
Voice Three: Stay!
Voice One: The crowd is cheering and throwing roses.
Voice Two: Cock the pistol.
John: Then I started to squeeze the trigger.
Voice Two: Bullet in the chamber.
Voice Three: Ready to fire.
John: Will?
Voice Two: He continued walking.
Voice One: Don José plunges the knife into Carmen.
John: I love you.
Voice Three: Bang! (100–102)

Yew creates a dizzying theatrical scene, combining John's spoken dialogue with his inner thoughts, both pleading ("Will?") and commanding ("Stay!"), "close-up" descriptions of the gun (the trigger, the chamber), and the bloody final scene of *Carmen,* which itself combines two worlds, both inside the bullring (the matador killing the bull) and outside it (Don José killing Carmen). After the shooting, John describes how he, like Stephen in *The Lisbon Traviata,* cradles his dying victim in his arms, creating a gay lover's pietà. From his prison cell, John explains the rationale behind his murder of William Hope: "He'll never be gone. Now I have him where I want him. I've finally got Will all to myself now" (110). Love is an uncontrollable force while it is alive, but a dead lover will never abandon you.

The result of the murder, which we've known from the beginning of the play, is that John is in prison and the tabloids are having a field day with his story. But by the end of the play, the hope is that the audience will no longer think of John as a character in a tawdry, sensationalized news story. The goal all along has been to humanize the "queer Chink killer" who looks for love in a place that many people find at best distasteful and at worst disgusting and immoral. Early in the play, John questions the emotional distance that the psychologist places between them: "Are you afraid of finding out that we're just the same as you? Have the same feelings and the same fears as you? How we are so much alike? You and I?" (33). By the end of the play, the cynical psychologist seems to have gained some genuine sympathy for John, even romanticizing John's love for Will: "Not all of us have the intense passion that John possessed—passion enough to kill the person he loved" (112).

Like the abandoned lover in Mae West's play nearly seventy years earlier, John killed him because he loved him, and the murder stands as a testament to the depth of that love, yet it also leaves John more alone than ever—sort of. After John folds his thousandth crane, the television reporter asks the psychologist what John wished for. The psychologist (as if giving the audience its cue) asks, "You mean you can't guess?" (112). In the final moment of the play, John holds that paper crane in his hand and extends it *to the audience* with a smile on his face. In my opinion, the thousandth crane does not represent John's wish for the love of William Hope or his ability to take back the murder or even for his freedom from prison. What John most wishes for is to be understood and accepted by the audience.

Judging from the critical response to the play, John partly got his wish. A handful of critics chose to interpret *Porcelain* as a sociological exposé of toilet sex and therefore found it unpleasant and unsatisfying. Taken literally, the main character's seemingly hysterical decision to kill a "trick" he met while "cottaging" might be difficult to accept (compared, for example, to Stephen's decision to kill the lover who shared his life for eight years). But taken more emblematically, John Lee's murder of William Hope resonates as a romantic cri de coeur against loneliness and abandonment, not just in the context of a brief affair but in the context of a young lifetime of isolation and rejection, exacerbated by differences in race, class, and sexuality. Certain critics recognized *Porcelain* as "a touching exploration of sexual and cultural alienation,"[54] and even "a cry of rage at (homo)sexual and racial rejection"[55] that "touches something which reaches beyond the homosexual world."[56] At its best, this is the balance, both minoritizing *and* universalizing, that *Porcelain* can achieve: it brings the audience to a deeper understanding of the specific emotional crises faced by a Chinese gay youth in a white heterosexual society, but the audience also recognizes that his feelings are not so different from their own.

In his author's introduction to the original publication of *Porcelain* in John Clum's anthology, Chay Yew writes that the play "is based largely on my teenage experiences of loneliness, identity, anger, and sexuality as a member of a racial minority in a Caucasian society."[57] The power of the play does not lie in the "authenticity" of its depiction of toilet sex—or, for that matter, of murder. Rather it lies in the emotional truths that Yew conveys in a highly theatricalized story. Toilet sex is not simply the play's sociological topic; it is the play's metaphor for the shame surrounding gay sexuality. Especially for Will Hope, the toilet serves as a sort of closet, a dirty place in which his homosexuality is kept, and it must be contained within that space.[58] Moreover, the play wrestles with the fear that gay lives and loves are devalued to such an extreme that they are the equivalent of excrement, unpleasant and unclean waste that should be flushed away from society. Gay love is not seen as healthy or reproductive, so all the organs of the social body (represented in the play by law, psychology, and the media) must work to discharge it.[59]

In *Porcelain* the motivation for murder is the desire to somehow legitimize gay love. Will Hope denies that any love exists between him and his attacker, and this rejection exists within the context of a society that also refuses to acknowledge or appreciate gay love. Feeling abandoned and alienated, yet insisting on the reality and legitimacy of his love, John Lee lashes out in frustration and anger, believing that he can empower himself and his love through violence. But this insistence on the existence of gay love is inevitably intertwined with a nihilistic fear of the impossibility of gay love. In killing his lover, John also kills any chance of achieving true love, since the object of his affection can no longer reciprocate. When he pulls the trigger six times on William Hope, John literally kills his "Hope" of finding love. The toilet is depicted as the location of both the fulfillment and the destruction of homosexual desire. Now in prison, the Hopeless John has made his physical reality correspond to his inner feelings of alienation and solitude—a fitting end to a boy originally named Lone Lee. Such feelings are perhaps not uncommon among queer youths, especially those who have yet to experience a loving relationship and have internalized homophobic fears about the impossibility of gay love and the inevitability of queer loneliness. For a killer like John, the only hope of reprieve is to win the sympathy of an audience, helping it understand what it feels like to be Lone Lee.

CHAPTER SIX

Queer Evil

In the homophobic imagination, queer people do not engage in a lifestyle but rather a "death style," one that chooses degeneracy over reproduction and decadence over regeneration. Homosexuality is imagined as a "dead end" that threatens to destroy individuals, relationships, families, and societies. Thus, the homicidal homosexual, who embodies the conflation of nonnormative sexuality and death, is a symbolically powerful figure in the homophobic worldview. Take, for example, the identity of Andrew Cunanan, a gay man who, over a three-month period in 1997, murdered five people, including fashion mogul Gianni Versace, before killing himself. To borrow the semiotic terms of C. S. Peirce, homophobes read the media image of Cunanan as not just *iconic* (representing Cunanan himself) but also *indexical* (indicating homosexuals as a group) and *symbolic* (representing concepts such as "murderousness" and death).[1] Indeed, the fight against homophobia often takes the form of a fight against such over-interpretations. When the tabloid media offered sensational portraits of Cunanan, the antihomophobic response insisted that Cunanan was an individual murderer who "happened to be" homosexual, not an indicator of the murderousness of *all* homosexuals.

Such over-interpretations make for bigotry and bad politics in the real world, but in the unruly realm of theatrical art, we welcome dramatic characters who are open to complex meanings and are "more than just themselves." Here a murderous queer character can both participate in and subvert the homophobic paradigm that denounces all queer people as dangerous and deadly, and characters can be understood as individuals, as representatives of a social group, *and* as embodiments of abstract concepts—all at the same time. Arguably, some plays encourage metaphorical and metaphysical interpretations more than others do. The codings of genre and style play a large role, as Marvin Carlson has shown in his analysis of "the iconic stage," which elucidates how realism tends toward iconic representation (e.g., a chair is a chair) while nonrealistic styles lend themselves to symbolic representation (e.g., a chair is a mountain).[2] For example, when Nicky Silver names a character Todd and then has another character break the fourth wall to inform the audience that the name means "death" in German, the playwright is encouraging the audience to engage in metaphysical interpretation—Todd *is* Death.

The plays in this chapter are rich sites of interpretation because they problematize conventions of realism by combining them with nonrealistic theatricality and intimations of the metaphysical, thus encouraging the audience to interpret the drama both literally and figuratively at the same time. While many elements of these plays are realistic, others are so abstracted, absurd, or surreal that they do not "make sense" within a strictly realistic, psychological narrative, so the audience is encouraged to look to the metaphysical and the symbolic. Thus, these plays position the homicidal homosexual as a character who exists simultaneously as a literal character and a symbolic representative of metaphysical forces. In doing so, these plays challenge the symbolic order that positions the queer as evil.

Queer Evil and the Destruction of the Good

Since evil is an abstract concept that has been described and applied in so many ways, it may be helpful to elucidate my working definition of the term, and then to examine some of the various ways that public discourse frames queer people as evil. At its most quotidian, evil can simply mean "morally reprehensible" or "causing harm." Many contemporary theorists of evil approach the subject from a psychoanalytic perspective. C. Fred Alford, author of *What Evil Means to Us,* bases his philosophy of evil on his experience interviewing people who have caused terrible harm—incarcerated murderers, rapists, and so forth. For Alford, evil is not an aberration but an impulse experienced by all humans, since we are all mortal and experience dread, that is, the feeling of being "vulnerable, alone in the universe, and doomed to die." Alford explains:

> Evil is an experience of dread. *Doing evil* is an attempt to evacuate this experience by inflicting it on others, making them feel dreadful by hurting them. Doing evil is an attempt to transform the terrible passivity and helplessness of suffering into activity.[3]

Evil, then, is enacting the opposite of the Golden Rule, which requires that we treat others as we ourselves would like to be treated. Evil consists of treating others in precisely the way we do *not* want to be treated, thrusting our suffering and pain onto the other in the hope of avoiding it ourselves. Alford goes on to describe some of the qualities of evil,

> Evil inflicts pain, abandonment, and helplessness on others, so that the evildoer does not have to experience them himself. . . . It is why torture is the paradigm of evil, master of all three terrors at once. . . . Hence, all evil has the quality of sadism, defined . . . as the joy of having taken control of an experience of victimhood by inflicting it on another.[4]

Here Alford hints at the idea that evil is not just about displacing dread but about controlling it. The sadist's joy comes not just from seeing someone else suffer but from feeling that he or she is in control of suffering, commanding and redirecting the force that threatens us with doom.

Alford offers a convincing thesis on the psychology of human cruelty and suffering, but another layer of meaning is necessary in order to understand how evil functions symbolically. He comes close to this layer when he refers to Melanie Klein, who focuses on *envy* as "the root of all evil, the desire to destroy what is good because one cannot have or be it."[5] Such envy is operating in Nietzsche's notion of *ressentiment,* in which weak people fabricate a system of "slave morality" that falsely characterizes the aristocratic man's will to power as "evil."[6] But envy is also, not coincidentally, one of the Seven Deadly Sins, and Alford touches on a crucial aspect of evil when he explores religious (and thus metaphysical) concepts, such as Saint Augustine's definition of evil as "the willful depletion of good."[7]

The greatest Willful Depleter of the Good is, of course, Satan. In Judeo-Christian cosmology, Satan, rejected by God and banished from Heaven, is filled with envy, vowing to destroy all that is Good by corrupting God's creations. The anonymous author of the medieval *Chester Mystery Plays* concisely states Satan's dramatic objective.

> *Lucifer:* And therefore I shall for His sake
> Show mankind great envy
> As soon as He can him make
> I shall him at once destroy.[8]

In this religious worldview, everything has metaphysical significance because everything plays a symbolic role in the battle between the Holy and the Unholy, the Good and the Bad. Even our modern, supposedly secular understanding of evil exists in the realm of the symbolic. More than ordinary violence or destruction, evil has symbolic value (i.e., it is more than just itself) because evil has an *agenda:* to destroy Goodness. To participate in this agenda is to be part of a Force of Evil that is larger than a single individual dealing with his or her psychological dilemma of dread. To call something evil is to assign metaphysical meaning to it. Evil is larger than the act of a single "bad" or "cruel" person. It is a manifestation of That Which Destroys the Good.

Evil, with all of its symbolic connotations, is applied to real people and actions in contemporary discourse. In *At Stake: Monsters and the Rhetoric of Fear in Public Culture,* Edward J. Ingebretsen explains that the label "monster" (i.e., the embodiment of evil) functions as a "metaphysical signifier" and "a perennially useful social tool" that teaches people what is "properly human" by separating and demonizing the "inhuman." Ingebretsen acknowledges that monsters make for compelling narratives *because* they appeal to a metaphysical understanding of reality, and, unsurprisingly, both the killer and the queer appear regularly in the role of monster.

> Like the homosexual, and often in the same terms and for many of the same political reasons, the killer is construed as a larger-than-life force, one who threatens not only private domesticity, but the entire fabric of national civility as well.[9]

In other words, the queer and the killer are monstrous because they are not "just themselves"; they are demonized as representatives of a Force of Evil whose goal is to destroy the Good (private domesticity, national civility, etc.). This may seem like a great deal of symbolic weight to put on the shoulders of your average queer person, or, for that matter, even a violent murderer. But when we make the queer and the killer into monsters, they take up residence in the realm of the symbolic, where they are endowed with extraordinary powers.

So how, exactly, are queer people—and queer characters—symbolically configured as evil? The religious right's response to the 9/11 terrorist attacks provides a telling instance. The *Washington Post*'s John F. Harris reported that within forty-eight hours of the attacks, televangelist Jerry Falwell was blaming homosexuals *as a group*—along with pagans, abortionists, feminists, and the American Civil Liberties Union—for the death and destruction.[10] Falwell was not claiming that homosexuals actually carried out the attack but rather that the mere presence of homosexuals in America creates an evil society that will not be protected by God. The underlying argument is that homosexuals must be removed from society, and gay historian Michael Bronski rightly points out the similarities between contemporary homophobic rhetoric and medieval anti-Semitic rhetoric, which successfully led to the expulsion of Jews from some European countries.

> [H]omosexuality functions on a primeval level as the great signifier of evil. Homosexuals have become to the modern world what the Jews were to the medieval world—they corrupt children, they spread disease, they stand outside the sanctified, secure boundaries of nationalism, and they seek the destruction of the state.[11]

The rhetoric of queer evil is based in a belief that queer people are detrimental to (1) the psychological and physical health of themselves and others; (2) family, including heterosexual monogamy and the production of children; (3) community, and the civic and religious systems that organize it; and (4) nation, and the political and military strength that defends it. Examples in each of these categories are numerous, but I will detail a few to elucidate the point.

Homophobic rhetoric has used AIDS as a means to inscribe queer people as dangerous to physical health. As Susan Sontag acknowledges in *AIDS and Its Metaphors,* the disease is more than "just itself" and takes on symbolic meanings, including "pollution" and "punishment." Moreover, AIDS has fostered a culture in which "illicit" sex is the equivalent of death, and the person who has sex is considered a murderer.[12] Since, despite so much evidence to the contrary, many people consider AIDS to be a "gay disease," homosexuality is symbolically the equivalent of murder. This conflation reached national prominence in 2003, when Jerry Thacker, a nominee to George W. Bush's Presidential Advisory Council on HIV and AIDS, called AIDS "the gay plague" and referred to homosexuality as a "death style" (as opposed to a lifestyle).[13] More than thirty years after the emergence of AIDS, a global phenomenon affecting millions of people of various societies and sexualities, some people still insist on using the disease as "proof" of the link between homosexuality and death.

In his book *No Future: Queer Theory and the Death Drive,* Lee Edelman explains how those whose sexuality exists outside the heteronormative reproductive family are constructed as inherently dangerous to "the Child" and the futurity that children represent within our society. If procreation is the key to the future, then "the death drive names what the queer, in the order of the social, is called forth to figure: the negativity opposed to every form of social viability."[14] In reality queer people might produce and raise or otherwise nurture children, but symbolically queerness signifies a threat to children, most often realized in the imagined conflation of homosexuality and pedophilia. Although Edelman warns queer people against participating in "the familiar familial narrativity of reproductive futurism,"[15] one of the social goals of legal battles over adoption and parental rights, as well as of groups such as Parents, Families, and Friends of Lesbians and Gays (PFLAG), is to reclaim LGBT people as members of families rather than threats to them.

Leo Bersani, in writing about "the gay outlaw," offers insight into how homosexuality is understood as an "anti-communitarian" threat to the social order. Symbolically, homosexuality has been constructed as infecundity, waste, and sameness (i.e., narcissism), and therefore it does not enact any "real" connection between people. Bersani looks to the French literary enfant terrible Jean Genet as the key example of the homosexual-criminal whose "demand that others find him hateful and unworthy of human society stands in sharp contrast to the tame demand for recognition on the part of our own gay community."[16] Indeed, while the current gay rights movement focuses on marriage as part of the battle for political (and, in many cases, religious) legitimization of same-sex relationships in the eyes of society, Bersani argues that Genet wants to be outside of society because only then can he be truly free from society. Bersani's argument relies not so much on an understanding of the different ways in which homosexuality is *actually* experienced in our culture, which can, in fact, be quite communitarian, as on a *symbolic* concept of homosexuality as anticommunitarian. Whether viewed positively by Bersani or negatively by homophobes, homosexuality is symbolically understood to represent a criminal act that destroys the bonds of community on which our law-abiding society is based.

Along with individual health, family, and community, queer people are imagined to be detrimental to the nation as a whole. Those who fueled the Red Scare of the McCarthy era expertly exploited the symbolic as they linked queers and communist subversives. In his book on sexual psychopath laws in the 1950s, Neil Miller quotes a *New York Post* interview with Nebraska senator Kenneth Wherry.

> You can hardly separate homosexuals from subversives. Mind you, I don't say every homosexual is a subversive, and I don't say every subversive is a homosexual. But a man of low morality is a menace to the government, wherever he is, and they are all tied together.[17]

Decades later Wherry's symbolic rhetoric was still potent and was used in the 1988 legal arguments of Jay S. Bybee, a lawyer for the Department of Justice, who in 2003 would become a George W. Bush appointee to the Ninth Circuit Court of Appeals. Richard Goldstein reported that Bybee

> argued for a Defense Department program that screened "all known or suspected" homosexuals seeking top-secret clearance. People who perform "acts of sexual misconduct or perversion," Bybee told the court, are guilty of "moral turpitude, poor judgment, or lack of regard for the laws of society."[18]

The important point here is not just that homosexuality is immoral. The point is that homosexuality is an *indicator* of "low morality" that can be detrimental to the national well-being.

It is no wonder that the battles of the gay rights movement have focused on AIDS, marriage and adoption, inclusion in schools and churches, and military service. All these battles have symbolic value in overturning the conception of queer people as detrimental to health, family, community, and nation. With the 2011 repeal of the Don't Ask, Don't Tell policy and an increasing number of states that recognize same-sex marriages, some commentators have argued that the gay rights movement can claim "victory." The rhetoric of the "gay threat" is crucial to understanding the cultural context in which the plays discussed in this chapter were written, and while the intensity and prominence of that rhetoric may have lessened, it has by no means disappeared. Furthermore, I'd like to join the critics who ask whether the goal of a queer movement is to change the position of queer people within the symbolic order or to change the order itself. If Evil is a metaphysical force whose goal is to destroy the Good, who gets to decide what constitutes the Good? Whose lives, loves, and values are allowed to occupy the charmed realm of the Good, and who, then, must be relegated to the abject status of Evil?

The plays in this chapter wrestle with queer evil, using the theater as a forum in which to confront and challenge the symbolic order. Theater can create its own world, one in which the values of Good and Evil, of human and monster, are questioned, challenged, or wholly reinvented. Being well versed in the power of the symbolic, theater artists can challenge the popular discourse with new symbolic meanings and significance. These plays enact the very evil of which queer people are often accused in homophobic discourse. But they do more than reiterate homophobic rhetoric through the use of camp or irony. They wrestle with the status of queer people by asking the questions that every queer person existing within a homophobic society must, at some time or another, ask himself or herself: *Am* I evil? How evil am I?

No Tragedy: Queer Evil in the Metaphysical Comedies of Nicky Silver

Nicky Silver began his career in the 1980s as a wildly prolific, self-produced playwright at the Vortex, a small gay theater on the fringes of New York's Chelsea neighborhood. By the mid-1990s, he had become one of the most widely produced American playwrights, regularly premiering his plays at more mainstream artistic homes such as the Woolly Mammoth Theatre in Washington, DC, and the Vineyard Theatre in New York. In 2012 Silver had his first Broadway success with *The Lyons,* which earned a Tony Award nomination for the star, Linda Lavin. Silver's work is notable for its combination of a wide variety of influences, from Greek tragedies to television sitcoms. David Savran locates Silver in the "black farceur" tradition of gay playwrights such as Oscar Wilde, Joe Orton, and Christopher Durang.[19] I would add that Silver has built his reputation largely on exploring the absurd nightmare of the dysfunctional American family, perhaps linking him most directly with Edward Albee. Like Albee, Silver is often concerned with the intertwining of sexual desire and death and how these elements play out in the Freudian family drama. Many of Silver's plays feature a prodigal gay son who returns home, bringing with him some shameful crime (incest, murder, pedophilia), and this transgression creates a rupture in the facade of familial stability and happiness. The queer criminal son forces a confrontation with the long-avoided truth, often involving sexuality, violence, addiction, and the dissolution of the family. In *Pterodactyls* (1993), one of Silver's most popular and critically acclaimed plays, the returning son forces his family, and the play's audience, to reckon with a much larger truth: the mortality of the entire human race.

Many of Silver's plays before *Pterodactyls* depict this disruptive queer son as a murderer. His early hit, *Fat Men in Skirts* (1988), centers on Bishop, a young man who is straight but "coded" as gay; he not only obsesses about an old movie queen (Katharine Hepburn), but he fears and feels the rejection of his family and then society because of his "sexual difference." In this play, the difference is not gayness but an incestuous relationship, usually described in animalistic terms, with his mother. Bishop acts out the oedipal fantasy and then some, killing his father, his father's mistress, and finally his mother.[20] In *Free Will & Wonton Lust* (1991), Philip is another young man who is sexually confused rather than actually gay—for example, when he loses his fiancée, he finds sexual solace in the embrace of his sister. But the climactic revelation of his act 2 soliloquy centers on same-sex attraction and murder. Philip reveals that, although he "wasn't gay," he was obsessed with a handsome young Englishman. When the object of his desire kindly refused him, Philip threw a brick at the Englishman's head, knocking him out, and most likely killing him, although Philip did not stick around to find out. Homosexual desire and the rejection of that desire both create a panicked rage that leads Philip to murder.[21]

The murderous queer son takes on greater symbolic significance in *Pterodactyls*.[22] Todd returns home to his upper-class Philadelphia family because he has AIDS and needs a place to live. His return interrupts the festive marriage arrangements of his sister and knocks down the tower of denial constructed by his alcoholic socialite mother and his distant fantasizing father. Todd refuses the melodramatic role of sympathetic AIDS victim as he confesses that he knowingly had unsafe sex, casually reminds other characters that they are going to die, and denies the existence of God. He seduces his sister's fiancé, which enacts one of the "evils" of which gay men are often accused: corrupting straight men and ruining the bonds of heterosexual marriage. His macabre statements and this sexual seduction, however, are just the quotidian tip of a much more metaphysical iceberg. Todd finds large dinosaur bones in the family's back yard and spends the remainder of the play constructing the skeleton of a giant tyrannosaurus in the living room. Between scenes Todd directly addresses the audience, giving somewhat twisted lectures on the deaths of species and civilizations, focusing particularly on the extinction of the dinosaurs and the ten plagues that destroyed the Egyptians in Exodus. The improbable existence of dinosaur bones in the back yard and these minilectures place the play's action within a historical field that covers millennia, as well as within a supernatural realm that includes divine retribution and plagues from God. Todd also creates a link between these awesome destructions and the destruction of the humble family: he reminds us that dinosaurs "lived as families, traveling in packs" (110) and announces that his "favorite" plague is the slaying of the firstborn of the family.

Todd shows his true dimensions at the end of act 1. Responding to his father, who insists on calling him Buzz, the name of some fictional, ideal son, Todd "*explodes in a rage which shocks the others,*" repeatedly shouting "MY NAME IS TODD!!" His sister helpfully points out to the audience that Todd's name "means 'death' in German." If this weren't enough to establish Todd as something other than "just himself," he responds to his mother's wail "MY SON IS DYING!!" with the following proclamation.

> I AM NOT DYING!! . . . I WILL NOT DIE! I WILL NOT! I WILL BE HERE FOREVER! WHEN YOU ARE DUST I WILL BE HERE! I WILL OUTLIVE THE TREES AND THE STARS AND THE SEAS AND THE PLANET! (114)

Todd *is* Death, an immortal force that visits all living things but will itself never die. Throughout the play, Todd is associated with darkness and coldness, but he brings act 1 to a fiery close with this awesome and terrifying pronouncement. He is the Angel of Death declaring his own magnificence and revealing himself in all his sublime horror. Furthermore, Todd will now play an active role in bringing death to almost all the play's characters. The play begins as a family comedy, in the summer with the planning of a wedding. The second half of the play slides into autumn and finally winter, the wedding replaced by funerals, family reunions replaced by abandonment and solitude, and sex replaced by death.

In act 2, death permeates the play. The sister's wedding seems absurdly doomed, as "all the rabbits had cervical cancer and the pâté is contaminated" (118) and the "violinist was killed this morning by a stray bullet during a bank holdup" (123). Todd's wedding present to his sister is a loaded gun, which she will use on herself (and her unborn child) once she learns that her fiancé will not marry her because he claims to be in love with Todd. The fiancé's confession of love for Todd is combined with the revelation that he, too, is now HIV positive. In the final scene, the fiancé's AIDS-ravaged corpse lies in the yard, frozen and unburied. The sister appears as a ghost, having found some peace and wisdom in death and thankful to Todd for providing her with the gun. The play reaches a chilling conclusion as the lights grow dim and Todd pours more and more alcohol into his mother's glass, until she finally dies. The final images of the play are Todd embracing his sister's ghost and the lights on the dinosaur skeleton growing brighter and brighter.

So by the final curtain Todd has been the source or provider of death for his sister (the gun), her fiancé (HIV), and his mother (alcohol). (The father does not die, but he abandons his position as father, leaving home and disowning the family.) Meanwhile, Todd shows no symptoms or manifestations of AIDS, and, true to his proclamation at the end of act 1, he remains after everyone else has died. In analyzing the desire to do evil, Alford writes, "When we are faced with intolerable, uncontainable dread, the natural tendency is to identify with the persecutor, becoming the agent of doom, as the only way of controlling it."[23] Todd avoids death by *becoming* Death. In this fantasy of empowerment, Todd takes control of the force that would destroy him and uses it to destroy others. In doing so, he enacts in real terms the evil of which gay men are often accused in symbolic terms: he literally destroys the family, ruins heterosexual marriage, spreads a fatal disease, and even kills the unborn. But Todd is not evil. The sister, fiancé, and mother each play a role in his or her own demise. They are not "innocent victims" of a sinister villain, as Silver successfully complicates such melodramatic categories. Furthermore, Silver repeatedly reminds the audience that death is part of a natural order, one that has no apparent cause or reason. The tyrannosaurus skeleton that dominates the stage is a "monument to the transience of everything" (116), and Todd's final speech reminds us that no one really knows how or why the dinosaurs died out.

> Some people think there was a meteor. Perhaps volcanic ash altered the atmosphere. Some think they overpopulated and the shell of their eggs became too thin. Or they just ran their course, and their end was the order of things. And no tragedy. Or disease. Or God. (150)

Todd may be Death, but he is not malicious or vindictive. Death simply *is*, an amoral natural force that takes individual lives and will one day take the entire human race.

In creating an amoral comedy of death, Silver accomplishes some interesting work within the symbolic order. His play dramatizes, even exaggerates, a homophobic fantasy of queer villainy, which can also be read as a dramatization of the homosexual's internalized homophobia and guilt. Homophobic discourse accuses queer people of the crimes that Todd performs, and queer people have been taught to feel guilty for those same crimes, whether they have performed them or not. Silver presents a literal enactment of the gay man as symbol of Death and Destruction—and then, shockingly, radically declares that death and destruction are *not* evil, just natural, perhaps even a comforting release from the neuroses and suffering of human existence. The play confronts the homophobic symbolic order head on and asks the question "What if gay men *were* to bring about the death of humanity?" Silver invokes the transhistorical view (it's happened to other species) and the philosophical view (death comes for us all eventually). Silver seems to argue that even if gay men were the walking embodiments of death and destruction, that would not mean they were evil. He lifts the symbolic weight heaped on queerness and AIDS by the homophobic imagination and reminds us that *all* living things are, ultimately, engaged in a "death style" and our deaths are part of the natural order. This is the truth that homophobes would deny by displacing their dread onto the queer, but Todd is there to remind us that mortality is the universal condition.

Nevertheless, *Pterodactyls* is undeniably a morbid play, one that embraces death and, disturbingly, finds more comfort there than in any human lover. Rather than refuting accusations of immorality with depictions of morality, it takes a chilly stance of amorality. As such the play hardly qualifies as an example of "gay pride." But Silver has done something remarkably brave, actually confronting the symbolic power of the homophobia that most queer people try to avoid or deny in their daily lives. For the relatively brief period of time the audience spends in the theater, the terrifying vision is given the spotlight, and we are asked to consider it for what it is and what it might mean. Taking on the role of Death, the gay man is empowered, taking control of forces that normally control him. He enacts revenge against the family and the social order, which ignore or reject him. His suffering is dramatized as the suffering of all creatures over the history of existence, and his death is dramatized as part of the cosmic and awesomely inevitable. Thus Todd's supposedly imminent death from AIDS does not mark him as monstrous but brings him into the circle of a frail, mortal humanity. The play bravely wrestles with queer fear and guilt created by the homophobic symbolic order, and it achieves a victory of sorts. For those who can find comfort in realizing that death does not discriminate and we are all equal and united in mortality, *Pterodactyls* is a cleansing ritual that exorcizes fears and anxieties over the queer's symbolic status as "bringer of death."

Pterodactyls is one of Silver's most acclaimed plays dealing with a homicidal homosexual, but it is not his last. In *Raised in Captivity* (1995), he changes focus to the masochistic "victim" of queer killers. Sebastian refuses to believe that anyone is truly bad or evil. He writes love letters to a convicted murderer, begs for the return of a hustler who has just cut and robbed him, and longs for his dead lover Simon, whom he believes "willfully" infected other people with HIV. The play asks the question "Are the men we love murderers?" In the end, Sebastian withdraws from sexual relationships and embraces his nurturing side, choosing to care for his sister's newborn baby, whom he names after his dead lover. The final note is both mournful and hopeful, with Sebastian perhaps being released from his romantic obsession with pain and death and finding comfort in his love for an innocent child.[24] In *Beautiful Child* (2004), the story of a gay man's love for an innocent child takes a sinister turn, but here Silver focuses on the guilt-ridden parents of the disruptive queer son. Isaac returns home, confessing his crime of pedophilia with an eight-year-old boy. Isaac's mother imagines that one of her son's previous victims has committed suicide, making her son guilty of murder. In the end, the family is reunited, but only in guilt and shame. The parents agree to protect Isaac, but they punish him by blinding him and imprisoning him in their home. The parents condemn Isaac as a criminal, but they also reclaim him as *their* criminal.[25]

In December 2006, Silver himself appeared onstage in a workshop production of his play *The Agony and the Agony* at the Vineyard Theatre.[26] Playing a mediocre middle-aged playwright named Richard who is writing a play about a mediocre middle-aged playwright, Silver presented his most self-reflexive work to date. Appearing onstage as the playwright's conscience and confidant is real-life killer Nathan Leopold, who with Richard Loeb famously murdered Bobby Franks in 1924. The Leopold and Loeb crime has been reimagined frequently in plays and films (see chapter 2), and Silver reiterates a popular interpretation of the case, positioning Leopold as a sympathetic gay man who participated in the killing in order to win the affections of the brutal sociopath Loeb. Through a farcical series of events, Richard has trapped in his apartment the theatrical producer he blames for ruining his career. As he contemplates killing the producer, Leopold serves as the voice of reason and morality, convincing Richard that if a villainous murderer like himself can turn over a new leaf and contribute to the good of society, then Richard's career is not hopeless, and murder is not a solution to his problems. Functioning as a Ghost of Gay Murderers Past, Leopold haunts the conscience of the playwright, even becoming his friend, and ultimately inspiring him to turn away from his own murderousness. By forming a bond with the gay murderer, the gay playwright avoids becoming a murderer himself.

Although these later plays do not have the same metaphysical dimensions as *Pterodactyls,* Silver is still appealing to the realm of the symbolic, with characters named after signifying figures: the homoerotic Christian martyr Sebastian, the Old Testament sacrificial son Isaac, and the archetypal and oft-represented homicidal homosexual Nathan Leopold. In each play, queer villainy in the form of the queer killer is confronted and psychically released (*Captivity*), pardoned (*Agony*), condemned (*Beautiful Child*), or proclaimed innocent (*Pterodactyls*). In all of them, the guilt and stigma of the criminal are inseparable from the guilt and stigma of the queer, struggling with shame, familial rejection, the loss of love, and so on. Silver's plays often seem informed by a Freudian perspective, with oedipal struggles, neuroses created by trauma, and symbolic dreams. A guiding principle behind Silver's dramaturgy is that the repressed will, inevitably, return. Much of the comedy in these plays comes from the farcical lengths to which neurotic characters will go to maintain a state of denial. Rather than pretending that the homophobic assertion of queer villainy does not exist or has no power, Silver confronts it head on. He does so in a dark comic universe that may be grotesque but is ultimately a realm in which the fear of queer evil can be fully, awfully realized and perhaps exorcized. As every Greek tragedian and Freudian therapist knows, the nightmare must be confronted if we are to be free of it.

Snap: Truth, Power, and the Killer Queen from Hell

"The Gospel According to Miss Roj" is a segment of George C. Wolfe's *The Colored Museum,* which debuted in 1986 at the Crossroads Theatre, a company dedicated to the culture of the African diaspora, located in New Brunswick, New Jersey. That fall the Public Theatre in New York mounted an off-Broadway production that ran for nearly two hundred performances and was later broadcast on PBS.[27] *The Colored Museum* presents "exhibits" of African American types and stereotypes, from the mammy to the disco diva, with a combination of satire and sympathy, exploring the cultural history that contributes to African American identity. The fifth vignette introduces Miss Roj, a trashy but fierce drag queen who addresses a monologue to the audience.[28] Although this queer character exists in our real world, she shows strong connections to otherworldly, spiritual, and mystical realms. Wolfe clues the audience in to his metaphysical intentions in a variety of ways. The very title of the segment invokes the rhetoric of religious testament and proclaims Miss Roj as a prophet, one who has extraordinary—perhaps even supernatural—powers of insight and wisdom in understanding the present and predicting the future. Wolfe locates his character in "The Bottomless Pit," which is both the name of a disco bar for black gay men in New York City and, of course, an allusion to Hell.

Miss Roj magically appears in a puff of smoke and introduces herself as a snap queen, explaining that when the truth is spoken it must be underscored by snapping one's fingers. This prophet of truth may be stuck drinking Bacardi and Cokes in Hell, but she alerts the audience to her more awesome origins.

> Snapping comes from another galaxy, as do all snap queens. That's right. I ain't just your regular oppressed American Negro. I am an extraterrestial [*sic*]. And I ain't talkin' none of that shit you seen in the movies! I have real power. (14–15)

The space alien as a fantasy figure of empowerment has a lineage in both black and gay culture. Cultural critic Mark Dery traces the trend of "Afro-futurism" in black music, including the cosmic jazz of Sun Ra, the interplanetary funk of George Clinton, and hits like "Planet Rock" (1982) by hip-hop pioneer Afrika Bambaataa.[29] All these performers embraced "far out" theatrical personas that incorporated space age costumes and songs with titles and lyrics that evoked otherworldly origins and interplanetary travel. African American science fiction writers like Samuel Delany and Octavia Butler also contributed to Afro-futurism, and John Sayles's 1984 film *Brother from Another Planet* imagined the black man as a space alien stranded in New York City, observing the strange ways of Planet Earth.

Miss Roj participates in this trend of "black alienation," which sociologist Paul Gilroy understands as a reaction to the historical and psychological circumstances created by the black diaspora and the legacy of slavery. Ken McLeod, in his reading of Gilroy, positions the black space alien as a utopian wish: "Black diasporic consciousness seeks to return to an inaccessible homeland—in some sense, an imaginary utopian homeland that outer space metaphorically represents."[30] The black alien, then, can imagine himself escaping the "earthly" racism that oppresses him and "rising above" it to a better world. Miss Roj gives voice to this desire when she, as an extraterrestrial being, proclaims her distance from "your regular oppressed American Negro."

Gay culture has also tapped into intergalactic fantasy for metaphors of liberation and empowerment. In the early 1970s, glam rock star David Bowie linked the alienated homosexual to the extraterrestrial to create an alter ego named Ziggy Stardust, a visitor to our doomed planet who warns that *Homo sapiens* will be replaced by "the homo superior." This moon age messiah, however, ultimately falls prey to the corruption of Earth and ends up a "Rock 'n' Roll Suicide."[31] The decade of the gay liberation movement also gave us the sexual renegades of *The Rocky Horror Show,* who are visitors from the planet Transsexual in a galaxy called Transylvania (see chapter 4). The cross-dressing Dr. Frank-N-Furter is an alien monster who promises freedom from the sexual restrictions and repression of our own planet—even though he is ultimately killed by his own kind for being "too extreme." The drag queen as queer alien, then, combines the liberating fantasy of a "homo superior" with the nihilistic trope of the doomed homosexual.[32] Wolfe's Miss Roj also participates in this apocalyptic fantasy, inviting the audience to mourn the deterioration of society and "dance your last dance with Miss Roj" (17). By proclaiming herself an extraterrestrial snap queen, Miss Roj claims a position of regality, dignity, and power, lifting herself above the squalor of this planet—but she is also in danger of succumbing to that same squalor.

Like other avatars of black and gay "alienation," Miss Roj combines the role of space alien with that of religious or spiritual prophet, warning humanity of its imminent demise. But unlike the prophets who appear as beneficent angels or mystics, Miss Roj seems to get her powers from darker realms, and these powers include the ability to kill. As she sits in The Bottomless Pit, consuming more and more Bacardi and Cokes, Miss Roj informs us that drinking alcohol releases her demons, and these demons avenge the racism and homophobia suffered by her. The weapon of vengeance is the snap.

> Everytime I snap, I steal one beat of your heart. So if you find yourself gasping for air in the middle of the night, chances are you fucked with Miss Roj and she didn't like it. (16)

Miss Roj then tells the story of "this asshole at Jones Beach who decided to take issue with my coulotte-sailor ensemble," calling her "monkey coon" and "faggit." With a rapid series of snaps, Miss Roj causes the racist, homophobic bully to have an immediate heart attack. The snap is both an indicator of truth and a weapon of justice, used against those who do not pay proper homage to the prophet. It is no coincidence that Miss Roj's favorite song is Aretha Franklin's "Respect."

Miss Roj's power lies in her ability to speak the truth and destroy the nonbeliever. At the end of her monologue, she recites a litany of contemporary urban horrors, from homelessness to drive-by shootings, while instructing the audience to dance and snap at each instance of suffering. The snap represents empowerment through naming and acknowledging the truth of this suffering, but Miss Roj's gospel is ambivalent at best. Rather than asking us to fight against our demise, she invites us to embrace it. She leads us in a danse macabre, announcing that the party is actually a wake, and it's in our honor. In the face of all this death and despair, Miss Roj escapes the fate of the "regular oppressed American Negro" by claiming the role of the Angel of Death, having supernatural insight and power over matters of life and death rather than being subjected to them. Questions remain. Is Miss Roj deluding herself with fantasies of empowerment? Does this killer queen actually have supernatural powers? Throughout history, many cultures have ascribed mystical powers to androgynous people because they exist outside the gender binary. Perhaps, like Tiresias, who changed from man to woman and back again, Miss Roj's genderqueer status has given her extraordinary insight.[33] As a black gay queen, this triply alienated observer of our "deteriorating society" has a grasp on the truth, and we ignore her gospel at our peril.

Dark Enlightenment: Universal Suffering and the Gay Soul

Many of Craig Lucas's most successful works, including his play *Prelude to a Kiss* (1987) and the screenplay of *Longtime Companion* (1990), incorporate a metaphysical vision of what happens to the soul of the beloved once it leaves the body. The main character in *The Dying Gaul* (1998) does not necessarily embody the metaphysical, but he is a gay man who wrestles with the metaphysical and, through the act of murder, tries to take control of suffering and death.[34] The play, set in Los Angeles in 1995, has a complex plot, which it is best to summarize before further analysis. Robert recently lost his lover Malcolm to AIDS and has written a screenplay (called *The Dying Gaul*) about the experience. Jeffrey is the married bisexual Hollywood executive who performs two morally questionable seductions at once: convincing Robert to rewrite and heterosexualize his screenplay for a million dollars (because Americans won't watch movies about gay people) and making Robert his lover.

Robert struggles with his guilt over "selling out" his memorial to his lover and over this secret affair, especially since he meets and genuinely likes Jeffrey's wife, Elaine. In treatment with a therapist named Foss, Robert also wrestles with his suicidal tendencies, caused by guilt and anger over Malcolm's death. Meanwhile, Elaine is charmed by Robert and intrigued by the online world of gay chat rooms that Robert describes. Pretending to be a gay man who has lost a lover to AIDS, Elaine goes online and chats with Robert, who confesses to this "stranger" that he helped kill his dying lover and is having an affair with his boss (i.e., Jeffrey). Intrigued by her husband's lover, Elaine pursues a duplicitous scheme. She breaks into Foss's office and copies Robert's files, and with this personal information she goes online under the guise of "Arckangell"—the spirit of Robert's dead lover Malcolm. The misspelling indicates that all is not quite right, that this angel is misshapen, as Lucifer was after the Fall. This angel is both male and female, lover and stranger, true and false, comforting and avenging. The simultaneous pain and joy, belief and disbelief of Robert at having his dead lover returned to him, is heartbreaking in its desperate need, made all the more so because the audience is fully aware of Elaine's duplicity.

The masquerade continues in act 2 as Elaine gives Robert messages of hope and encouragement. Robert continues to wrestle with his rage, which is sometimes still directed toward himself but also begins to turn outward, as he becomes more hostile to Foss in particular and the world in general, fantasizing about global destruction. He continues his affair with Jeffrey, even though he becomes disturbed when Jeffrey "jokes" about killing his wife—a fact that Robert reveals to Arckangell/Elaine in their final online conversation. Humiliated, angry, and afraid, Elaine confronts Jeffrey and threatens to leave him. She then confronts Robert and deals a devastating blow when she confesses that she was masquerading as Malcolm. Frenzied and furious about losing his lover again, Robert first tries to poison himself but then decides to put the poison in Elaine's food, an act that may or may not be responsible for a subsequent accident in which Elaine crashes her car, killing herself and her two children. Jeffrey is devastated by the senseless death of his family, but Robert feels no remorse.

When *The Dying Gaul* premiered at the Vineyard Theatre, it received qualified praise, since many people, as Craig Lucas puts it, "liked it up to the point it turned violent."[35] In this *The Dying Gaul* has much in common with *The Lisbon Traviata* (see chapter 5). Both plays present a main character who despite some ethically dubious acts, is basically sympathetic because he has suffered great losses. But in the play's final moments, this character sheds the role of victim to become the perpetrator of murderous violence, and this "switch" is criticized as gratuitous, unearned, and unpleasant. But, as with *The Lisbon Traviata,* a more thorough analysis of the play shows that the murderous act is actually integral to the character's arc and organic to the play's thematic concerns, which have been skillfully laid out by the playwright in the words and actions leading up to the violence. While some might accuse Lucas of failing to convince the audience of the "necessity" of the violence, I would argue that the violence is necessary to the play and the character, in part because, paradoxically, it brings about a death that lacks any "necessary" cause or reason.

One of the play's main concerns is how we attempt to make sense of seemingly arbitrary suffering and death. As they struggle with this issue, the play's characters explore and express metaphysical perspectives on the world, borrowing from no fewer than four different philosophical systems: Buddhist, Freudian, ancient Greek, and Judeo-Christian. Throughout the play, Robert addresses the audience with quotes from "Twelve Principles of Buddhism," proclaiming tenets of "self-salvation," "becoming what you are," and being responsible for one's own suffering. Robert is learning this Buddhism in part through Foss, the Freudian analyst who encourages him to understand his psychological response to suffering by analyzing his repression and expression of rage, particularly in his dreams and fantasies. Lucas himself has written about how the play is informed by the ancient Greek concept of *Ate,* the "ruinous impulse" or "rash action," perhaps brought on by an external supernatural force. Finally, the play wrestles with Judeo-Christian concepts of divine retribution and the afterlife of the soul, particularly in the form of an "arckangell" who serves as a spiritual guardian to Robert.[36] The angel exists in an Internet chat room, which Robert describes as "like life after death" because it is a place that "doesn't even exist, really" filled with "disembodied souls" (22–23).

Yet *The Dying Gaul* often plays with these belief systems in complex and critical ways. The Internet chat room may be a metaphysical realm for disembodied souls, but they are all focused on the physical, seeking to satisfy their sexual desires and fantasies. Another compelling contradiction emerges in relation to Robert's belief in the Arckangell, which is moving partially because Robert is having an experience of the sublime and also because of the dramatic irony created by the audience's knowledge that Robert is being deceived and the angel is an earthbound imposter. In another ironic twist, the audience is forced to ask itself whether "becoming what you are" is the road to enlightenment if "what you are" is a rage-filled murderer. If the play's metaphysical philosophies are meant to serve as guideposts for the characters' spiritual journeys, then these shifting and bending guideposts create a twisted path on which all the characters make ethically dubious choices—most of all Robert, whose journey ends with murder.

The play deftly shows the forces and events that propel Robert in his path to becoming a murderer.[37] Robert expresses much guilt over killing his dying lover Malcolm, first by administering poison to him in his hospital bed and then by writing him out of *The Dying Gaul*, "eliminating" his character in the script of the film he promised Malcolm he would create as a memorial to him. This guilt is linked to anger, and when we see Robert in therapy, Foss's first question, in relation to Robert's dream about a Nazi death camp, is "Who do you want to kill?" (33). Robert is not sure if he is the Nazi or the Jew in this scenario, still unsure whether to turn his aggression inward or outward and hinting at his own confusion as to whether he is a victim or an aggressor. But by the second act, after describing the terrible shout Malcolm made just before he died, Robert is able to articulate to Foss his anger.

> You ask how big my rage is. That's . . . Everyone should—World War Three, that's what I want. Not just Auschwitz . . . not . . . The whole planet. All of us . . . I want the world, all mankind. We should all . . . hear that. We should all know what that's like. (58–59)

This fantasy of universal suffering is central to Lucas's play. In the first scene, when Jeffrey convinces Robert to alter his screenplay, one of Jeffrey's arguments is that a story about two gay men cannot be universal (14). Robert, in his fantasy of mass annihilation, expresses his desire for the rest of the world to experience what he and Malcolm have experienced. Since Jeffrey prevents Robert from making the film that would express his suffering as universal (something that everyone can relate to), he has fantasies of literally making his suffering universal (something that everyone experiences).

Of course Robert is not alone in his murderous impulses. Foss also feels some guilt about having supplied the morphine with which Robert intended to kill Malcolm (even though we learn that the morphine didn't work, so Robert used the potassium chloride provided by a nurse's aide instead). Jeffrey admits to fantasies of killing his wife Elaine because his infidelity would not hurt her if she were dead. Robert, out of concern for Elaine, wonders how seriously to take Jeffrey's "fantasy," perhaps causing the audience also to wonder if this duplicitous bisexual will kill his wife. Once Elaine reveals that she knows about the affair, one of the tactics Jeffrey uses to win back her trust is to offer to kill Robert. As with the bisexual husbands of *Deathtrap* and other thrillers (see chapter 3), Jeffrey is depicted as duplicitous, without loyalty, and potentially dangerous to whichever partner is "in the way." While Jeffrey's threats carry weight because we know he is a powerful and rather unscrupulous man, Elaine also displays the murderous impulse. She acknowledges that part of the thrill of pretending to be Malcolm is that she has control over Robert, including the power to make him commit suicide (52). Near the end of the play, when she gives Jeffrey an ultimatum about their marriage, Elaine grimly announces that she wants Jeffrey to bring her lobsters because "I want to boil something alive" (66). But her real act of violence is in creating and then killing Arckangell. As part of her revenge against Robert, she tells him the truth.

> Arckangell is dead. Robert. He died. He had to be deleted from his hard drive. He doesn't even have a floppy anymore, he doesn't have anything. No corporeal being. No spirit. (70–71)

By revealing to Robert her role as the creator of Arckangell, she "murders" Malcolm once again, taking Robert's lover away from him a second time. If Malcolm's first death was a physical death, Elaine's confession announces Malcolm's spiritual death. Elaine's words mock Robert for believing that his lover's spirit could exist in some technological system, and she cruelly takes away the hope that she herself implanted: that the soul of the beloved can exist even after death.

Robert's response to this crushing revelation seems like disbelief and despair. Alone onstage, he vainly, pleadingly calls out Malcolm's name, then tries to commit suicide by ingesting poisonous monkshood from the garden. Then, in a moment without any explicit explanation, Robert instantly changes his mind. He spits out the poison and, in an instance of *Ate*, puts fresh monkshood in Elaine's food. He refuses complete responsibility for his murderous actions by explaining to the audience, "I gave it all, everything over to god" (72). Whether Elaine actually eats the food, whether it actually kills her, whether Robert will be caught—all these things he says he leaves to a higher power. But Robert also explains that the second death of Malcolm resulted not only in his despair but in the loss of his moral compass.

> There was no Malcolm, none I could see. To lose him again . . . Maybe he was there, beside me screaming: NO! Stop!, don't, life, every breath of it is precious, you mustn't kill so much as an *ant* . . . NO! ROBERT! Maybe. But I couldn't hear. (72)

Robert has suffered a terrible loss, and rather than suffering making him more sensitive to the value of life, suffering has made him deaf to it. The playwright directly addresses this situation, autobiographically linking it to his own experiences of loss, in his afterword to the published edition of the play.

> Where did so many of us learn to believe that the victims of terrible loss are ennobled by their suffering? Though I'm sure some people are ennobled—me, I've come out of the experience rather the worse for wear.[38]

Robert's suffering does not make him stronger, wiser, or kinder. His suffering has made him someone who does not recognize the precious dignity of each life. It has made him a murderer.

But what does Robert truly accomplish with this murder? When Jeffrey learns of the destruction of every member of his family, he is distraught. Robert remains cool and explains to the audience:

> They died . . . senselessly . . . his children, the woman he loved . . . slammed into a concrete divider at seventy miles an hour . . . dead for no reason . . . Reaching out to stop it, nothing he or anyone could do . . . Maybe now someone understands. No one to take the blame for these terrible deaths . . . Dead for no reason . . . And this time I'm god. (74)

By referring to the deaths of Elaine and the children as "this time," Robert reminds the audience that there was a "last time"—that is, the death of

Malcolm. There was no reason for Malcolm's death, nothing Robert could do about it, and no one to blame. The senselessness of Malcolm's death, combined with Robert's feeling that no one else truly understands his suffering, has made Robert crave a scenario in which (1) he has control over life and death and (2) he will not be alone in his dreadful mourning. At the beginning of the play, Jeffrey does not understand or respect Robert's suffering. The movie executive convinces the screenwriter to alter his memorial to his dead lover because Robert's experiences and suffering—that is, his *gay* experiences and suffering—are not "universal." At the end of the play, Robert has made Jeffrey experience that same suffering. He has shown Jeffrey that his experiences of pain, abandonment, and helplessness are universal.

This theme directly relates to the title of the play, and it finds visual representation in the film version, which Lucas directed in 2005. Lucas's film of *The Dying Gaul* is even more meta, since it is about Robert's film of *The Dying Gaul,* in which two characters discuss the significance of a statue called *The Dying Gaul.* This statue, made by a Roman and depicting a soldier killed by a Roman, represents art's capacity to awaken our compassion, especially the compassion of the victor for the victim. Lucas's film shows photographs of this statue to the audience, and therefore in the film's final image, after Jeffrey learns of his family's deaths and falls to the ground, we recognize that he has taken the same position as the dying Gaul—sitting on the ground, propped up on his right arm, left hand on bent right knee causing the torso to slightly twist, and head bowed. The Roman and the Gaul have switched places, and the man who did not truly understand Robert's memorial to the fallen victim now must mourn his own fallen victims. This "sympathy" is not created through art, but through experience. Lucas questions Robert's idealistic hope that his screenplay for *The Dying Gaul*—and by extension *any* work of art—can cause an aggressor to feel compassion for his own victim. Will the powerful and the comfortable ever truly identify with the suffering of others, no matter how beautiful the artistic monument to that suffering?

Empathy is necessary in order to enact the Golden Rule of treating others as we ourselves would be treated. Once Jeffrey convinces Robert that straight moviegoers will never empathize with a gay man, Robert realizes that his work of art will not achieve the goals he had hoped. Rather than finding an outlet through art, his dread takes a more twisted path. Robert is motivated by a desire to alleviate his own suffering by inflicting it on another; he is motivated by the envious desire to destroy what he cannot have or be; and he is motivated by a desire to make the world reflect, rather than deny or silence, his own tragic state. If we accept the definitions of evil set out by Alford, Klein, and Augustine, then Robert has, in fact, become evil. Evil is a sort of empowerment that Robert has attained by the end of the play. At the beginning of the play, he is largely meek and deferential, but in his final speech to the audience, he proclaims, "There are no limits to what I can accomplish" (75). Robert has lost his dread and become a master over life and death. It is a dark enlightenment, in pursuit of which Robert has gone on a spiritual journey to "become what he is," but what he has become is evil. Robert finally emerges from his spiritual quagmire of guilt and anger by turning from Gaul to Roman.

Perhaps Robert, much like Silver's Todd, enacts a cool revenge against a heterosexual union and a family—that is, that which occupies the position of the Good in the heterosexist symbolic order. But viewing Robert and his motives as "evil" should not obscure the play's most disturbing ambiguity, namely, that Robert kills Elaine and the children *because* he has no good reason to do so. For the play to make sense, their deaths must be as terrible and inexplicable as Malcolm's. From this perspective, Robert is also like Todd since he sees himself as simply an agent within an amoral universe in which suffering is random and senseless. He does not see himself as evil but as someone who has finally given up on morality and accepted the fundamental amorality of human pain and death.

Especially since the advent of AIDS, antigay religious rhetoric has often blamed gay people for their own suffering since the punishment for "sin" is death. But the authors of *Pterodactyls,* "Miss Roj," and *The Dying Gaul* present another perspective on queer suffering. They depict death and destruction as horrifyingly amoral and universal forces with which we *all* must reckon. They attack the symbolic order that insists on seeing the suffering of queers as "deserved" and "not universal" because the Good are protected from such suffering. And they imagine a scenario in which gay men escape being victims of destructive forces by taking control of those forces.

The homicidal homosexuals discussed in this chapter might be described as evil, but they exist in complex dramas that force the audience to question simple notions of good and evil. Confronting the symbolic order, these plays wrestle with accusations of queer villainy and the supposed deadliness of homosexuality. Since the plays are, to varying degrees, nonrealistic in their performance style, thus eschewing any "objective" reality, the audience member must also wrestle with the ambiguities of symbolic values, perhaps fluctuating between identification with and condemnation of the evildoer and thus questioning the very use of the notion of evil in our society. Just as "doing evil" may be a method of taking control of terrifying forces, perhaps enacting queer evil on the stage is a method of controlling homophobia, accusations of villainy, and the fear of death faced by queer people in a homophobic society. Within the artful realm of the theater, these plays simultaneously liberate the nightmare and control it, setting it free but also making it perform in ways not normally realized in mainstream discourse. By wresting queer evil out of the hands of the homophobes and giving it a new script, these plays allow for the possible creation of new meanings and understandings of the queer and the evil. Given the continuing use of homophobic rhetoric in cultural and political discourse, which positions queer people as monstrous threats to the Good, the need to understand and challenge the symbolic uses of "queer evil" remains crucial.

CHAPTER SEVEN

Serial Killers

Gratifying Monstrous Desires

Serial killers are part of modern American folklore, having become characters in our national narratives about good and evil. The term *serial killer* describes someone who murders a number of people over a period of time, often motivated to kill for "psychological gratification." Within American culture, many serial killers have become celebrities—supercriminals whose names and faces are known by millions, with aficionados who pore over the details of their lives and extraordinary crimes in countless magazine articles, web pages, books, films, and television programs. Popular discourse typically frames these killers as "monsters," aberrations outside the sphere of humanity. As David Schmid notes in *Natural Born Celebrities: Serial Killers in American Culture* (2006), "Positioning serial killers as gothic monsters represents our attempt to salvage and locate a (national) community by defining what stands outside that community."[1] But the parameters of community and humanity are never absolute, and the dominant culture is often in conflict about the position of the supposed "other." Thus, Schmid argues, "[T]hese monsters exert equal parts repulsion and attraction, a fact that ensures their simultaneous abjection from and ingestion into the social."[2]

Both the homosexual and the serial killer have occupied this position of "monster" in the public imagination, and the "gay serial killer" has been a particularly compelling and problematic monster, especially since the early 1990s, when the conflation of homosexuality and homicidal violence found new resonance in popular culture. In 1991 America was both repulsed and fascinated by the fictional gay male/transgender serial killer in Jonathan Demme's film *The Silence of the Lambs,* and by the arrest of real serial killer Jeffrey Dahmer, who murdered seventeen young men, often engaging in necrophilia and cannibalism. Diana Fuss observed how popular discourse of the time reified the connection "between homosexuality and pathology, between perversion and death,"[3] and Philip Jenkins noted that "the gay-killer connection is so frequent . . . as to be overwhelming."[4]

Homophobic discourse symbolically connects serial killers with queer people, equating their crimes with sexual lust. Serial killers usually do not murder for financial gain or out of emotions like love or hate. Rather, they possess a pathological, even physical urge to kill that must be satisfied on a regular basis. As Joyce Carol Oates put it in her 1994 profile of Jeffrey Dahmer, the serial killer operates "with no apparent motive for his monstrous crimes except the gratification of desire."[5] The homophobic imagination equates this murderous desire with homosexual desire, viewing it as physical lust, removed from the romantic or social ideals attributed to heterosexuality. Both homosexual and murderous "lusts" are imagined as abnormal, unhealthy, monstrous desires that exist because of a lack of proper morality. And both are subject to much speculation and debate about causation: what internal or external forces make someone gay, and what makes someone a psychopathic killer?

In his analysis of narratives about serial killers, David Schmid argues that true crime writers inevitably focus on some "deviant" aspect of the killer's life as an explanation for his or her murders, since the public needs to be able to exclude the killer from the realm of the "normal." But they enforce a double standard when it comes to sexually motivated crimes. So true crime writers represent Ted Bundy, who murdered and engaged in necrophilia with numerous women, as "an aberration that told us nothing about heterosexuality at all," while they attribute Jeffrey Dahmer's crimes to homosexuality itself. Indeed, Schmid finds in these narratives "the assumption that extreme violence is a normal part of homosexuality."[6]

In their attempts to explain the murders of Jeffrey Dahmer, many true crime writers place the blame on *internalized homophobia*—that is, the gay man's loathing of his own homosexuality. While this assertion may be correct, Schmid maintains that true crime writers use it to support, rather than challenge, the homophobia of their readers, since they never address the origin of the loathing. The implication, then, is that "to be homosexual is so disgusting and traumatic that of course one would murder again and again in order to assuage one's guilt about being gay." And here Schmid imagines an alternate possibility for the exploration of internalized homophobia.

> A more productive, and less homophobic, aim for true crime would be to explain why Dahmer felt ambivalent about his homosexuality or why he hated other homosexuals. Examination of these issues in true crime has the potential to correct some of the biases of the genre, but rarely does, simply because gay self-hatred can be acknowledged but never analyzed in detail . . . To explore the sources of Dahmer's conflicted homosexuality would involve acknowledging both the familial (Dahmer's father was virulently homophobic) and social context of widespread homophobia.[7]

In other words, rather than naturalizing internalized homophobia as a psychological response to homosexuality, Schmid challenges true crime writers to examine the social origins of this homophobia, thus implicating American society itself as the source of Dahmer's self-loathing.

The plays discussed in this chapter have the potential to take up that challenge. My examination of plays and performances about queer serial killers focuses on how these works may challenge the homophobia so often found in other media, articulating a critical perspective on causation and the supposed conflation of violence and homosexuality. Additionally, many of these plays engage critically with other issues surrounding narratives of queer serial killers, including the role of the media in creating celebrity serial killers, ambivalence about the innocence of their victims, and the public's interest in the gruesome physical details of sadistic murders. Compared to many other plays discussed in this book, plays about queer serial killers include more carnage, using different theatrical techniques to enact or relate the gory particulars of the act of murder. But certain ambiguities surround each of these subjects. Can a play critique the sensationalism inherent in marketing serial killers without contributing to it? Can a play represent grotesque violence in an effort to condemn our culture's hunger for spectacles of such violence?

These ambiguities are further complicated by the gay rights movement's history of combating this particular archetype. Obsessed with the serial killer and the homosexual as monstrous threats, our culture often links the two in fictional narratives, much to the dismay of the gay rights movement. Much has been written about the homophobia—and the protests against the homophobia—surrounding the representations of queer serial killers in films such as *Cruising* (1980), *The Silence of the Lambs* (1991), and *Basic Instinct* (1992).[8] The protests aimed to call attention to the way these Hollywood narratives vilified a minority group, and also to challenge the symbolic order that consistently positions the queer as a violent threat. These protests accomplished important work in challenging and perhaps changing the field of representation, but the queer serial killer is an unstable signifier, and he or she is not necessarily always a homophobic construction.[9] The plays discussed in this chapter create new narratives for the queer serial killer, confronting and reimagining one of the most repellent archetypes in the field of queer representation.

In many cases, queer playwrights and theater artists have wrested the representation of the queer serial killer away from the homophobic dominant culture, staging their revisions in LGBT theaters or other alternative venues. They employ theatrical conventions other than realism to explode the supposedly objective realities constructed by the news and other nonfiction media. While films like *Cruising, The Silence of the Lambs,* and *Basic Instinct* ask the audience to identify with the normative detective-hero, making the homicidal homosexual simply the object of the hero's hunt, these plays tend to give the killers a greater degree of subjectivity, allowing them to express their own fears and desires. Plays can take advantage of the differences in systems of production, genres, and narrative conventions to construct new meanings for the queer serial killer, but audiences must also play a role in this endeavor. An audience eager to confront and challenge queer villainy ultimately constructs its own meanings.[10] These plays replace the homophobic melodrama of the queer villain with complex narratives that allow the audience to imagine a variety of possible interpretations for the relationship between queer sex and violence in our lives and our culture.

Jeffrey Dahmer Superstar

Jeffrey Dahmer is one of the most famous serial killers in recent American history, and his sexually motivated murders of young men have inspired a number of plays and theatrical performances. As a teenager, Dahmer was an antisocial alcoholic who enjoyed dissecting dead animals.[11] He committed his first murder in 1978, at the age of eighteen, when he invited a hitchhiker back to his home, then struck him on the head with a dumbbell, supposedly because he desired the young man and did not want him to leave. Living in Milwaukee in the 1980s, Dahmer would meet men in gay bars, drug them, and then rape them; he also had convictions for indecent exposure and child molestation. He committed sixteen murders in Milwaukee between 1987 and 1991. In many cases, he would drug his victim—many of whom were African American, Latino, or Asian American—then drill a hole in the young man's skull and inject hydrochloric acid in order to turn him into a "zombie." He would engage in sex with the incapacitated body, then murder and dismember the victim, in some cases eating parts of the body or keeping them as souvenirs. In July 1991, one of Dahmer's potential victims, Tracy Edwards, fought him off, escaped, and led the police back to Dahmer's apartment. Dahmer's murder trial, which was televised, resulted in fifteen life sentences. A fellow prisoner beat Dahmer to death in 1994.

The first theatrical production about Jeffrey Dahmer was perhaps the most stunning—and the most open to diverse interpretations. In February 1992, avant-garde theater maker Reza Abdoh staged his production of *The Law of Remains* in the abandoned ballrooms of the Diplomat Hotel in Manhattan. The *New York Times* heralded this world premiere by proclaiming, "The *enfant terrible* of sex and death has created yet another demonic work of experimental theater."[12] As a writer and director, Abdoh eschewed realist notions of character and plot to create dense and layered performances with viscerally affecting sounds and images.[13] Critic Stephen Holden described *The Law of Remains* as "a blood-soaked pageant of contemporary Grand Guignol depicting mass murder, sexual mutilation, necrophilia, and cannibalism."[14] Abdoh's postmodern aesthetic intersperses found materials, including interviews and news reports about Dahmer, with scenarios inspired by the S & M club scene, African dances, and invocations from the Egyptian *Book of the Dead*. These scenes are joined by the story of Andy Warhol creating a movie about Dahmer, here named Jeffrey Snarling.[15] Abdoh's fourteen actors push the audience to different sections of the hotel, witnessing seven stations in the journey of Snarling's soul through scenes of sex and violence, until the performance ends in Heaven.

Critics differed about the meaning and merit of the production, but most agreed that it was, in the words of *New York Times* critic Stephen Holden, "one of the angriest theater pieces ever hurled at a New York audience." While Holden seemed to admire Abdoh's skill, he complained that "the sheer density of the noise and tumult make it hard to follow" and that the production "seems to want to punish as much as to enlighten" the audience.[16] Alisa Solomon in the *Village Voice* also found the performance elusive in its frenzy and assaultive in its "high pitch of rage."[17] Yet certain elements of Abdoh's nightmare vision did resonate for both critics, and these elements speak to the ways in which Dahmer, as a gay serial killer, has functioned in American culture.

Along with noting the fury at the heart of *The Law of Remains,* both Holden and Solomon acknowledge the play's commentary on a culture that turns murderous criminals into celebrities. But rather than focusing on mass media, Abdoh depicts Andy Warhol—the master of Pop Art who died in 1987—as the avatar of America's obsession with fame and celebrity. By putting the serial killer Jeffrey Snarling into a movie, Abdoh's Warhol is exploiting him as a commodity, creating him in a "factory" and selling him like a can of soup. Warhol and Snarling are not protagonist and antagonist as much as they are two sides of the same coin: two gay men who gain celebrity in America, one for works of art (creation), one for acts of murder (destruction). Perhaps Warhol can also be seen as a stand-in for Abdoh, the auteur who offers an artistic representation of a celebrity serial killer that is somewhat different from the mass media image, but still attached to the culture of commodity and consumption.[18]

While playing himself in Warhol's film, Snarling asks, "Andy, what's gonna happen to me at the end of the movie?" Warhol cannot, of course, give a legitimate answer to the query, since Dahmer's story had not yet come to an end when the play was performed in the winter of 1992. But Snarling's metatheatrical question also highlights his anxiety about being a "character" who is giving a "performance." Earlier in the play, during an interview, Snarling relates how he would "act up" in high school, pretending to be "retarded" and "epileptic" in order to amuse his classmates (39). This odd detail from Dahmer's youth is also depicted by the writer and artist Derf Backderf in *My Friend Dahmer* (2012), his autobiographical graphic novel about being high school classmates with Jeffrey Dahmer in Ohio in the 1970s. Backderf and his friends encourage Dahmer in his strange act, and in one incident they pay Dahmer to give a "command performance" at a shopping mall, twitching and shouting at unsuspecting patrons.[19] The teens laugh at Dahmer's grotesque shenanigans, but once the show is over they don't invite Dahmer to be part of their evening plans. The incident highlights how Dahmer, as an awkward outsider, performed a comically exaggerated version of his "freakishness" in order to win the attention of his peers; but this attention does not translate into actual friendship, and Dahmer remains nothing more than an amusing yet creepy spectacle for the other teens. *The Law of Remains* re-creates this dynamic, showing Dahmer's complicity in his own exploitation as a celebrity monster, but also implicating the audience as the consumers of this grotesque performance.[20]

Another key element of *The Law of Remains* mentioned by critics is the specter of AIDS, which, by 1992 had been in the news for a decade and killed over one hundred thousand Americans. With approval of life-extending protease inhibitors by the Food and Drug Administration still three years away, Americans considered AIDS a death sentence that disproportionally affected men who had sex with men. *The Law of Remains* and the figure of Jeffrey Dahmer were invariably seen through this lens, and as Solomon noted, "In the theater, this mass murderer of gay men can hardly be represented without evoking that other mass murderer of gay men: AIDS." Reflecting on Abdoh's representation of a real incident in which one of Dahmer's victims escaped only to be returned to him by the police, Holden commented that the event "becomes a metaphor for governmental indifference to the AIDS crisis." Abdoh, who was HIV-positive and died in 1995, told Glenn Collins of the *New York Times* in 1992 that HIV "can't help but color my work, the idea of life as a clock ticking."[21] *The Law of Remains,* then, might encourage the audience to interpret Dahmer as a theatrical personification of the AIDS crisis, presenting sex as erotic and seductive, but also fatal.

The "use" of Dahmer to convey the warped values of America's celebrity-obsessed culture or the devastation of the AIDS crisis, however, should not overshadow the theatrical force inherent in depicting Dahmer's acts of brutality in and of themselves. Abdoh seems to distrust the mass media's attempt to make sense of Dahmer's violence by containing it within rational discourses of psychology, forensic science, and law. Like the French theatrical theorist and visionary Antonin Artaud, Abdoh rejects psychological realism and linear narrative in favor of an avant-garde theater that shocks the audience with visceral sensations, appealing not to intellectual understanding but to the audience's capacity for irrational, spiritual, and physical experience. Abdoh's assaultive use of loud noises and bloody images outside a traditional theater space is very much in line with Artaud's notions of a "theatre of cruelty," intended to shock and provoke the audience. In this way, Abdoh uses a form of theatricality that does not offer enlightenment or catharsis but rather demands that the audience experience the brutality of Dahmer's crimes on a physical and visceral level.

Yet, within all of this brutality, Abdoh also finds space to mourn, paying significant attention to Dahmer's victims. *The Law of Remains* dedicates an entire segment to a litany of the dead, with an actress reciting the name, age, and ethnicity of each murder victim (82–83). More than many other works, Abdoh's production highlights the fact that many of Dahmer's victims were men of color and makes explicit the racism swirling around the crimes. Snarling remarks that he "was chopping up nigger boys and chinks" (25), and the play suggests that he escaped detection for as long as he did because the police did not take seriously the disappearance of young African American, Latino, and Asian American men. Some true crime writers blamed these men for their own deaths—just as the culture at large often blamed gay men with AIDS for their own deaths—claiming that they were engaged in a "risky lifestyle" and courting danger. Furthermore, the mass media's focus on Dahmer as a spectacular monster often relegated his victims to the background, making them nameless men who created a statistic: seventeen victims. By invoking the victims' individuality while Dahmer stands before the audience, *The Law of Remains* effectively shifts attention from the celebrity monster to the absent victims of his crimes.

As I argued in chapter 2, contemporary theatrical portraits of real life homicidal homosexuals tend to offer their audiences multiple perspectives and possible responses to their subjects rather than presenting a single coherent ideological position. *The Law of Remains* is no exception, and this deliberate confusion is reflected in the mixed critical response to Abdoh's production, especially when it comes to the conflation of homosexuality and murderous violence. The play shows gay male characters as the perpetrators of violence, the victims of violence, and the exploiters of narratives about that violence. But it recognizes the larger social forces in which these characters exist, encouraging the audience to understand Dahmer's murders not as the expression of a pathological homosexuality but rather as the product of society's homophobia, which Abdoh further contextualizes within America's nationalism and racism. In particular, Abdoh's Dahmer embodies the brutality behind the indifference and inaction that allowed so many deaths during the first decade of the AIDS crisis. As a character wracked by internalized homophobia, Dahmer is both the perpetrator and the victim of antigay brutality, producing an unresolved struggle between the audience's sympathy and condemnation.

In 2003, about a decade after the premiere of *The Law of Remains,* About Face Theatre in Chicago produced Jim Grimsley's *Fascination,* a lyrical drama loosely based on Jeffrey Dahmer's life and crimes. Aside from differences in the dramaturgical styles of Abdoh and Grimsley, their plays are also separated by a decade of change. Dahmer himself was dead, having been killed by a fellow prisoner in 1994, and while his fame persisted in the popular culture of the twenty-first century, much of the media hysteria surrounding him had faded. His potency as a metaphor for AIDS had also diminished, since the approval of the first protease inhibitors in 1995 caused many to no longer consider AIDS a "death sentence," but rather to see HIV infection as a chronic but manageable condition. Gay and lesbian characters appeared much more frequently in mainstream media, with shows like *Will & Grace* (1998) and *Queer as Folk* (2000) bringing palatable depictions of gay people into America's living rooms. The rage and confrontational tactics of activist groups like ACT UP and Queer Nation gave way to the "insider" lobbying of organizations like the Human Rights Campaign. And in 2003 the US Supreme Court declared that antigay sodomy laws were unconstitutional, thus decriminalizing gay sex, even while a major political party continued to use the "threat" of same-sex marriage as a scare tactic to rally voters and create more homophobic legislation.

Grimsley's *Fascination* offered a new representation of a gay serial killer to this much-changed culture. Grimsley is a gay writer whose novels and plays often deal with young gay men in the American South struggling to find a safe place. His acclaimed 1995 novel *Dream Boy,* about a gay youth who is severely beaten—perhaps to death or perhaps rescued by the object of his desire—was successfully adapted for the stage by the gay-oriented About Face Theatre in Chicago in 1996.[22] Subsequently, About Face worked collaboratively with Grimsley to develop *Fascination,* a play about a serial killer of over forty young men, which premiered in the spring of 2003. The character of Randall Bartelman seems loosely based on Jeffrey Dahmer, but the play is neither journalistic fiction nor crime drama. Rather, *Fascination* is a moody, dreamlike play, which, in a series of juxtaposed scenes, explores the thoughts of the killer, his first victim, the parents of both the killer and the victim, and others who are "fascinated" by the crimes, including a journalist, a local busybody, and a Christian woman who wants to redeem the killer through marriage.[23]

When interviewing Randall, the journalist reminds him of all the products created by the culture of celebrity surrounding serial killers: books, television movies, playing cards, and so on. The journalist insinuates that Randall committed his crimes in order to gain fame, that he was "a sad sick nobody looking for a way to get [himself] in the headlines" (15). Randall denies the assertion, claiming that he never expected to get caught. The journalist then searches for another explanation and presents the theory that Randall's murders were the result of self-hatred and internalized homophobia. Again, Randall deflects the ready-made explanation for his murders, complicating the very notion of what constitutes homosexuality. "I had sex with their corpses," he explains. "They're not boys when they're dead. They're just corpses. Don't you get it?" (26). In Randall's view, the corpse is ungendered, and therefore not a partner in a "homosexual" act. Necrophilia trumps homosexuality.

The play allows the audience to ponder this notion by flashing back to the encounter between Randall and his first victim, Victor. More than many other plays about murder, *Fascination* gives almost equal voice to the victim and the murderer. The teenage Victor has been kicked out of his home because he is gay, and the play puts no small amount of blame on the homophobia of Victor's parents, showing how their abandonment of their gay son turned him into easy prey for the likes of Randall. Indeed, Randall explains that he "picked boys I thought nobody cared about. Who I thought nobody would miss" (15). Grimsley counters a dominant trope in true crime writing that blames the gay victim as somehow complicit in his own death because of "risky behavior" and instead shows how the parents or communities that reject gay youths are responsible for endangering them. After meeting Randall in a bar, Victor takes the "aggressive" role, if such a term can be used for so mild and sweet a seduction, as he makes the first overtures to Randall, offers to go home with him, and then tries to talk to and touch his reticent companion. Randall responds awkwardly, perhaps because he is so deeply repressed or filled with self-loathing, or perhaps because he is not really gay. In either case, Randall seems not to believe his good fortune with Victor, as if the lamb was simply offering itself to the lion.

After Randall has murdered Victor, he keeps a small photograph of him in his wallet, as one might do with the photograph of a sweetheart. This evocative detail again raises the question of the relationship between homosexuality and murder. But Randall insists that he "didn't really like" sex (52) and craved murder as a sensual experience, the way others might crave sex. Indeed, while Abdoh aimed to assault his audience with the brutality of murder, Grimsley instead offers poetic descriptions that focus on the gruesome yet sensual aspects of murder, going into detail about the sounds ("the crack of that bone") and smells ("this incredible aroma of the inside of him") of the act (52). The penultimate scene plays with horrific irony as the audience watches Victor, all the while knowing that his expectation of sex will be replaced with Randall's plans for murder. At the climax, Grimsley replaces one sensual experience with another, creating a murderer who is not physically attracted to another man but eroticizes the act of murder and the corpse as the object of desire. Whether this displacement is caused by Randall's internalized homophobia is left open to interpretation, but the play creates a clear distinction between the erotics of same-sex desire expressed by Victor and the erotics of death expressed by Randall.

Fascination further deconstructs the homophobic conflation of homosexuality and murder by including the character Holly, a deeply Christian woman who sees Randall on television and decides that she can save him. She proposes marriage to Randall, since getting married would prove that he is not gay, and if he is not gay, then he would not be a gay serial killer, and then he would be innocent and free (33). Holly's strange proposal exposes the homophobic narrative that constructs gay as guilty and not gay as innocent, since she seems to believe that evidence of heterosexual normalcy can erase all other evidence of homosexual deviance, including murder. This heterosexual marriage, condoned by the state and legitimized by society, is a sham, and Grimsley employs subtle satire to expose Holly's delusions about love, as well as her deluded morality.

The play contrasts the superficial bond between Randall and Holly as legal husband and wife with the more ambiguous and haunted bond between Randall and Victor. *Fascination,* like *The Law of Remains,* delves into the metaphysical and spiritual realm surrounding death. In the fantastic world of the play, the spirit of Victor now "lives" in the ground under Randall's house, keeping watch over his killer. As a spirit, Victor has great powers of insight, and he describes Randall's thoughts and feelings, his rage and fear, to the audience. The connection between Victor and Randall is more profound now than it ever was in life, and this contrast serves not so much to romanticize relationships with the dead as much as it highlights the sad lack in the relationships of the living. Indeed, in depicting the afterlife onstage, *Fascination* transforms the theater into an ethereal limbo between the living and the dead, and it also imagines the possibility for comfort and community among the dead. Victor tells us of his interactions with all the other murdered boys, serving as a guide for each of the victims as he passes from life into death. He is joined by Randall's dead mother, who was physically unable to care for Randall when she was alive and now turns to caring for the spirits of his victims. Grimsley's afterlife is disturbing but also comforting, allowing us to imagine that death is not an absolute end and might be a place where a murderer's dead mother can bake cookies for the boys murdered by her son (41).

Chicago critics gave mixed reviews to this ninety-minute play, which alternates between the carnal and the spiritual, the poetic and the prosaic, the beautiful and the horrifying. Most recognized that, as Jonathan Abarbanal stated in the *Windy City Times*, "*Fascination* is not so much about Randall as how others respond to him in this life and the next."[24] The critics themselves, then, became part of the cast of characters responding to the representation of the gay serial killer. Abarbanal thought the portrayal was too restrained to offer deeper insight, while Tony Adler of the *Chicago Reader* complained that by showing the reporter, nosy neighbor, and religious fanatic as caricatures the play ran the danger of making Randall seem like a sympathetic victim.[25] The strongest detraction, however, came from Chris Jones of the *Chicago Tribune*, who declared that "the annals of dramatic literature need no more portraits of serial killers. Period."[26] For Jones the subject matter itself is the problem, and he's further offended that a gay theater company would present the stereotype of the gay murderer, describing the production as "gimmicky, grant-funded irresponsibility" and presuming that it will "irritate greatly" About Face's gay audience.

The theater critics for the alternative and gay newspapers of Chicago did not seem to share Jones's outrage over the "irresponsibility" of representing a gay serial killer onstage. Indeed, even when they found fault with the script or the production, nearly all critics took seriously the play's attempt to illuminate the phenomenon of the queer serial killer as a figure of fascination in American culture. Randall is fascinating to his victims and the audience in part because he cannot be fully explained—we bring our own ideologies and feelings about sex and death to fill in the tantalizing void at the heart of his character. Thus Grimsley's play simultaneously fascinates and frustrates, not resolving the contradictions and ambiguities of the queer serial killer but reflecting them.

Acting Alone: The Serial Killer Solo

At the end of the first decade of the twenty-first century, the Dahmer-inspired gay serial killer appeared onstage in yet another theatrical form. Bill Connington wrote and performed the one-man show *Zombie* as part of the New York International Fringe Festival in the summer of 2008 and, on the strength of many positive reviews, remounted the show, directed by Thomas Caruso, for an extended run at a small midtown theater in 2009. Adapted from the novella by Joyce Carol Oates, *Zombie* takes the form of a monologue delivered by seemingly ineffectual but deeply sinister Quentin P.[27] Although it does not literally represent Dahmer, the play clearly uses him as a model, creating Quentin as a midwestern homosexual sociopath who kidnaps young men (mostly black young men) so he can perform do-it-yourself lobotomies and turn them into his "zombie" sex slaves. If Abdoh's theatricality was noisy and assaultive, and Grimsley's lyrical and mournful, then Connington's theatricality was cold and clinical, presenting the killer as an object of study.

The redacted last name of Quentin P. might suggest that we are studying a psychological case file, and Quentin relates episodes from his life in an understated manner, with as little commentary as possible. In his cheap slacks, collared shirt, and large plastic-frame glasses, Quentin could easily be mistaken for an accountant. His manner of speaking is overly precise—and as oily as his thinning hair—but his ominously smooth tones are occasionally disturbed by bursts of psychopathic fury. He offers a portrait of the killer as a loser, rejected by peers at school, unloved by his father, and ashamed of his homosexuality. This constant sense of alienation causes Quentin to want to create objects of desire who cannot reject him.

Like *The Law of Remains* and *Fascination, Zombie* asks its audience to consider horrific acts—including raping, killing, and disposing of people—but it does so with chilling detachment. The production underscores this detachment by using a mannequin to represent Quentin's victims in his "restaging" of events. The actor playing Quentin is alone onstage, which emphasizes his alienation, but he also enacts certain scenes with a life-size cloth mannequin with barely discernible and completely immobile facial features on its Styrofoam head. *Zombie* becomes highly metatheatrical, with Quentin as a performer staging his acts by manipulating this dummy. This theatricality is consistent with Oates's theory that "the psychopathic serial killer is a deep fantasist of the imagination, his fixations cruel parodies of romantic love and his bizarre, brutal acts frequently related to cruel parodies of 'art.'" In particular, Oates describes the killer's "seemingly insatiable need to orchestrate, and reorchestrate, a drama of hallucinated control."[28] By turning Quentin into a puppet master, the play creates a striking metaphor for the killer's "drama of control."

As the title *Zombie* suggests, Oates is most interested in how the necrophiliac "exerts control over the dead body as, he believes, he could never exert control over the living."[29] In Connington's theatrical version, Quentin the loser becomes the "puppet master" of an incapacitated lover who can never reject or leave him—or expose him as homosexual or force him

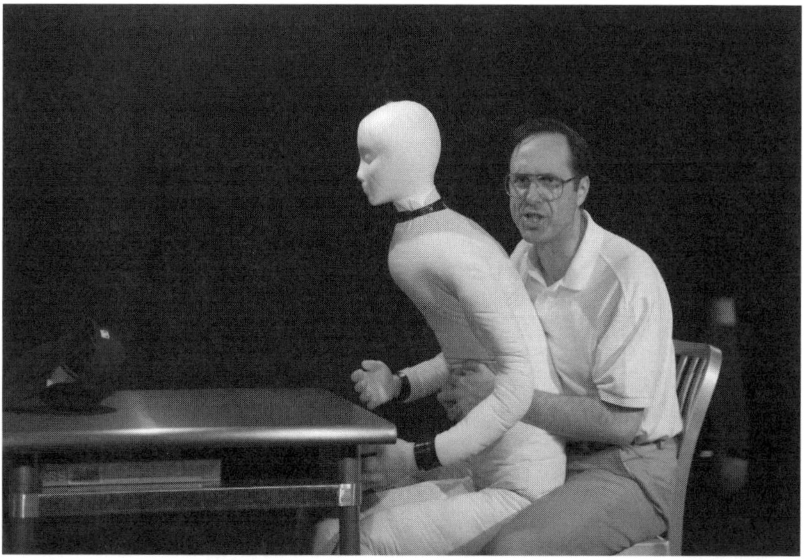

Bill Connington plays serial killer Quentin in his adaptation of Joyce Carol Oates's novella *Zombie*, produced at the Studio Theatre in New York in 2009. Photo: Dixie Sheridan.

to confront his own homosexuality. The use of a life-size mannequin onstage also creates an experience of the *uncanny*—which Freud theorized as that which is at once familiar and strange, human-seeming and yet not human.[30] While the sociopathic Quentin sees a human being as no more than a puppet, the audience's imagination can endow the inanimate puppet with humanity, recognizing that this stage prop is meant to represent an actual human being that suffered and died.

The serial killer as puppet master was also imagined by Dennis Cooper in his 1993 short story *Jerk,* which was re-created as a stage play in 2010, performed by French actor Jonathan Capdevielle and directed by Gisèle Vienne.[31] Cooper's literary novels often explore the darker shades of the homoerotic imagination, with characters who engage (or fantasize about engaging) in brutal acts of sexual violence. *Jerk* focuses on David Brooks, who, as a teenager in Texas in the 1970s, joined his classmate Wayne and an older psychopath named Dean in the murder of other teenage boys.[32] Presumably as part of his therapy, David has come to a theater to perform a puppet show about those events for students at the University of

Jonathan Capdevielle performs in *Jerk*, adapted by Gisèle Vienne from Dennis Cooper's short story, staged as part of the Under the Radar Festival at P.S. 122 in New York in 2010. Photo: Alain Monot.

Texas. Through his performance with puppets, David reenacts scenarios in which the murderers treat their victims like puppets, manipulating the bodies of—and giving voice to—the corpses in a drama of sexual fantasy.

As Wayne explains to Dean as they abuse a corpse, "Who cares what the fucker was really like? Killing's just about *power,* man. You can make up whoever you want and like . . . imagine that person in this fucker's body" (19). So Dean imagines he's having sex with a teenage star from the TV show *Flipper,* and later Wayne will imagine another dead boy as Jimmy Page of the rock band Led Zeppelin. In Cooper's scenario, sexualized murder is rooted in a fantasy of power, forcing the corpses to play the roles of famous and desirable men whom the murderers, in reality, could never dominate. But Cooper also suggests that these murderous fantasies are the result of an inability to love created by internalized homophobia. Wayne calls one corpse a "faggot," but with another he's filled with regret and cries, "Jamie, I loved you, man. I could never tell you" (27). It's only when the object of affection is a corpse, an inert mass manipulated by the killer, that the killer can admit his same-sex romantic desire. The living lover is fickle and cannot be so easily controlled, so when Dean rejects Wayne, Wayne kills Dean, and when Wayne rejects David, David attacks Wayne.

If Connington's Quentin is the killer as dorky loser, Capdevielle's David is the killer as brooding hipster. The actor appears as a handsome but disheveled young man—with a neck tattoo, bed head, and a few days' worth of stubble—and he speaks with a heavy French accent. He wears blue jeans, black boots, a black leather jacket, and a hoodie that says "JERK," which he strips off to reveal a sleeveless t-shirt. During his puppet show, David uses different voices to portray the other characters, and his puppets are Bunraku-like dolls, complete with legs and shoes, although "Dean" and "Wayne" initially have animal heads (panda and otter, respectively). At times the performance is excruciating, with the performer making repetitive guttural sounds and/or drooling spit as he imitates at great length Dean fisting a corpse, David snogging Wayne, and other acts of sex and violence.

As in *Zombie,* the corpses in *Jerk* are played by puppets, conveying a creepy lifelessness. The production becomes a meta–puppet show when the actor playing David is giving voice to the puppets playing the killers, who in turn give voice to the puppets playing the corpses. Puppets, like corpses, are uncanny because they resemble humans but are not actually alive. In the final scenario, though, David abandons his puppets and does all the voices, including his own, as a ventriloquist, not moving his lips, as if he is also losing his humanity, becoming increasingly inanimate. In the story, David is ultimately alone in a house of corpses, and in performance he is alone on an empty stage, with only lifeless puppets sharing the space.

Our culture's fascination with serial killers exists in part because, as Oates put it in her analysis of Dahmer, we recognize "connections between extremes of psychopathic behavior and behavior considered 'normal.'"[33] But these connections do not necessarily lead to an easy understanding or explanation of the serial killer. Indeed, Oates finds that "Dahmer remains a riddle" and "we understand him, finally, no better than we understand ourselves."[34] One of the traditional claims about theatrical performances is that they "humanize" their subjects, eliciting the audience's empathy for even the most monstrous characters. Yet both *Zombie* and *Jerk* present performances that can be deliberately repulsive, challenging the audience's ability to empathize. In his portrait of British serial killer Dennis Nilson, Brian Masters writes that the most disturbing aspect of his subject is not his terrible crimes but his capacity for "inhuman detachment" in the face of those crimes.[35] The serial killers of *Zombie* and *Jerk* are themselves uncanny because we recognize the "connections" between their humanity and ours, but their "detachment"—their ability to treat other humans as no more than mannequins or puppets—marks them as "inhuman." Both Oates and Cooper imagine serial killers as warped versions of theater artists, creating dramas of power and control by manipulating their victims like characters in a play. To perform these killers in the theater, then, is to turn them into puppets as well, opening up for the audience the possibility of human connection and empathy, but also forcing us to confront our potential for detachment and repulsion.

Aileen Wuornos: Acting in Self-Defense

In the same year in which America witnessed the release of *The Silence of the Lambs* and the arrest of Jeffrey Dahmer, the arrest of Aileen Wuornos also caused a sensation. Wuornos, a hitchhiking prostitute who killed seven men in Florida before her arrest, was (inaccurately) branded as "the first female serial killer." The media also sensationalized her romantic relationship with Tyria Moore to construct Wuornos as a "man-hating lesbian murderer." As an "unnatural monster," the lesbian serial killer may share certain features with the gay male serial killer in the public imagination, but she also occupies a position uniquely her own, constructed by homophobic *and* sexist ideologies. Just as a discussion of the homicidal homosexual in queer theater would be incomplete without analysis of lesbian representation and production (see chapter 4), an examination of representations of Aileen Wuornos is necessary to understand more fully the construction of the queer serial killer in American culture.

Representations of the lesbian serial killer have already received much critical attention, particularly from Lynda Hart in *Fatal Women: Lesbian Sexuality and the Mark of Aggression* (1994). Hart argues that female prostitutes are often the victims of violence, including rape and murder, but since the patriarchal order condones violence against women, it cannot acknowledge Wuornos's claims of self-defense. For Hart, Wuornos's murders were acts of resistance, not only against the men who attempted to rape and murder her but also against a symbolic order that denies women any subjectivity, making them figures for men's objectification, and therefore victims of their violence.[36] Indeed, Hart writes about Wuornos as the actualization of a paranoid male fantasy of the murderous woman. Those belonging to the patriarchy "eroticize their worst nightmares" about the femme fatale in order to "preclude their actualization," and Wuornos has to be executed because she "has violated that barrier" between fantasy and reality, taking a role as an active subject in her own defense.[37] The State of Florida found Wuornos guilty of murder and executed her on 8 October 2002.

After the initial media frenzy and a well-regarded documentary by Nick Broomfield, Wuornos's story moved into the realm of dramatic narrative, with an off-Broadway play and a major Hollywood film inspired by her story.[38] In both works, female creators retell the case and express sympathy for Wuornos—and the play, first produced when Wuornos was still alive, mounts a vigorous defense for her. Carson Kreitzer's play, *Self Defense, or Death of Some Salesmen* (2001), imagines Wuornos as consciously enacting vigilante justice against men who would abuse women.[39] Kreitzer wrote the play as part of her *Women Who Kill* triptych, which also includes *Valerie Shoots Andy* (1993), about Valerie Solanas's attempt to kill Andy Warhol, and *Heroin/e* (1995), about Ellie Nesler, who shot and killed the man accused of molesting her son. After the play's premiere at the Perishable Theatre in Providence, Rhode Island, in 2001, and a subsequent production at the Playwrights' Center in Minneapolis, *Self Defense* received its New York production at New Georges, a company founded in 1992 dedicated to the work of women theater artists. The New Georges production at HERE Arts Center, a downtown venue known for experimental theater, opened in May 2002—just five months before Wuornos's execution.[40]

Self Defense is a well-researched play that accurately relates the events of Wuornos's murders and her trial, although (in the tradition of Meyer Levin's *Compulsion*) Kreitzer renames her characters in order to allow for some dramatic license and perhaps also to create some critical distance from the familiar media representations of Wuornos, whom Kreitzer renames Jolene Palmer. Furthermore, in her desire to explore the true causes and significance of the murders from many perspectives, Kreitzer explodes theatrical realism, allowing many characters, including Jo, to address the audience directly, often juxtaposing conflicting opinions and ideologies. Along with Jo's inner monologues and fantasies, which grant her a high degree of subjectivity rather than constructing her as an object for forensic study, the play also includes a chorus of other women—prostitutes and strippers, a coroner, a lawyer, a scholar—who articulate feminist perspectives on the broader contexts for Jo's violent acts.

The play presents evidence that Jo did indeed act in self-defense in all seven cases, although much of this evidence was not placed before the jury at the time of her trial. A prostitute named Daytona gives the most pointed explanation for the fact that no one, including the jury, believes that Jo murdered in self-defense.

> An' I'll tell you why they're not buying that Self Defense. What Self? Plain an' simple. Ask any one of 'em. They don't see a self there to defend. They even say—she sold herself for money. Sold her Self. No right to fuckin' defend it now. (317)

Jo's social status as a prostitute condemns her—as does her status as a lesbian, with prosecutors painting her as "this man-hating lesbian" (311). Kreitzer's Jo, however, is highly cognizant and articulate about social inequalities based on gender and class, countering these condemnations by exposing the hypocrisy and double standards by which she will be convicted. In what amounts to the play's call to arms, Jo explains her notion of feminist vigilante justice.

> There are, y'know, there are certain . . . activities that are just known to carry a Death Sentence. I'm not talking about Law here, I'm not talking about being illegal. I'm talking about the list of activities that, if you

> pursue them, these could very easily lead to death. . . . All's I'm saying is that *I want killing women to be added to that list.* And I'm not talking about a court of law, getting Caught. I'm talking about right there, at the time. Knowing, this is an activity that, if you engage in this activity, you could easily wind up dead. 'Cos killing women is not on that list right now. (302)

Kreitzer's play represents the facts of this real life case, but in this dramatic version Jo is allowed to mount her own stirring defense before the audience. Just as she acted in order to defend herself, she is now acting to defend the *meaning* of her self. Even the well-intentioned characters in the play do not really understand the significance of Jo's actions, so Jo herself must explain them to make sure that her acts are not misconstrued. While Kreitzer satirizes all the characters who would appropriate Jo's story, her sharpest dart is saved for Annie Ames, a Hollywood producer who wants to tell and sell Jo's story. As soon as the case unfolds in the tabloid press, Annie gleefully announces, "It's *Silence of the Lambs* meets *Thelma and Louise!*" (291). Thus the play tries to distance itself from the commercial exploitation inherent in the "based on a true story" appropriation of famous murder cases.

Shortly after the debut of *Self Defense*, the 2003 film *Monster,* written and directed by Patty Jenkins, earned much publicity because of the performance of its lead actress. The former ballerina and model Charlize Theron, who regularly appears on lists of the "Sexiest Women in the World," acquired fat, splotchy skin, stringy hair, and bad teeth in order to impersonate Wuornos (here named Lee).[41] Theron's performance garnered numerous awards, including the Oscar for Best Actress. The film is much more concerned than the play with Lee's sexuality and the difficulty of categorizing her as a lesbian. Like many of the later Leopold and Loeb retellings, *Monster* is framed as a love story, beginning with Lee's first meeting with Shelby (Christina Ricci), the young woman who will be her lover, and ending with Shelby testifying against Lee in court. Rather than showing the lesbian relationship as "man-hating," the film shows that Lee does not initially identify as a lesbian: when Shelby tries to flirt with her, she calls Shelby a "dyke" and insists that she isn't gay. But Lee's desire for Shelby grows, and soon Shelby is the only person for whom she feels love in her bleak existence.

The film is also much more explicit about acts of violence, showing the audience how Lee was tortured, raped, and threatened with death by one of her johns. This horrific scene ends with Lee shooting the john—and then taking his car, his clothes, and his red trucker hat, which she will wear in the next few scenes. One of the tropes found in the crime narratives describing the real life Wuornos is that she killed "like a man": using a gun (rather than poison), killing strangers (rather than family members), and taking pleasure in having power over someone else's life.[42] Jenkins's film highlights this "cross-gendered" dynamic by emphasizing Lee's appropriation of the car and clothes of her first male victim, potentially playing into the heterosexist fear that lesbians eradicate men by taking "the masculine position," effectively making men superfluous. At the same time, if an audience member reads this aggressive woman who wears men's clothes and wields a phallic gun as a "male" figure, then her murders can be symbolically read as acts of violence *between two men*, once again playing into the violence associated with male homosexuality. In this instance, the fear of the lesbian as "phallic woman" and the fear of male homosexuality collapse in on each other. In both cases, Lee's gender transgressions mark her as "monstrous."

But the film also elicits the audience's sympathy for this monster. Lee has a miserable life, and her good intentions and attempts to better herself meet with rejection and degradation, largely because of society's sexism and classism. *Monster* does not condemn Lee for being a prostitute or in love with a woman, although it does show both situations as the result of desperation more than desire. And Jenkins leaves no doubt that Lee is guilty of murder. The film presents her first murder as legitimate self-defense, but she then becomes irrationally vengeful, looking at all men as guilty until proven innocent, assuming that all men want to abuse women and therefore should be killed, in order to justify crimes actually committed for material gain. Unlike Kreitzer's Jo, Jenkins's Lee does not express a sophisticated analysis of social inequalities based on gender and class. She acts out of ego and greed, unable to understand why she has suffered so much and still not achieved the American Dream of luxury and property that she deserves.

The film's title raises the question of whether Lee is in fact a "monster." Especially in emphasizing the transformation of Theron from "beauty" into "beast," the film presents Lee as monstrous, with the actor's physical deformation mirroring the character's moral deformation. But, like the beast of the fairy tale, Lee earns our sympathy because it is not her fault that she is a beast. While *Self Defense* rails against Wuornos's circumstances and the social order that created them, the film presents her circumstances as unchangeable, the cruel context that will inevitably lead to her undoing. While the play demands that society change, *Monster* shows how poor women are fated to suffer in this society. The love Lee feels for Shelby may give her some temporary solace from her suffering, but ultimately she will be alone in the swampy Florida landscape, howling like an animal and committing murder, because that is all that she can do. *Monster* shows us the personal tragedy surrounding Wuornos's actions; *Self Defense* shows us the social injustice surrounding the way society determined the meaning of her actions.

Ridiculously Sensational: The Comedy of the Gay Serial Killer

Murder is a serious subject, and, historically, most plays that have included murder belong to serious genres, particularly tragedy. Yet nearly all the plays discussed in this book include humor to some extent, ranging from the grim to the witty to the outrageous. It might be argued that the modern theater is tragicomic, not simply interweaving tragic and comic elements but producing plays that encourage the audience to see the tragic and the comic in a single instance. Leaving aside the neoclassical argument that such genre mixing is aesthetically "monstrous," the use of murder within wholly comic plays may still raise ethical issues for a contemporary audience. Do we feel guilty for laughing at murder? And, if queer killers are, as I have been arguing, to be understood in relation to factors such as the closet, homophobia, and AIDS, can these social and political contexts also be laughing matters?

These ethical qualms may hover around all plays that deal with serious subjects, but they are more pronounced in comedy, because the audience's laughter functions as an outward sign of pleasure. Is it right to take pleasure in creating or viewing murderous violence? One of the American theater's most popular satirists, Christopher Durang, has written plays that reflect on their own status as violent comedies, questioning the ethics of creating and viewing comedies that include murder. Durang's depiction of a gay serial killer in *Betty's Summer Vacation* (1999) can make an audience laugh while also making them think about why they are laughing.

Christopher Durang earned his reputation in the 1980s as one of America's eminent satirists with comedies that confronted religious dogma (*Sister Mary Ignatius Explains It All for You*), psychoanalysis (*Be-*

yond Therapy), and dysfunctional families (*The Marriage of Bette and Boo*).[43] The 1990s were not as successful for Durang, but when Playwrights Horizons produced *Betty's Summer Vacation* at its off-Broadway theater in 1999, critics hailed it as his comeback hit and it won four Obie Awards.[44] Although the play has sometimes met with mixed critical reception and inspired some audience members to flee the theater, it remains popular, with numerous amateur and professional productions. In the summer of 2011, the Bay Street Theatre staged a revival directed by Trip Cullman, with Tony-nominated actors Veanne Cox, Celia Keenan-Bolger, and (in the role of the gay serial killer) Bobby Steggert.

Betty's Summer Vacation is a pitch black comedy. In this bloody and hysterical play, Durang includes the figure of the gay serial killer to satirize the madness of America's tabloid culture, inviting the audience to find both horror and humor in increasingly sensational acts of indecent exposure, rape, castration, and murder. Durang's critique of a puerile culture that has "gone too far" is ultimately about the *audience* for sex and violence, forcing us to question our own culpability as the consumers of such entertainment—including the play *Betty's Summer Vacation*.

The play takes place in the living room of an East Coast beach house, where Betty and her friend Trudy hope to find rest and relaxation but instead find themselves caught in a whirlwind of madness and mayhem. A collection of kooky characters interrupt Betty's vacation: Mrs. Siezmagraff, the landlady who declares Auntie Mame is her role model; Buck, a sexually insatiable surfer dude; Mr. Vanislaw, a derelict who keeps exposing himself; and Keith, a "sensitive" young man who carries a shovel and a hatbox that may contain body parts. Surreally, the house also seems to be home to a trio of "voices," supposedly coming from the ceiling, who laugh and occasionally make comments, much like a television studio audience. The sitcom-style zaniness, which in Durang's world always contains a hint of menace, becomes full-blown horror at the end of act 1, when the derelict rapes Betty's friend Trudy. Trudy avenges the rape by cutting off the derelict's penis, and then serial killer Keith cuts off his head.

In act 2, the Voices, who have grown increasingly demanding in their need to be constantly entertained, materialize onstage as a trio of menacing aliens who insist that Trudy and Keith be put on trial for their crimes à la Court TV. Mrs. Siezmagraff acts as the defense attorney, and by painting both Trudy and Keith as sympathetic victims of abuse rather than violent perpetrators, she convinces this jury of Voices to find them not guilty. But the Voices still aren't satisfied and want more sex and violence. They goad

Trudy and Keith into doing it again, this time castrating and beheading the surfer dude, Buck. Finally, the Voices convince Trudy and Keith to blow up the house and everyone in it—except for Betty, who escapes to the beach.

Although Keith is not the central character of *Betty's Summer Vacation,* he is crucial to the play's plot and themes. Keith is a strange young man, modeled in part on Robert Montgomery's charming murderer in the classic thriller *Night Must Fall* (1937), but also inspired by two of the media's favorite gay serial killers, Jeffrey Dahmer and Andrew Cunanan—with perhaps a dash of Norman Bates from *Psycho* (1960). He gets upset if he is around people for too long, so he spends most of his time alone in his room with his "collection" of body parts. When Keith does emerge, he takes particular interest in the other men in the house, although Durang describes this interest as "oddly innocent," as if Keith were a naive young man, unsure of why he is so attracted to Mr. Vanislaw and Buck. Keith makes sexual invitations to both men, but there are no same-sex relations in this play because Keith is ultimately more interested in beheading other men than sleeping with them.

When he is put on trial for murder, Mrs. Siezmagraff defends Keith by arguing that he was "molested," "treated really badly," and "unrelentingly criticized" by his large family, and that this terrible childhood is what caused him to murder. The Voices, acting as the jury, sympathize with Keith's pain, and so they set him free, although as soon as they do Keith admits that he killed people not only in "self-defense" but "also because I *like* to cut heads off" (55). So how does the audience judge Keith? He is the most violent character onstage, but he is also the "nicest"—he is boyish, shy, and generally polite unless he feels that his personal space is threatened. Trudy and Keith bond over their shared status as victims, and even Betty is surprised to find that she prefers the company of this sensitive sociopath to the other men in the house. But part of Durang's point is that a sympathetic person is not the same as an innocent person and no amount of victimization is an excuse for violent acts.

In his notes to the play, Durang explains that he wrote *Betty's Summer Vacation* in response to the explosion of tabloid television culture in the 1990s, the result of twenty-four-hour cable news channels such as CNN and Court TV. With the televised trials of O. J. Simpson, Lorena Bobbitt, and the Menendez Brothers, America existed under a constant bombardment of information about sensational legal cases. Arguably, in the age of the Internet, our culture's desire for constantly updated infotainment has grown even stronger. It is no wonder that Durang places Keith at the center of his satire of tabloid culture, since the queer serial killer satisfies the audience's desire for tales that involve "deviant" sex and violence. The main thrust of the play, however, is not to judge the gay serial killer but to judge the viewers of tabloid media who take pleasure in consuming such lurid characters and stories. The ultimate target of Durang's satire is the audience sitting in the theater, and those three grotesque, childlike creatures onstage demanding sex and violence are stand-ins for us. The Voices' constant demand for sensational entertainment creates a world in which nothing—from family relations and sexual desire to rape and murder—really has much significance. It is all just fodder for cheap thrills and even cheaper sentiment. As the Voices escalate their demands, Durang's play gets increasingly dark and bloody, and the climax is Keith blowing up the house and killing everyone inside, including the Voices, who are urging Keith along. In Durang's hyperbolic farce, the logical result of out-of-control tabloid sensationalism is suicidal nihilism, and the entire world of the play explodes into oblivion. Only Betty, the voice of reason throughout the play, escapes the house. Alone on the beach, unsure if she has had a breakdown or a breakthrough, she is comforted by the relaxing sound of the waves, which had been obscured by all the play's previous noise.

Betty's Summer Vacation has the potential to be extremely unsettling because it invites the audience to find entertainment in increasingly disturbing incidences of sex and violence, and the play is designed to make us feel at best queasy and at worst actually guilty about enjoying the play itself.[45] We are complicit in this performance, not just because Durang puts a ridiculous version of the audience onstage but because live theater always implicates its audience in a way that television, for example, does not. The play encourages a variety of responses—from sympathy to laughter to horror—while also challenging the audience to interrogate those responses. How do we balance our desire for stories of sex and violence with our sense of morality? By laughing at something, are we trivializing it, condoning it, or criticizing it? And if Durang can get us, members of the audience, to laugh at our own monstrosity, will we change our behavior?

In the final analysis, nearly everything about Durang's gay serial killer escapes analysis. His mysterious nature encourages our inquiries, but in the end he remains unknowable, since the play short-circuits all attempts to truly understand Keith through, for example, psychology, social context, medical and legal discourse, systems of morality, or genre convention—in short, through all of the methods I have attempted to apply to other homicidal homosexuals. Durang seems to throw his hands up and say that there is no explanation for Keith; he is simply a gay young man who enjoys cutting off people's heads. We would do better to explain ourselves as a culture, our penchant for tales of sex and violence, and our fascination with the likes of Keith. Laughing at Keith may be cathartic, because he is both ridiculous and terrifying, and at the end of the play the homicidal homosexual is swept off the stage and into oblivion. But the audience remains, and we are left to question our own complicity in creating and encouraging Keith, goading him on to more and more horrific crimes for our entertainment. If we laugh at those ridiculous Voices onstage, we are in fact laughing at our own excesses, and the laughter catches in our throats.

Nevertheless, I would argue that taking pleasure in the character of Keith is not a crime. Certainly any appetite taken to extremes is ridiculous, and Durang's critique of tabloid culture is trenchant: representations of sex and violence can be consumed excessively and thoughtlessly. But I believe his play works to engage the audience's critical response, and I read it as more provocative than condemnatory. We can take pleasure in Keith, but the play urges us to have a deeper understanding of how and why we enjoy this comical queer killer. Watching this character onstage can provoke our sympathy, horror, and even laughter, and all those feelings can be pleasurable for an audience. If these responses also lead to greater insight, not just into the character but also into ourselves, then this is one of the greatest pleasures to be had in the theater.

Afterword

> *Ghost:* Revenge his foul and most unnatural murder.
> *Hamlet:* Murder!
> *Ghost:* Murder most foul, as in the best it is;
> But this most foul, strange and unnatural.
>
> *Hamlet,* I.v.25–28

When considering the variety of factors that have inspired both the creators of and audiences for homicidal homosexual characters, it seems likely that such characters will continue to be created and find a home in the theater. The fears and desires grounded in the personal, social, and political realities of queer people are not, of course, universally shared or unchanging. Yet consider the many factors that persist in shaping the lives of many queer people, and therefore shape our understanding of the homicidal homosexual character: the imagined link between sexual deviance and criminal deviance, the fantasy of empowering queer people by shedding the role of victim in favor of the role of perpetrator, the desire to legitimize same-sex love, the fear that same-sex love cannot exist in a homophobic society, an identification and fascination with other queers (including real life killers), the secrecy and shame of the closet, the urge to express rage and other repressed emotions, the devastation of AIDS and its symbolic meanings, and the need to confront accusations of queer evil. Even as the political and social status of LGBT people shows signs of improvement, it seems to me that all of the above-mentioned factors maintain a powerful influence over queer lives.

Indeed, I expect that homicidal homosexual characters will continue to flourish as long as queer people must wrestle with their own status as "criminals" within our society. Clearly it is not enough that the US Supreme Court has legally decriminalized homosexuality or that same-sex marriage is recognized in some states. For many, queer people continue to pose a "threat" against which some Americans feel they must "protect" and "defend" themselves. If one can imagine a world where queer people are not treated as criminals—and do not have to struggle with their own sense of themselves as criminals—then perhaps the dramatic narrative of the homicidal homosexual will have less power. If the status of queerness changes to become simply a variation of human existence that carries no stigma, no shame or fear, no social or psychological repression, no victimization or criminalization, and no association with disease or evil—then perhaps the character of the homicidal homosexual will fade from the stage.

In her influential book *Terrorist Assemblages: Homonationalism in Queer Times* (2007), Jasbir K. Puar writes about this time of transition for LGBT American citizens, warning that acceptance and full citizenship "is contingent upon ever-narrowing parameters of white racial privilege, consumption capabilities, gender and kinship normativity, and bodily integrity."[1] Those who do not fit within these narrow parameters, then, are still vilified as deviant and deadly. Is it possible that the American theater will increasingly see murderous characters who represent those queer people still criminalized or pathologized in the popular imagination, including (but certainly not limited to) people who are poor, youths of color, immigrants, and persons who are transgender or nonmonogamous? If, as Puar argues, homonormativity relies on removing the deviant deadliness from the queer and placing it on the Arab or Muslim "monster-terrorist-fag," then this vilified conflation of religious, racial, national, and sexual difference will, inevitably, find its way to the stage in the figure of a queer killer. The archetype of the homicidal homosexual thrives not when queers are fully accepted or rejected but when we as a society are navigating the turbulent waters of uncertainty. Despite the rise of homonormativity, those struggles continue, and the theater remains a key venue for enacting and debating the uncertainties.

Yet, even as I hope for and work toward that world free of homophobia and other criminalizing prejudices, I do not desire the disappearance of the homicidal homosexual. I have argued that these characters wrestle with some of the most complex and often difficult aspects of queer existence. In doing so, they expand the discourse surrounding queer issues and themes. They may reiterate homophobic paradigms, and they may confront and challenge those paradigms—often they do both. My goal in this book has been to expose and explore the diverse and often contradictory readings that these representations can provoke. I have also tried to enrich our understanding of homicidal homosexuals as compelling characters who appear in an entertaining variety of theatrical forms and genres. Plays with homicidal homosexuals often defy easy categorization since they incorporate the realistic and the fantastic, the optimistic and the nihilistic, the reactionary and the progressive, the serious and the frivolous. The complexities and contradictions of homicidal homosexuals, simultaneously reflecting realities and realizing fantasies, make them exciting theatrical figures, and plays featuring them constitute a portion of our theatrical culture that I consider vibrant, challenging, and insightful in a manner rarely found in other representations of queer lives. They deserve a place on our stages, in our scholarship, and in the discourse that shapes our understandings of ourselves, our relationships, and our society.

Appendix: Plays with Homicidal Homosexuals

In writing this book, I have necessarily focused on some plays more than others, and some homicidal homosexual plays were left out altogether. The entries below, while not exhaustive, are an attempt to account for the great number of plays with homicidal homosexuals that inspired this book.

Each play's title is followed by the author, the year of its premiere, and a brief annotation. If the play is discussed in this book, I've noted in parentheses the chapter in which it appears.

Accomplice. Rupert Holmes, 1989. A thriller featuring not one but two same-sex conspiracies to kill off an unwanted spouse. (3)

The Agony and the Agony. Nicky Silver, 2006. A struggling playwright writes Nathan Leopold into his play, much to Leopold's dismay. (2)

All the Kings' Men. Glenn Kessler and Brian Salveson, 2003. Teen killer Alex King in prison and missing his forty-year-old lover.

Angry Fags. Topher Payne, 2013. Two gay men become vigilantes in response to a gay bashing, but their acts of violence have unforeseen repercussions.

Atta Boy. Brian Bowman, 2011. A white gay teenager and a middle-aged Pakistani American man have an affair, eroticizing each other as murderous outlaws. (2)

Beautiful Child. Nicky Silver, 2004. A pedophile's mother imagines that her son is guilty of murder. (6)

Becket. Jean Anouilh, 1960. King Henry loves Thomas, but Thomas loves God more, so Henry kills Thomas.

Betty's Summer Vacation. Christopher Durang, 1999. A sweet and gentle serial killer ruins Betty's quiet vacation at the beach. (7)

Beyond Therapy. Christopher Durang, 1981. Bruce is going to leave Bob to marry a woman, so Bob decides to shoot Bruce—with a starter's pistol. (7)

Blacklips. 1992–95. East Village "performance cult" with queers of every sort enacting gory deaths each week. (4)

Bluebeard. Charles Ludlam, 1970. A wicked doctor tries to create a new gender, but he destroys his failed creations. (4)

Burning Habits. Blair Fell. Gay vampires in a serialized soap opera staged in New York in the 1990s.

Busted Jesus Comix. David Johnston, 2003. A gay teenager gets in trouble for creating a comic book filled with sex and violence, and his own past involves a gruesome murder.

Carrie. Erik Jackson, 2006. Stephen King's outsider revenge fantasy gets a queer spin with a drag queen portraying the telekinetic teen whose prom goes to Hell. (4)

The Castle. Howard Barker, 1985. The "witch" Skinner leads a lesbian feminist revolution in medieval England, and she kills a builder to stop the construction of a patriarchal castle.

The Children's Hour. Lillian Hellman, 1934. Little Mary claims that her two female schoolteachers plan to murder her. False alarm, since in the end the lesbian Martha kills herself.

Cock-Ups. Simon Moss, 1981. Kenneth Halliwell murders his lover, playwright Joe Orton.

The Colored Museum. George C. Wolfe, 1986. In the segment "The Gospel According to Miss Roj" a snap queen from Hell suffers no fools. (6)

Compulsion. Meyer Levin, 1958. Leopold and Loeb as juvenile delinquents in need of help. (2)

Conquest of the Universe, or When Queens Collide. Charles Ludlam, 1967. The evil Tamberlaine makes his conquered foes his sexual slaves and is especially fond of the King of Mars. (4)

Corpse! Gerald Moon, 1984. A gay actor impersonates his twin in order to kill him. (3)

Deathtrap. Ira Levin, 1978. Two lovers plot to kill an unwanted wife and then try to kill each other in Broadway's longest-running thriller. (3)

Diary of a Somebody. John Lahr, 1986. Based on the Orton diaries, recounting the playwright's murder by his lover, Kenneth Halliwell.

Dickie & Babe: The Truth About Leopold & Loeb. Daniel Henning, 2007. Docudrama retelling of the classic case. (2)

Die! Mommie! Die! Charles Busch, 2001. Busch stars as a woman with an evil past. (4)

The Drag. Mae West, 1927. West's banned play features a bevy of drag queens, a duplicitous queer cad, and an abandoned lover who commits murder. (1)

The Dying Gaul. Craig Lucas, 1998. A widower seeks spiritual peace but turns his rage loose on the world. (6)

Entertaining Mr. Sloane. Joe Orton, 1964. A middle-aged brother and sister blackmail the murderous Mr. Sloane into splitting his "attentions" between the two of them.

Fascination. Jim Grimsley, 2003. A sometimes gory, sometimes surreal look at our fascination with a Dahmer-like killer and his victims. (7)

Fat Men in Skirts. Nicky Silver, 1988. An oedipal nightmare with queer tendencies. (6)

Feeling. Paul Cameron Hardy, 2013. The ghost of Jeffrey Dahmer discusses life and love with a distraught graduate student.

Free Will and Wonton Lust. Nicky Silver, 1991. A confused young man kills the object of his desire. (6)

Gin & "It." Reid Farrington, 2010. Stagehands creating Hitchcock's *Rope* get caught in their own story of desire and brutality. (2)

Golden Age. Roberto Aguirre-Sacasa, 2005. Nathan Leopold dates Archie Andrews, the all-American teen of comic book fame. (2)

Hothead Paisan. Donna DiMassa, 2004. The cult comic books about a "homicidal lesbian terrorist" become a musical at the Michigan Women's Festival.

The House of Von Macrame. Joshua Conkel, 2013. A world-famous fashion designer stays young by bathing in the blood of his slain models in this camp parody of horror films.

Jeffrey Dahmer Live! Avner Kam, 2011. A solo cabaret features the serial killer singing songs and telling the story of his life while in prison. (7)

Jerk. Dennis Cooper, adapted by Gisèle Vienne, 2010. David Brooks performs a puppet show, reenacting his serial murders in Texas in the 1970s. (7)

Judith of Bethulia. Charles Busch, 2012. Busch creates biblical camp as Judith, who murders the tyrannical Holofernes. (4)

The Killing of Sister George. Frank Marcus, 1965. The childlike Alice fears that her butch lover June, an actress, will murder her. False alarm, since in the end June's rival for Alice's affections, BBC executive Mercy Croft, "kills" June's character, Sister George.

The Law of Remains. Reza Abdoh, 1992. Jeffrey Dahmer meets Andy Warhol in an avant-garde nightmare. (7)

Leopold and Loeb: A Goddamn Laff Riot. Laural Meade, 2003. The Leopold and Loeb case performed as a deconstructed vaudeville. (2)

Lesbians Who Kill. Deb Margolin, 1992. Split Britches' exploration of the desire to kill, inspired by Aileen Wuornos. (4)

Lilies. Michel-Marc Bouchard, 1987. Unrequited love and an obsession with Saint Sebastian lead to murder in a Quebec boys' school in the 1890s.

The Lisbon Traviata. Terrence McNally, 1985. The loss of love drives an opera queen to kill. (5)

The Maids. Jean Genet, 1948. Two sisters fantasize about killing the lady of the house. Based on the Papin sisters.

The Martyrdom of St. Sebastian. Gabriel D'Annunzio, 1911. The saint is imagined as the victim of an unrequited lover, Emperor Diocletian.

Most Wanted. Michael Greif and Jessica Hagedorn, 2007. Andrew Cunanan sings.

The Mousetrap. Agatha Christie, 1952. One of us is a killer, and the masculine woman and feminine man seem like prime suspects. (3)

Murder among Friends. Bob Barry, 1975. A husband and a wife are both having an affair with the same bisexual man, and each has involved him in a plot to kill the other. (3)

My Sister in This House. Wendy Kesselman, 1981. The murderous Papin sisters seen through a feminist lens.

The Neon Woman. Tom Eyen, 1978. Divine stars as a murderous burlesque performer. (4)

Never the Sinner. John Logan, 1998. Leopold and Loeb as a love story. (2)

Non-Scene. Brian Fillis, 2003. A gay killer enacts scenarios of domestic happiness with his corpses.

Paradise. David Foley, 2006. Robbie loses his faith in God and love, as inner turmoil turns to violence.

The Paris Letter. Jon Robin Baitz, 2005. A youthful love affair sours when one man chooses to repress his homosexuality, with deadly results much later in life.

Pieces. Chris Phillips, 2012. A kept boy murders his sugar daddy in West Hollywood, and his defense attorney indicts the values of the gay community.

Poison Apple. Sean Galuszka, 2012. Wild Jerry invades the apartment of fastidious Paul. Each seems threatened by and attracted to the other, until one is revealed as a murderer.

Porcelain. Chay Yew, 1992. William Hope abandons John Lee, so John shoots his lover dead in a public restroom. (5)

Psycho Beach Party. Charles Busch, 1987. A teenager has a split personality: good girl versus murderous sexual dominatrix. (4)

Pterodactyls. Nicky Silver, 1993. Todd avoids death by becoming Death in this darkly comic exploration of mortality. (6)

Raised in Captivity. Nicky Silver, 1995. The objects of desire for a lonely gay man are all dangerous, including an imprisoned murderer who becomes his pen pal. (6)

The Rocky Horror Show. Richard O'Brien, 1973. A glam rock musical about a transvestite mad doctor trying to create the perfect man and killing his failed experiments. (4)

Rope. Patrick Hamilton, 1929. Two upper-class Englishmen kill a friend for fun. Loosely based on Leopold and Loeb. (2)

Rope Enough. Sky Gilbert, 2005. Two young men suspected of murder claim Leopold and Loeb as their role models. (2)

The Secretaries. Five Lesbian Brothers, 1993. Secretaries murder men in a monthly ritual, and a "good girl" unleashes her bad side. (4)

Self Defense. Carson Kreitzer, 2001. Aileen Wuornos as feminist vigilante. (7)

Shanghai Moon. Charles Busch, 2001. Another of Busch's tough-talking dames faces the jury over the murder of her Chinese lover. (4)

Silence! The Musical. Hunter Bell, Jon Kaplan, and Al Kaplan, 2011. This camp version of Jonathan Demme's *Silence of the Lambs* makes *all* performances of gender and sexuality rather ridiculous, so the perversion of the killer is actually "normalized." (7)

Sleuth. Anthony Shaffer, 1970. There's something queer about Andrew wanting to live with Milo and play murder games with him. (3)

Strangers in Paradox. Kate Bornstein, 2004. A transsexual-lesbian duo goes on a killing spree. (4)

Streamers. David Rabe, 1976. "Rough trade" turns brutal in a barrack room as an African American soldier kills the straight white soldier who interferes with his same-sex relations.

Surveillance, Punishment, and the Black Psyche. M. Lamar, 2013. A solo performance song cycle inspired by the actual murder case of Willie Francis, a black teenager who killed his white boss and lover in Louisiana in 1947.

The Talented Mr. Ripley. Phyllis Nagy, 1999. A stage adaptation of Patricia Highsmith's novel, with Ripley motivated by unrequited love for Dickie Greenleaf.

Thrill Me: The Leopold and Loeb Musical. Stephen Dolginoff, 2003. Leopold and Loeb sing. (2)

The Toilet. Amiri Baraka, 1964. Foots refuses to acknowledge his love for Karolis, so Karolis tries to kill Foots in the boys' bathroom at school.

Unidentified Human Remains and the True Nature of Love. Brad Fraser, 1989. A homoerotic friendship creates a serial killer and tests the limits of sex and love.

Vampire Lesbians of Sodom. Charles Busch, 1984. Two rivals seduce and suck the blood of young maidens over the centuries. (4)

Voyage to Lesbos. Five Lesbian Brothers, 1990. Bonnie is going to get married and leave the lesbian sisterhood behind, but one of her ex-lovers murders the groom. (4)

The Well of Horniness. Holly Hughes, 1983. A killer lesbian is on the loose in this "dyke noir" from the WOW Café Theatre. (4)

Zombie. Joyce Carol Oates, adapted by Bill Connington, 2008. Quentin P. abducts, lobotomizes, and kills young men in an attempt to create a sex slave. (7)

Notes

Introduction

1. Jonathan Ned Katz, *Gay American History* (New York: Thomas Y. Crowell, 1976). See also National Museum and Archive of Lesbian and Gay History, *The Gay Almanac* (New York: Berkley Books, 1996).

2. An exhaustive catalog of recent antigay rhetoric would be overwhelming, but a few pertinent examples will show how homosexuality is criminalized and vilified in American society. In July 2013 police in Baton Rouge, Louisiana, used sodomy laws to arrest men who discussed engaging in private consensual sexual relations. In 2009 the attorney general of Virginia, Ken Cuccinelli, stated his desire criminalize homosexual acts, since they do not "comport with natural law." Oklahoma state legislator Sally Kern gained national attention in 2008 (and received a standing ovation from her fellow Republican legislators) when she stated, "I honestly think [homosexuality is] the biggest threat our nation has, even more so than terrorism or Islam. . . . It will destroy our young people, it will destroy this nation!" Internationally, homosexuality is illegal in seventy-six countries, and American antigay activists such as Scott Lively have publicly championed the criminalization of homosexuality in Nigeria and of "homosexual propaganda" in Russia. Jim Mustian, "Gays in Baton Rouge Arrested under Invalid Sodomy Law," *Advocate,* 28 July 2013, http://theadvocate.com/home/6580728–125/gays-in-baton-rouge-arrested; Caitlin Dickson, "Fringe Factor: Should Oral Sex Be a Crime?," *Daily Beast,* 21 July 2013, http://www.thedailybeast.com/articles/2013/07/21/fringe-factor-should-oral-sex-be-a-crime.html; Ruth Fine, "Oklahoma Rep. Sally Kern Says Gays Are a National Threat, Worse Than Terrorism," *LGBT Weekly,* 12 September 2011, http://lgbtweekly.com/2011/09/12/oklahoma-rep-sally-kern-says-gays-are-a-national-threat-worse-than-terrorism/; Joe Jervis, "Scott Lively Again Takes Credit for Russia's Ban on Homosexual Propaganda," *Joe.My.God,* 22 July 2013, http://joemygod.blogspot.com/2013/07/scott-lively-again-takes-credit-for.html; Lucas Paoli Itaborahy and Jingshu Zhu, "State-Sponsored Homophobia," International Lesbian, Gay, Bisexual, Trans, and Intersex Association, May 2013, http://old.ilga.org/Statehomophobia/ILGA_State_Sponsored_Homophobia_2013.pdf.

3. Nina Auerbach, *Our Vampires, Ourselves* (Chicago: University of Chicago Press,

1995); Harry M. Benshoff, *Monsters in the Closet: Homosexuality and the Horror Film* (Manchester: Manchester University Press, 1997); Lynda Hart, *Fatal Women: Lesbian Sexuality and the Mark of Aggression* (Princeton, NJ: Princeton University Press, 1994); Vito Russo, *The Celluloid Closet: Homosexuality in the Movies,* rev. ed. (New York: Harper & Row, 1987).

4. Sean Griffin, *Tinker Belles and Evil Queens: The Walt Disney Company from the Inside Out* (New York: New York University Press, 2000).

5. For more on GLAAD, see its website, http://www.glaad.org/about/history.php.

6. For example, this narrative is reiterated in the documentary film based on Vito Russo's groundbreaking book *The Celluloid Closet,* directed by Rob Epstein and Jeffrey Friedman (Sony Pictures Classics, 1995).

7. Larry P. Gross, *Up from Invisibility: Gay Men, Lesbians, and the Media in America* (New York: Columbia University Press, 2001).

8. Vito Russo, *The Celluloid Closet: Homosexuality in the Movies,* rev. ed. (New York: Harper & Row, 1987).

9. Brent Hartinger, "Ask the Flying Monkey," After Elton (blog), 19 August 2008, http://www.afterelton.com/askmonkey/08-19-08?page=0%2C1.

10. See John M. Clum, *Still Acting Gay: Male Homosexuality in Modern Drama* (New York: St. Martin's Griffin, 2000); Alan Sinfield, *Out on Stage: Lesbian and Gay Theatre in the Twentieth Century* (New Haven, CT: Yale University Press, 1999); and Alisa Solomon and Framji Minwalla, eds., *The Queerest Art: Essays on Lesbian and Gay Theater* (New York: New York University Press, 2002).

11. Here I am echoing Roland Barthes's famous assertion that "a text's unity lies not in its origin but in its destination." See Roland Barthes, "The Death of the Author," in *Image-Music-Text,* trans. Stephen Heath (New York: Hill and Wang, 1978), 142–48.

12. See Jill Dolan, *The Feminist Spectator as Critic* (Ann Arbor: University of Michigan Press, 1991) for an influential work that theorizes and exemplifies this kind of interpretive practice.

13. Stanley Cavell, "The Avoidance of Love," in *Disowning Knowledge in Six Plays of Shakespeare* (New York: Cambridge University Press, 1987), 118.

14. Oscar Wilde, "The Decay of Lying," in *The Complete Works of Oscar Wilde* (New York: Harper & Row, 1989), 978.

15. Georges Bataille, *Erotism: Death and Sensuality,* trans. Mary Dalwood (San Francisco: City Lights Books, 1991), 68.

16. Ibid., 17–18. Note, however, that Bataille's insistence on the violence of sex contains a crucial exception: "If eroticism leads to harmony between the partners its essential principle of violence and death is invalidated" (167).

17. For example, Sissela Bok, in *Mayhem: Violence as Public Entertainment* (Reading, MA: Perseus Books, 1998), rails against the dangers of media violence until the final segment of her book, where she focuses on educating impressionable children in "media literacy."

18. Hart, *Fatal Women,* 26.

19. One way to understand victimization is through the prevalence of violent crimes against gay people, although statistics on antigay violence are troubled by the underreporting of such crimes and the difficulty of categorization when it comes to sexual identity. The US Department of Justice recorded 1,706 incidents of sexual-orientation

bias in 2008, accounting for 17.6 percent of all hate crime offenses that year. The majority of these crimes (57.5 percent) are categorized under "anti-male homosexual bias," and 72 percent of hate crimes against gay, lesbian, and bisexual people involved physical violence, including rape and murder—a much higher rate than in crimes of racial and religious bias. http://www2.fbi.gov/ucr/hc2008/victims.html.

20. Eve Kosofsky Sedgwick has helped define *queer* as a term that interrogates assumptions about empirical categories of identity and acknowledges that the actual qualities and components of individual identities cannot always "be made to line up neatly together." Eve Kosofsky Sedgwick, *Tendencies* (Durham, NC: Duke University Press, 1993), 13.

21. In her groundbreaking book *Fatal Women: Lesbian Sexuality and the Mark of Aggression,* Lynda Hart illuminated how misogynistic understandings of female sexuality coded the lesbian as murderous within cultural narratives, and Lisa Duggan's *Sapphic Slashers: Sex, Violence, an American Modernity* (Durham, NC: Duke University Press, 2000) revealed how newspapers in the 1890s "portray[ed] romance between women as dangerous, insane, and violent," thus diminishing women's struggles for equality (2). My own interpretations of lesbian killers in chapters 4 and 7 are particularly indebted to Hart's excellent work in the field of lesbian representation.

22. Eve Kosofsky Sedgwick, *The Epistemology of the Closet* (Berkeley: University of California Press, 1990), 44.

23. As David M. Halperin has pointed out, actual practices of same-sex relationships have varied greatly over the course of history, and changing social concepts structure our understanding of sexuality. Nevertheless, nearly all the characters in this study exist in a world informed by the relatively recent concept of homosexuality, which Halperin describes as an "unstable conjunction" of the psychiatric notion of lifelong orientation, the psychoanalytic notion of sexual object choice, and the sociological notion of sexually deviant behavior. David M. Halperin, *How to Do the History of Homosexuality* (Chicago: University of Chicago Press, 2002), 131.

Chapter 1

1. Mae West, *The Drag,* in *Three Plays by Mae West,* ed. Lillian Schlissel (New York: Routledge, 1997). All page references in parentheses refer to this edition.

2. Michel Foucault, *The History of Sexuality, vol. 1: An Introduction,* trans. Robert Hurley (New York: Vintage Books, 1990).

3. Hubert Kennedy, *Ulrichs: The Life and Work of Karl Heinrich Ulrichs, Pioneer of the Modern Gay Movement* (Boston: Alyson Publications, 1988).

4. Vern Bullough, *Science in the Bedroom: A History of Sex Research* (New York: Basic Books, 1994). See also Jonathan Ned Katz, *The Invention of Heterosexuality* (New York: Plume, 1995).

5. When Sigmund Freud published "Three Essays on the Theory of Sexuality" (1905), he rejected the notion of inversion, noting that gender behavior and sexual object choice are not necessarily linked. Although he continued to write of homosexuality as an "aberration," he did not believe that it was "caused" either by congenital degeneration or by moral turpitude. Sigmund Freud, *Three Essays on the Theory of Sexuality,* trans. James

Strachey (New York: Basic Books Classics, 2000). See also the widely reprinted 1935 "Letter to an American Mother," in *Come Out Fighting: A Century of Essential Writing on Gay and Lesbian Liberation*, ed. Chris Bull (New York: Thunder's Mouth Press, 2001).

6. Karen Halttunen, *Murder Most Foul: The Killer and the American Gothic Imagination* (Cambridge, MA: Harvard University Press, 1998), 32.

7. Ibid., 58.

8. Ibid., 239.

9. Ibid., 244.

10. Eve Kosofsky Sedgwick, *The Epistemology of the Closet* (Berkeley: University of California Press, 1990), 44–48.

11. George Chauncey, *Gay New York: Gender, Urban Culture, and the Making of the Gay Male World, 1890–1940* (New York: Basic Books, 1994), 5.

12. Ibid., 48.

13. Ibid., 57.

14. Ibid., 69–70. Chauncey notes the changing use of the term, initially "the customer of a fairy prostitute" and later "straight-identified men who worked as prostitutes serving gay-identified men." But *trade* does not necessarily indicate a financial transaction. *Rough trade* can refer to an "unpolished" heterosexual who has the potential to become violent with a gay partner.

15. As Chauncey explains, sex was something you did to someone, not with someone, and the choice of an effeminate male partner for sexual release did not necessarily carry the stigma of abnormality. "The most striking difference between the dominant sexual culture of the early twentieth century and that of our own era is the degree to which the earlier culture permitted men to engage in sexual relations with other men, often on a regular basis, without requiring them to regard themselves—or to be regarded by others—as gay" (ibid., 65).

16. Ibid., 61.

17. Ibid., 72.

18. Ibid., 133.

19. Ibid., 7.

20. West exposed and attacked duplicity, especially sexual duplicity, as a villainous trait in other plays, including *Sex* (1926), in which a prostitute challenges the hypocrisy of a slumming society dame, and *The Pleasure Man* (1928), in which a young man avenges his innocent sister, who was seduced and abandoned by a dapper vaudeville star. Among the show's vaudeville performers, *The Pleasure Man* also features a female impersonator named Paradise Dupont, who is the sympathetic voice of reason and honesty, extolling the virtues of plain speaking and "being oneself." In West's world, the issue is not so much what kind of sex one has (homosexual, extramarital, or professional) but whether one is honest about it. Gay men and prostitutes are not the villains; snooty socialites and lying libertines are. Both *Sex* and *The Pleasure Man* can be found in Mae West, *Three Plays by Mae West,* ed. Lillian Schlissel (New York: Routledge, 1997). For more on West's dramatic works, see Richard Helfer, "Mae West on Stage: Themes and Persona" (PhD diss., City University of New York, 1990).

21. Indeed, Chauncey points out that gay men in this era did not use the term *coming out* to refer to emerging from a closet and being recognized as gay by family, coworkers,

and friends; rather they came out *into* homosexual society, in the way a debutante comes out in high society (*Gay New York,* 7).

22. Ibid., 172–73.

23. Ibid., 140.

24. Ibid., 200.

25. West does not treat David's heroin addiction as a dramatic revelation or a major plot point; the characters speak of it in passing in a matter-of-fact way. Rather, the addiction is simply one of many justifications for David's "hysterical" behavior, an indication of the weakness of his character and perhaps a sign of his generally tawdry "low life" existence.

26. For an account of how West constructed this scene, including her use of the drag performers she found in nightclubs, see Jill Watts, *Mae West: An Icon in Black and White* (New York: Oxford University Press, 2001); and Kaier Curtin, *"We Can Always Call Them Bulgarians": The Emergence of Lesbians and Gay Men on the American Stage* (Boston: Alyson Publications, 1987).

27. West gives Rolly a single moment, just before his death, when it is possible to have some sympathy for him: after the end of the party, when he is alone with his butler, he "stands at center, lost in thought and repeats Grayson's name" (134). It is a small detail, but for the first time Rolly has the chance to show his sensitive side and perhaps convince the audience that he genuinely loves Grayson. Nevertheless, within the dramatic framework of the play, Rolly is undeniably cast as the villain.

28. *Zit Theatrical Newspaper, Variety,* and *New York Graphic,* all cited in Curtin, *"We Can Always Call Them Bulgarians,"* 81–82.

29. Marybeth Hamilton, *When I'm Bad, I'm Better: Mae West, Sex, and American Entertainment* (New York: Harper Collins, 1995), 97.

30. "Confidential Performance of 'Drag' for Endorsement," *Variety,* 9 February 1927, cited in Curtin, *"We Can Always Call Them Bulgarians,"* 87–88.

31. Curtin, *"We Can Always Call Them Bulgarians,"* 99.

32. Chauncey, *Gay New York;* Curtin, *"We Can Always Call Them Bulgarians";* Hamilton, *When I'm Bad, I'm Better;* West, *Three Plays by Mae West,* edited by Lillian Schlissel; and Watts, *Mae West* all support this interpretation.

33. Watts, *Mae West,* 92.

34. Curtin, *"We Can Always Call Them Bulgarians,"* 102. A few plays featuring gay and lesbian characters skirted the law, as long as they functioned as cautionary tales, usually ending with the death of the queer character. Martha, near the end of Lillian Hellman's *The Children's Hour* (1934), confesses her lesbian desires and immediately kills herself. Tennessee Williams's gay characters—Alan in *A Streetcar Named Desire* (1947), Skipper in *Cat on a Hot Tin Roof* (1955), and Sebastian in *Suddenly Last Summer* (1958)—are dead (victims of suicide or murder) before the curtain rises and never appear onstage. See Jordan Schildcrout, "Drama and the New Sexualities," in *The Oxford Handbook of American Drama* (New York: Oxford University Press, 2014).

35. Curtin's own groundbreaking research helped to remedy this situation, as did Lillian Schlissel's publication of the play's text in West, *Three Plays by Mae West,* in 1997.

36. Although the play's publication in 1997 has not yet inspired a major production, there have been public presentations of the play by the Lambda Players in Sacramento, California, and New Village Productions in New York City.

Chapter 2

1. Paul Cameron, "Violence and Homosexuality," Family Research Institute, 1993, accessed 25 April 2010, http://www.familyresearchinst.org/2009/02/violence-and-homosexuality/.

2. "Gay Secret That Made Snipers Kill," *National Enquirer,* 12 November 2002, 34–37.

3. "Killer's Secret Gay Life," *Globe,* 7 May 2007.

4. See Lothar Machtan, *The Hidden Hitler* (New York: Basic Books, 2001); Corey Robin, "The Way We Live Now: Closet-Case Studies," *New York Times Magazine,* 16 December 2001, 23. See also Jasbir Puar, *Terrorist Assemblages: Homonationalism in Queer Times* (Durham, NC: Duke University Press), 2007. Puar argues that with the "normalization" of many gay Americans, the perverse sexuality of the queer is now attached to the terrorist—and to the Middle East and Islam in general. Puar also directly addresses the case of Mohamed Atta (58–59). The post-9/11 relationship between homophobia and xenophobia was the theme of the performance piece *Atta Boy,* by Brian Bowman (staged off-off-Broadway in January 2011), which imagined a hotel room assignation between a white gay teenager and a middle-aged Pakistani American man, both queer outsiders who eroticize the murderous outlaw.

5. Eve Kosofsky Sedgwick, *The Epistemology of the Closet* (Berkeley: University of California Press, 1990), 44.

6. Much has been written about Leopold and Loeb, and I have relied on the following sources for information about the facts of the case. In order of publication: Frederick A. Mackenzie, *Twentieth Century Crimes* (Boston: Little, Brown, 1927); Francis X. Busch, *Prisoners at the Bar: Notable American Trials* (Indianapolis: Bobbs-Merrill, 1952); Hal Higdon, *The Crime of the Century: The Leopold and Loeb Case* (New York: G. P. Putnam's Sons, 1975); Paula S. Fass, "Making and Remaking an Event: The Leopold and Loeb Case in American Culture," *Journal of American History* 80, no. 3 (December 1993) 919–51; and Gilbert Geis and Leigh B. Bienen, *Crimes of the Century: From Leopold and Loeb to O. J. Simpson* (Boston: Northeastern University Press, 1998).

7. Patrick Hamilton, *Rope: A Play* (London: Constable, 1929). All page references in parentheses refer to this edition.

8. For a thorough discussion of how homosexuality is constructed through connotation in Alfred Hitchcock's 1948 film adaptation of *Rope,* see D. A. Miller, "Anal Rope," reprinted in *Inside/Out,* ed. Diana Fuss (New York: Routledge, 1991); and Robin Wood, "The Murderous Gays: Hitchcock's Homophobia," reprinted in *Out in Culture: Gay, Lesbian, and Queer Essays on Popular Culture,* ed. Corey K. Creekmur and Alexander Doty (Durham, NC: Duke University Press, 1995).

9. Alan Sinfield, *Out on Stage: Lesbian and Gay Theatre in the Twentieth Century* (New Haven, CT: Yale University Press, 1999), 170. Sinfield also notes that these differences are less pronounced in Hitchcock's film version, and John M. Clum argues that the film uses the similarity between John Dall and Farley Granger to construct homosexuality as narcissism. John M. Clum, *He's All Man: Learning Masculinity, Gayness, and Love from American Movies* (New York: Palgrave, 2002), 116–17.

10. Robert Littell, "The New Play," *World News,* 20 September 1929.

11. *Rope,* directed by Alfred Hitchcock, screenplay by Arthur Laurents, from the play by Patrick Hamilton (Warner Bros., 1948). Hitchcock's film, which relocates the action to New York in 1948, is also famous for its single setting and long takes, which were often edited to create the illusion of one continuous, "unblinking" take.

12. This choice of actors carries its own significance, since both had been famous as child movie stars, McDowall (1928–98) in films such as *How Green Was My Valley* (1941) and *Lassie Come Home* (1943) and Stockwell (b. 1936) in *Gentleman's Agreement* (1947), *The Secret Garden* (1949), and *Kim* (1950). Thus the casting emphasizes the growth from childhood innocence to maladjusted adolescence, reminding the audience that these troubled teens were once adorable kids.

13. Meyer Levin, *Compulsion: A Play* (New York: Simon and Schuster, 1959). All page references in parentheses refer to this edition.

14. *Compulsion,* directed by Richard Fleischer, screenplay by Richard Murphy, from the novel and play by Meyer Levin (Twentieth Century Fox, 1959).

15. David Savran, *Communists, Cowboys, and Queers: The Politics of Masculinity in the Work of Arthur Miller and Tennessee Williams* (Minneapolis: University of Minnesota Press, 1992), 53.

16. Ibid., 41.

17. Although the film version also uses the names Steiner and Strauss, it never raises the fact of the boys' Judaism, going so far as to imply that the Ku Klux Klan has burned a cross in front of the defense attorney's home because he is defending "rich boys" (as opposed to Jewish boys). Furthermore, the name of the female lead character is changed from Ruth Slimovitsky to Ruth Evans.

18. Sander Gilman, *The Jew's Body* (New York: Routledge, 1991).

19. Hamilton's *Rope* also deals, albeit less self-consciously, with notions of "failed masculinity," using factors of wealth, intellectualism, and refinement among the Oxbridge set as indicators of moral corruption. Hamilton, a dedicated Marxist, shows less sympathy for his upper-class characters than Levin does.

20. See Neil Miller, *Sex-Crime Panic: A Journey to the Paranoid Heart of the 1950s* (Los Angeles: Alyson Books, 2002). Miller sums up the prevalent attitude of the times: "Despite their good intentions, sexual psychopath laws invariably took a catch-all approach to sexual offenses. The intended targets may have been rapists and murderers, but in almost every state with a sexual psychopath law, little or no distinction was made between nonviolent and violent offenses, between consensual and nonconsensual behavior, or between harmless 'sexual deviates' and dangerous sex criminals. An adult homosexual man who had sex with his lover in the privacy of his bedroom was as deviant as a child murderer" (81–82).

21. John Logan, *Never the Sinner: The Leopold and Loeb Story* (Woodstock, NY: Overlook Press, 1999). All page references in parentheses refer to this edition. The play won the Outer Critics Circle Award for Outstanding Off-Broadway Play, and Logan has gone on to even greater success as an Oscar-nominated screenwriter of Hollywood films such as *Gladiator* (2000), *The Aviator* (2004), and *Hugo* (2011). His Broadway play *Red* won the 2010 Tony Award for Best Play.

22. D. J. R. Bruckner, "Leopold and Loeb as Everymen," *New York Times,* 2 December 1997, E5.

23. *Swoon,* directed and written by Tom Kalin (American Playhouse/Fine Line, 1992).

24. John M. Clum, *He's All Man: Learning Masculinity, Gayness, and Love from American Movies (*New York: Palgrave, 2002), 123.

25. Janet Maslin, Film Review: *Swoon, New York Times,* 27 March 1992, C8.

26. Also Leopold is played by Craig Chester, one of the very few out gay actors at the time, thereby bringing a concept of modern gay identity to the role in the minds of viewers. See Craig Chester, *Why the Long Face? The Adventures of a Truly Independent Actor* (New York: St. Martin's, 2003). For more on the queer activism of the early 1990s, see chapter 4 in this volume.

27. Stephen Dolginoff, *Thrill Me: The Leopold and Loeb Musical,* Abingdon Theatre, New York, 19 July 2003.

28. Laural Meade, *Leopold and Loeb: A Goddamn Laff Riot.* Videotape of live performance, Los Angeles, 2003.

29. Reid Farrington. *Gin & "It."* Wexner Center for the Arts, Columbus, Ohio, 7 March 2010.

Chapter 3

1. Gay political activism and gay theater, of course, existed before the Stonewall Riots of 1969, and the cultural influence of the gay liberation era extends beyond the 1970s and into the current day. Nevertheless, here I'm focusing on this era to highlight the radically different modes of theatrical production and representation that coexisted during this particular moment of heightened awareness about gay identities and civil rights.

2. For chronicles of the riots and analysis of their impact, see Martin Duberman, *Stonewall* (New York: Plume, 1994); and David Carter, *Stonewall: The Riots That Sparked the Gay Revolution* (New York: St. Martin's Griffin, 2005).

3. Eve Kosofsky Sedgwick, *The Epistemology of the Closet* (Berkeley: University of California Press, 2008), 71, 73–74.

4. *Deathtrap* is also Broadway's fifth-longest-running nonmusical, topped only by, respectively, *Life with Father* (1939), *Tobacco Road* (1933), *Abie's Irish Rose* (1922), and *Gemini* (1977).

5. Marvin Carlson, *Deathtraps: The Postmodern Comedy Thriller* (Bloomington: Indiana University Press, 1993), 12.

6. Sedgwick, *Epistemology of the Closet,* 3.

7. Alisa Solomon, "Great Sparkles of Lust: Homophobia and the Antitheatrical Tradition," in *The Queerest Art: Essays on Lesbian and Gay Theatre,* ed. Alisa Solomon and Framji Minwalla (New York: New York University Press, 2002), 13.

8. Ibid.

9. Agatha Christie, *The Mousetrap and Other Plays* (New York: Bantam, 1981).

10. Alan Sinfield, *Out on Stage: Lesbian and Gay Theatre in the Twentieth Century* (New Haven, CT: Yale University Press, 1999), 174.

11. Anthony Shaffer, *Sleuth* (London: Marion Boyers, 1971), 83. Note that the 2007 film adaptation of *Sleuth,* with a screenplay by Harold Pinter, makes "gay baiting" a more explicit part of the plot.

12. Patrick Hamilton, *Angel Street (Gaslight)* (New York: Samuel French, 1942). Ham-

ilton is, of course, also the author of *Rope* (see chapter 2). The Broadway production of *Angel Street* (1941) starred Vincent Price, Judith Evelyn, and Leo G. Carroll. It ran for 1,295 performances. Ingrid Bergman earned an Academy Award in George Cukor's 1944 film version of *Gaslight,* which also starred Charles Boyer and Joseph Cotten.

13. Ira Levin, *Rosemary's Baby* (New York: Random House, 1967); Ira Levin, *The Stepford Wives* (New York: Random House, 1972). Both novels have enjoyed success as films: Roman Polanski's *Rosemary's Baby* (1968) starred Mia Farrow and is routinely judged one of the best thrillers ever made (e.g., number nine on the American Film Institute's list of the one hundred best thrillers); Bryan Forbes's *The Stepford Wives* (1975) starred Katharine Ross and has become a cult classic; and Frank Oz remade *The Stepford Wives* (2004) with a screenplay by gay playwright Paul Rudnick, starring Nicole Kidman.

14. *Veronica's Room* was performed on Broadway at the Music Box Theatre between 22 October and 29 December 1973, for a total of seventy-three performances. Under the direction of Ellis Rabb, the cast included Eileen Heckart and Arthur Kennedy, and Regina Baff earned a Tony Award nomination for her performance as The Girl. The play was revived off-Broadway at the Provincetown Playhouse in 1981 for a total of ninety-seven performances.

15. *Les Diaboliques*, directed and written by Henri-Georges Clouzot, from the novel by Pierre Boileau and Thomas Narcejac (Filmsonor, 1955).

16. For more on the lost lesbian relationship, see Susan Hayward, "Literary Adaptations of the 1950s: *Thérèse Raquin* (1953) and *Les Diaboliques* (1955)," *Studies in French Cinema* 3, no. 1 (2003): 5–14.

17. Bob Barry, *Murder among Friends* (New York: Samuel French, 1976). The play was directed by Val May, who was best known for staging the British lesbian drama *The Killing of Sister George* in the 1960s. Also worth mentioning is Janet Leigh's first and only Broadway performance in the role of the wife. After being so famously killed by Norman Bates in the shower in Alfred Hitchcock's *Psycho* (1960), again Leigh portrays a sympathetic woman of less than perfect morality, but this time she narrowly escapes being the victim. The critics were not very kind to Ms. Leigh, although they praised Jack Cassidy in the role of her vain and villainous husband.

18. Christopher James, "Denying Complexity: The Dismissal and Appropriation of Bisexuality in Queer, Lesbian, and Gay Theory," in *Queer Studies: A Lesbian, Gay, Bisexual, and Transgender Anthology,* ed. Brett Beemyn and Mickey Eliason (New York: New York University Press, 1996), 218.

19. Brendan Gill, Review: *Murder Among Friends, New Yorker,* 12 January 1976; Martin Gottfried, "They Called It Murder, but It's Just Hot Air," *New York Post,* 29 December 1975.

20. "The New Bisexuals," *Time,* 13 May 1974; "Bisexual Chic: Anyone Goes," *Newsweek,* 27 May 1974.

21. An excellent source on bisexuality, including its history, culture, and theory, is Marjorie Garber, *Bisexuality and the Eroticism of Everyday Life* (New York: Routledge, 2000).

22. Fritz Klein, *The Bisexual Option: A Concept of One Hundred Percent Intimacy,* excerpted in *Bisexuality: A Critical Reader, edited by Merl Storr* (London: Routledge, 1999), 41.

23. "For most bisexuals, same-sex desire is a sideline, more a fetish, and people of

their own sex never seem to qualify for potential life partners." Dan Savage, "Savage Love 2.0," Planetout.com, 30 May 2004, http://www.planetout.com/health/sexuality/qanda.html?sernum=1050 (no longer posted online).

24. Benoit Denizet-Lewis, "Double Lives on the Down Low," *New York Times Magazine,* 3 August 2003.

25. Sedgwick argues that "the now chronic crisis of homo/heterosexual definition" has made such categorical binaries crucial to our understanding of individual identity and social organization. Sedgwick, *Epistemology of the Closet,* 11. The bisexual, then, is regarded as sinister because he or she threatens the stability of those dichotomies.

26. Ira Levin, *Deathtrap* (New York: Dramatists Play Service, 1979). All page references in parentheses refer to this edition.

27. Moore's previous work had well prepared him to direct a comedy thriller with queer characters. He directed Mart Crowley's landmark gay play *The Boys in the Band* (1968), as well as the film *Murder by Death* (1976), a comic murder mystery with a screenplay by Neil Simon.

28. Richard Eder, Review: *Deathtrap, New York Times,* 27 February 1978, C15. In response, Ira Levin wrote the following bit of verse, which was initially posted on the Music Box Theatre's backstage bulletin board and later reprinted for the general public in *Playbill.*

> We made it through the Blizzard,
> We made it through the flu;
> We'll make it just as easily
> Through Eder's foul review.
> With Barnes and Kerr applauding
> I've a feeling in my gut
> That our 'Trap will still be open
> After Eder's trap is shut.

Indeed, Eder ended his stint as the *Times* drama critic in August 1980, while Levin's play ran through June 1982. See "A Theatregoer's Notebook," *Playbill,* May 1982, 23–24.

29. Erika Munk, "Death and Transfiguration," *Village Voice,* 20 March 1978, 81.

30. "Brady Bunch Dad's Secret Gay Life: The Shocking Untold Story," *National Enquirer,* 3 June 1992, cover; Farley Granger, *Include Me Out: My Life from Goldwyn to Broadway* (New York: St. Martin's Griffin, 2008). See also Arthur Laurents, *Original Story By: A Memoir of Broadway and Hollywood* (New York: Applause Books, 2001).

31. William Henry III, "*Deathtrap:* A 'Comedy with Screams' Becomes Broadway's Longest-Running Thriller," *New York Sunday News,* 29 March 1981, Leisure section, 3.

32. *Deathtrap,* directed by Sidney Lumet, screenplay by Jay Presson Allen, from the play by Ira Levin (Warner Bros., 1982), DVD. Allen also wrote the screenplay for Bob Fosse's *Cabaret* (1972), which included the bisexuality found in Christopher Isherwood's original stories but not depicted in the Broadway musical.

33. Vito Russo, *The Celluloid Closet,* rev. ed. (New York: Harper & Row, 1987), 295.

34. Both actors, however, had previously played queer characters. Caine was a gay husband (also named Sidney) in the film of Neil Simon's comedy *California Suite* (1978) and was a transgender serial killer in Brian DePalma's thriller *Dressed to Kill* (1980).

Reeve starred as a gay war veteran in the 1980 production of Lanford Wilson's play *Fifth of July,* although he is best known for his onscreen role as Superman in *Superman* (1978). At a screening of *Deathtrap* attended by this author in Youngstown, Ohio, in 1982, a young woman reacted to the Caine-Reeve kiss by screaming, "No, Superman, don't do it!"

35. Gerald Moon, *Corpse!* (London: Samuel French, 1985). Directed by John Tillinger and with a cast that included Keith Baxter and Milo O'Shea, the play ran in the West End in 1984 and then on Broadway in 1986 for 149 performances.

36. Rupert Holmes, *Accomplice* (New York: Samuel French, 1991). Directed by Art Wolff and with a cast that included Michael McKean and Jason Alexander, the play ran on Broadway for seventy-five performances.

37. Mark Shenton, "Reviews: *Deathtrap,*" *The Stage,* 8 September 2010, http://www.thestage.co.uk/reviews/review.php/29533/deathtrap. I would note, however, that there are signs of life in the genre. Christie's *The Mousetrap* still runs in London's West End, and *Perfect Crime,* by Warren Mazi, has run off-Broadway since 1987. Samuel French maintains and regularly adds new titles to the "Murder Mystery" section of its catalog, and the Mystery Writers of America still gives an Edgar Award for Best Play every year.

38. Chris Jones, Review: Road—*Deathtrap, Variety,* 14 October 1996, 73.

39. Alvin Klein, "*Deathtrap* Can't Get Away with Murder," *New York Times,* 5 March 2000, section 14 (New Jersey), 3.

40. Roderick A. Ferguson, "Of Our Normative Strivings: African American Studies and the Histories of Sexuality," *Social Text* 23, nos. 3–4 (October 2005): 85–100; Marlon B. Ross, "Beyond the Closet as a Raceless Paradigm," in *Black Queer Studies: A Critical Anthology,* ed. E. Patrick Johnson and Mae G. Henderson (Durham, NC: Duke University Press, 2005), 161–89.

Chapter 4

1. Mae West (*The Drag*), Patrick Hamilton (*Rope*), Meyer Levin (*Compulsion*), and Ira Levin (*Deathtrap*) are all, as far as we know, heterosexual.

2. Susan Sontag, *Against Interpretation and Other Essays* (New York: Farrar, Straus & Giroux, 1966); Stefan Brecht, *Queer Theatre* (London: Methuen, 1986).

3. Brecht, *Queer Theatre,* 9.

4. Andy Medhurst, "Camp," in *Lesbian and Gay Studies: A Critical Introduction,* ed. Andy Medhurst and Sally R. Munt (London: Cassell, 1997).

5. All of Ludlam's plays are published in Charles Ludlam, *The Complete Plays of Charles Ludlam* (New York: Harper & Row, 1989), and are not cited individually in the notes and bibliography. All page references in parentheses refer to this volume.

6. For more on Ludlam's life and work, see David Kaufman, *Ridiculous! The Theatrical Life and Times of Charles Ludlam* (New York: Applause Theatre & Cinema Books, 2002).

7. Charles Ludlam, *Ridiculous Theatre, Scourge of Human Folly: The Essays and Opinions of Charles Ludlam,* ed. Steven Samuels (New York: Theatre Communications Group, 1992), 228.

8. Ibid., 229.

9. Ibid., 230.

10. The 1975 Broadway production ran for a mere 45 performances, but the 2000 revival ran for 437 and was nominated for four Tony Awards. For more on the *Rocky Horror* phenomenon, see David Evans and Scott Michaels, *Rocky Horror: From Concept to Cult* (London: Sanctuary Publishing, 2002).

11. *Pink Flamingoes,* directed and written by John Waters (Dreamland, 1972).

12. *Women Behind Bars* was originally produced in 1974, then remounted with Divine in 1976 at the Truck and Warehouse Theater, where it ran for nine months. Though out of print, *Women Behind Bars* maintains some cult status and is occasionally revived: San Francisco's seminal LGBT theater, Theatre Rhinoceros, produced the play in 2002 with women playing all the women's roles. See www.therhino.org and http://www.talkinbroadway.com/regional/sanfran/s188.html.

13. Brecht, *Queer Theatre,* 154.

14. Writing about Babs Johnson years later, John Waters positioned the character against both mainstream cinema (Disney) and mainstream social values (the family): "I'm against the Disney-ization of drag queens. I think families should run in fear at the sight of my heroine, not want to cuddle up to her like *Mrs. Doubtfire* or *Tootsie.*" See John Waters, "Introduction to an Introduction—1996," in *Trash Trio: Three Screenplays by John Waters* (New York: Thunder's Mouth Press, 1996), v.

15. Busch acknowledges the influence of Ludlam: "My fantasy was to emulate The Ridiculous Theatrical Company with myself as a North side Chicago Charles Ludlam." From Busch's notes on *Myrtle Pope, The Story of a Woman Possessed, Charles Busch.com,* www.charlesbusch.com/Myrtle%20Pope.htm. It should be noted, however, that most of Ludlam's roles were not, in fact, drag performances.

16. Charles Busch, *Vampire Lesbians of Sodom,* in *The Tale of the Allergist's Wife And Other Plays* (New York: Grove Press, 2001).

17. Another addition to the roster of murderous theatricals is a minor character, the butler Etienne, who is revealed to be "Baby Kelly Ambrose, the hatchet wielding vaudeville child star," who dismembered six people and "scattered their body parts along the entire Keith-Orpheum circuit" (ibid., 13).

18. Charles Busch, *Psycho Beach Party,* in *The Tale of the Allergist's Wife and Other Plays* (New York: Grove Press, 2001), 88.

19. *Psycho Beach Party,* directed by Robert Lee King, screenplay by Charles Busch (Strand Releasing, 2000).

20. Laurie Stone, "Sand Blast," *Village Voice,* 28 July 1987.

21. For a typical example of the genre, see *The Cheat,* Cecil B. DeMille's 1915 film in which Sessue Hayakawa's character blackmails, brands, and attempts to rape a married white woman. *The Cheat,* directed by Cecil B. DeMille, screenplay by Hector Turnbull and Jeanie Macpherson (Kino Video 2002).

22. Charles Busch, *Shanghai Moon* (New York: Samuel French, 2000), 27.

23. Ibid., 56.

24. Anonymous Queers, "Queers Read This: I Hate Straights," reprinted in *The Columbia Reader on Lesbian and Gay Men in Media, Society, and Politics,* ed. Larry Gross and James D. Woods (New York: Columbia University Press, 1999), 588–94.

25. David Savran, *A Queer Sort of Materialism: Recontextualizing American Theatre* (Ann Arbor: University of Michigan Press, 2003), 79–80.

26. See Emily L. Sisley, "Notes on Lesbian Theatre," *The Drama Review* 25, no. 1 (1981): 47–56, reprinted in *A Sourcebook of Feminist Theatre and Performance,* ed. Carol Martin (New York: Routledge, 1996), 52–60.

27. See Alisa Solomon, "The WOW Café," *The Drama Review* 29, no. 1 (1985): 92–101, reprinted in *A Sourcebook of Feminist Theatre and Performance,* ed. Carol Martin (New York: Routledge, 1996), 42–51. See also Split Britches, *Split Britches: Lesbian Practice/Feminist Performance, ed. Sue-Ellen Case* (New York: Routledge, 1996); and Jill Dolan, *Theatre and Sexuality* (New York: Palgrave Macmillan, 2010).

28. Kate Davy, *Lady Dicks and Lesbian Brothers: Staging the Unimaginable at the WOW Café Theatre* (Ann Arbor: University of Michigan Press, 2011), 8, 88, 124.

29. C. Carr, "The Lady Is a Dick: The Dyke Noir Theater of Holly Hughes," *Village Voice,* 19 May 1987.

30. Holly Hughes, *The Well of Horniness,* in *Out Front: Contemporary Gay and Lesbian Plays,* ed. Don Shewey (New York: Grove Press, 1988), 221–51. The original cast featured Peggy Shaw (of Split Britches), Maureen Angelos (who would later become one of the Five Lesbian Brothers), and Alina Troyano (who would later gain acclaim as Carmelita Tropicana).

31. Ibid., 251.

32. Kate Davy, "From *Lady Dick* to Ladylike: The Work of Holly Hughes," in *Acting Out,* ed. Lynda Hart and Peggy Phelan (Ann Arbor: University of Michigan Press, 1993), 57.

33. Split Britches, *Split Britches: Lesbian Practice/Feminist Performance,* ed. Sue-Ellen Case (New York: Routledge, 1996), 30. *Lesbians Who Kill,* written by Deb Margolin in collaboration with Peggy Shaw and Lois Weaver, is published in this book (185–223).

34. Lynda Hart, *Fatal Women: Lesbian Sexuality and the Mark of Aggression* (Princeton, NJ: Princeton University Press, 1994), 156.

35. Split Britches, *Split Britches: Lesbian Practice/Feminist Performance,* 223.

36. Five Lesbian Brothers, *The Secretaries,* in *The Five Lesbian Brothers: Four Plays* (New York: Theatre Communications Group, 2000). All page references in parentheses refer to this edition.

37. Euripides, *The Bacchae,* in *Euripides V,* trans. William Arrowsmith, ed. David Grene and Richmond Lattimore (Chicago: University of Chicago Press, 1959).

38. Hart, *Fatal Women,* 14.

39. See the introductory comments to each play in Five Lesbian Brothers, *The Five Lesbian Brothers,* 3, 119.

40. Sara Warner makes a compelling argument that, as female laborers in a service economy, the secretaries are subjected to physical and emotional regulation and exploitation. Thus these women are not "liberated" by working in the capitalist system but rather become enslaved to it, and their murders of lumberjacks serve the owners of the mill more than they serve the women's own desires. Sara Warner, "Rage Slaves: The Commodification of Affect in the Five Lesbian Brothers' *The Secretaries,*" *Journal of Dramatic Theory and Criticism* 23, no. 1 (Fall 2008): 21–45.

41. *The Secretaries* has also fared well in revivals performed by companies other than the Five Lesbian Brothers, including a New York production by TOSOS and a San Francisco production by Boxcar Theatre, both in 2010.

42. This author attended two performances by Blacklips at the Pyramid Club in New

York during the summer of 1993. The definitive history of this troupe has yet to be written. Information on Blacklips can be found at its website, www.blacklips.org.

43. Robert O'Haire, interview with Kabuki Starshine, originally published in *Juicy Zine,* Winter 1994, reprinted at Blacklips, www.blacklips.org/interview/interv.html.

44. Poison Eve, "Blacklips: Its Life and Its Many, Many Deaths," Blacklips, www.blacklips.org/essay/essay.html.

45. Another version of this analysis of Theatre Couture's *Carrie* originally appeared in Jordan Schildcrout, "Performance Review: *Carrie,*" *Theater Journal* 59, no. 3 (October 2007): 519–20.

46. The musical version of *Carrie* was revised and revived as an off-Broadway production by the Manhattan Class Company in 2012. The production, directed by Stafford Arima, received mixed reviews but earned nominations for Best Revival of a Musical from the Drama Desk, Drama League, and Outer Critics Circle Awards.

47. For a collection of Bornstein's theatrical and theoretical writings, see Kate Bornstein, *Gender Outlaw: On Men, Women, and the Rest of Us* (New York: Routledge, 1994).

48. Kate Bornstein, *Strangers in Paradox,* staged reading at La MaMa Theatre, New York, 12 June 2004.

Chapter 5

1. Terrence McNally, *Master Class* (New York: Dramatists Play Service, 1995), 43.

2. Arthur Jacobs and Stanley Sadie, *The Limelight Book of Opera* (New York: Limelight Editions, 1985), 15.

3. In fact, both *Traviata* and *Butterfly* are based on plays that are themselves based on prose fiction: Dumas fils' *La Dame aux Camélias* originally appeared as a novel, and Belasco's Madame *Butterfly: A Tragedy of Japan* is based on a short story by John L. Long. Still, I would argue that both stories achieved greater popularity as stage productions, largely because their dramatic and social values were well matched to the melodramatic conventions of their time. In each case, it is also the stage version, not the printed prose version, that is credited as the basis for the opera.

4. Catherine Clément, *Opera: The Undoing of Women,* trans. Betsy Wing (Minneapolis: University of Minnesota Press, 1988), 62.

5. Ibid., 28.

6. Ibid., 22.

7. Wayne Koestenbaum, *The Queen's Throat: Opera, Homosexuality, and the Mystery of Desire* (New York: Da Capo, 2001), 44. Michael Bronski puts forth a similar thesis in his chapter on opera queens in *Culture Clash: The Making of Gay Sensibility* (Boston: South End Press, 1984), 134–43.

8. Koestenbaum, *The Queen's Throat,* 40.

9. Terrence McNally, *The Lisbon Traviata* (rev. 1990) (New York: Dramatists Play Service, 1992), 58.

10. David Savran, *The Playwright's Voice: American Dramatists on Memory, Writing, and the Politics of Culture* (New York: Theatre Communications Group, 1999), 119–20.

11. John W. Pereira, *Opening Nights: 25 Years of the Manhattan Theatre Club* (New York: Peter Lang, 1996), 235.

12. Mel Gussow, "*Lisbon Traviata:* Tale of Two Opera Fans," *New York Times,* 14 June 1985, C14.

13. John Simon, Review: *The Lisbon Traviata, New York,* 15 July 1985, 68–69.

14. Clive Barnes, "McNally's Guide to Opera," *New York Post,* 18 June 1985, 23.

15. Anonymous, Review: *The Lisbon Traviata, Variety,* 3 July 1985, 76.

16. Pereira, *Opening Nights,* 229–94.

17. Michael Feingold, Review: *The Lisbon Traviata, Village Voice,* 13 June 1989, 97.

18. Terrence McNally, *The Lisbon Traviata* (1985), in *Out Front: Contemporary Gay and Lesbian Plays,* ed. Don Shewey (New York: Grove Press, 1988), 401.

19. Clive Barnes, "Operatic Obsession," *New York Post,* 7 June 1989, 23.

20. Mel Gussow, "Agony and Ecstasy of an Opera Addiction," *New York Times,* 7 June 1989, C21.

21. John Simon, "Anti-Romances," *New York,* 19 June 1989, 71.

22. Laurie Winer, Review: *The Lisbon Traviata, Wall Street Journal,* 9 June 1989, A8.

23. Mimi Kramer, "The Manhattan Traviata," *New Yorker,* 19 June 1989, 75–76.

24. John Horvath, Review: *The Lisbon Traviata, Show Business,* 21 June 1989, 11.

25. John S. Patterson, Review: *The Lisbon Traviata, New York Native,* 15 July 1985, 39–40.

26. John Hammond, Review: *The Lisbon Traviata, New York Native,* 26 June 1989.

27. Pereira, *Opening Nights,* 274.

28. Louis Botto, "A Night at the Opera," *Playbill,* November 1989, 66–73.

29. Terrence McNally, *The Lisbon Traviata* (rev. 1989) (New York: Dramatists Play Service, 1990), 81–83.

30. Pereira, *Opening Nights,* 274–75. In his interview with Louis Botto in *Playbill,* Heald admits that he was initially "unhappy" with the new ending, but "we kept refining it, and after we played it nine times, we all realized that this was the right ending for this play." Botto, "A Night at the Opera," 72.

31. Mel Gussow, "A New, Nonviolent Ending for *Lisbon Traviata:* A Lesson Learned, Life Isn't Opera," *New York Times,* 1 November 1989, C22.

32. Linda Winer, Review: *The Lisbon Traviata, Newsday,* 1 November 1989, 5.

33. Howard Kissel, "*Traviata*: A Magnificent Obsession," *Daily News,* 1 November 1989, 35.

34. Koestenbaum, *The Queen's Throat,* 45.

35. Clive Barnes, "Fat Lady Sings New Tune," *New York Post,* 1 November 1989, 29.

36. John Simon, Review: *The Lisbon Traviata, New York,* 13 November 1989, 131–32.

37. Steven Winn, "Unsettling Extremes in *Lisbon:* Comedy Turns to Tragedy in Tale of Gay Opera Fans," *San Francisco Chronicle,* 23 September 1990.

38. Jackson R. Bryer, ed., *The Playwright's Art: Conversations with Contemporary American Dramatists* (New Brunswick, NJ: Rutgers University Press, 1995), 187.

39. Ray Loynd, "Getting to the Heart of *Lisbon Traviata,*" *Los Angeles Times,* 28 November 1990, F8.

40. Pereira, *Opening Nights,* 281.

41. Gerald Nachman, "Slicing and Dicing the Divas," *San Francisco Chronicle,* 27 September 1990. Nachman complains that the second act is a sexually graphic gay soap opera, but he still praises the play and gives it four stars. See also Sylvie Drake, "*Traviata:* McNally's Tragic Torch Song," *Los Angeles Times,* 30 November 1990, F6. Drake has a

couple of "minor quibbles" but calls *Traviata* "a masterful play." See also Bryer, *The Playwright's Art,* 191.

42. McNally, *The Lisbon Traviata* (rev. 1990), 83. All subsequent references to the play are from this edition.

43. McNally copies Don José's lines from the opera.

Ainsi, le salut de mon âme	And so, every hope of salvation
Je l'aurai perdu pour que toi,	Now I shall have lost all for you.
Pour que tu t'en ailles, infâme!	For you to go running, you harlot,
Entre ses bras, rire de moi.	Into his arms, laughing at me.

Georges Bizet, Henri Meilhac, and Ludovic Halévy, *Carmen: Opera Guide 13,* trans. Nell Moody and John Moody (London: John Calder Press in association with the English National Opera, 1982), 124.

44. Mendy's rhetoric often links passion and death. For example, he celebrates the artistry of Maria Callas with the phrase "it's to die" (10); he theorizes that Callas' passionate dedication to every performance ultimately killed her (17); he imagines that upon meeting his true love he will "die just a little bit" (40). When Mendy first hears about Mike's new boyfriend Paul, he fantasizes that Paul could be an attractive Italian tenor who could be his lover. But when Paul reveals that he has no interest in opera and no appreciation of Maria Callas, Mendy is furious: "You heard the greatest singer who ever lived and you don't even remember it. Yes, she's dead, thanks to people like you! Murderer!" (35). Mendy interprets Paul's lack of love for Callas as the equivalent of murder, especially since it kills his own romantic fantasy of having Paul as a lover.

45. David Román, *Acts of Intervention: Performance, Gay Culture, and AIDS* (Bloomington: Indiana University Press, 1998), 93.

46. Ibid., 90.

47. Clément, *Opera,* 64.

48. Ibid., 9.

49. Yew's subsequent career includes the plays *A Language of Their Own* (1995) and *Red* (1999), as well as his work as an award-winning director. He served as the director of the Asian Theatre Workshop at the Mark Taper Forum in Los Angeles, and in 2011 he became the artistic director of the Victory Gardens Theatre in Chicago.

50. Chay Yew, *Two Plays by Chay Yew: Porcelain and A Language of Their Own* (New York: Grove Press, 1997). The play can also be found in John M. Clum, ed., *Staging Gay Lives: An Anthology of Contemporary Gay Theater* (Boulder, CO: Westview Press, 1996). Unless otherwise stated, all references are to the Grove Press edition.

51. Nicholas de Jongh, Review: *Porcelain, Evening Standard,* 6 August 1992.

52. George Chauncey, *Gay New York: Gender, Urban Culture, and the Making of the Gay Male World, 1890–1940* (New York: Basic Books, 1994), 200.

53. David Eng, *Racial Castration: Managing Masculinity in Asian America* (Durham, NC: Duke University Press, 2001).

54. Claire Armistead, Review: *Porcelain, Guardian,* 13 August 1992.

55. Antonia Denford, Review: *Porcelain, City Limits,* 28 May 1992.

56. Jane Langdon-Davies, Review: *Porcelain, What's On,* 20 May 1992.

57. Clum, *Staging Gay Lives,* 347.

58. A similar use of the public restroom as a space of desire, shame, and danger can be seen in *The Toilet* (1964) by LeRoi Jones (later known as Amiri Baraka), a one-act play about a homosexual relationship between two high school students, one black and one white.

59. In the homophobic imagination, gay male sex is disgusting because it touches shit. In 1869 an anonymous critic in a German medical journal responded to the theories of Karl Heinrich Ulrichs:

> What does this poor unfortunate man name as the temple of nature? The final ending of the intestine, which in humans received from the Almighty no other purpose than to release the rawest dregs, the last waste of the animal economy—the unfortunate "private scholar" will have this foul-smelling hole honored as a sacred temple of love. (Quote from *Medizinishche Press,* cited in Hubert Kennedy, *Ulrichs: The Life and Work of Karl Heinrich Ulrichs, Pioneer of the Modern Gay Movement* [Boston, Alyson Publications, 1988]).

Leo Bersani reverses this equation in his analysis of Jean Genet's *Funeral Rites* (1953), arguing that the "flowers" of Genet's writing are what grows out of the "waste" of homosexuality: "the anus produces life, waste is fecund, from death new landscapes emerge." Leo Bersani, *Homos* (Cambridge, MA: Harvard University Press, 1995), 179.

Chapter 6

1. I borrow the semiotic terms *iconic, indexical,* and *symbolic* from philosopher C. S. Peirce, as cited in Terry Eagleton, *Literary Theatre: An Introduction* (Minneapolis: University of Minnesota Press, 1983), 100–101.
2. Marvin Carlson, *Theatre Semiotics: Signs of Life* (Bloomington: Indiana University Press, 1990), 75–91.
3. C. Fred Alford, *What Evil Means to Us* (Ithaca, NY: Cornell University Press, 1997), 3.
4. Ibid., 52.
5. Melanie Klein, paraphrased in ibid., 70.
6. Friedrich Nietzsche, *On the Genealogy of Morals,* trans. W. Kaufmann and R. J. Hollingdale (New York: Vintage, 1969).
7. Saint Augustine, paraphrased in Alford, *What Evil Means to Us,* 71.
8. Maurice Hussey, ed., "The Fall of Lucifer," *The Chester Mystery Plays* (New York: Theatre Arts Books, 1957), 9
9. Edward J. Ingebretsen, *At Stake: Monsters and the Rhetoric of Fear in Public Culture* (Chicago: University of Chicago Press, 2001), 75.
10. John F. Harris, "God Gave U.S. 'What We Deserve,' Falwell Says," *Washington Post,* 14 September 2001, http://www.washingtonpost.com/wp-dyn/articles/A28620-2001Sep14.html. Certain Christian leaders regularly blame gay people for natural disasters, such as the destruction caused by Hurricane Sandy in 2012. See, for example, Mary Elizabeth Williams, "Pastor: Blame Gays for Hurricane Sandy," *Salon,* 29 October 2012, http://www.salon.com/2012/10/29/pastor_blame_gays_for_hurricane_sandy/.

11. Michael Bronski, "Closet Drama," *Boston Phoenix,* 15 November 2001.

12. Susan Sontag, *AIDS and Its Metaphors* (New York: Farrar, Straus & Giroux, 1989), 72.

13. Thacker withdrew his nomination after the gay press reported his statements, which were decried by gay rights groups and AIDS activists. Elisabeth Bumiller, "Under Fire, Conservative Withdraws from AIDS Council," *New York Times,* 28 January 2003.

14. Lee Edelman, *No Future: Queer Theory and the Death Drive* (Durham, NC: Duke University Press, 2004), 9.

15. Ibid., 17.

16. Leo Bersani, *Homos* (Cambridge, MA: Harvard University Press, 1995), 161.

17. Neil Miller, *Sex-Crime Panic: A Journey to the Paranoid Heart of the 1950s* (Los Angeles: Alyson Books, 2002), 106.

18. Richard Goldstein, "What Gay Friendly Republicans?," *Village Voice,* 4 June 2003. In 2009 the Department of Justice's Office of Professional Responsibility cited Bybee for "professional misconduct" and "poor judgment" due to his role in creating the infamous "torture memos" of the Bush administration.

19. David Savran, *The Playwright's Voice: American Dramatists on Memory, Writing, and the Politics of Culture* (New York: Theatre Communications Group, 1999), 213.

20. Nicky Silver, *Fat Men in Skirts,* in *Etiquette and Vitriol: The Food Chain and Other Plays* (New York: Theatre Communications Group, 1996), 217–300.

21. Nicky Silver, *Free Will & Wanton Lust,* in *Etiquette and Vitriol: The Food Chain and Other Plays,* (New York: Theatre Communications Group, 1996), 151–216.

22. Nicky Silver, *Pterodactyls,* in *Etiquette and Vitriol: The Food Chain and Other Plays* (New York: Theatre Communications Group, 1996), 69–150. All page references in parentheses refer to this edition

23. Alford, *What Evil Means to Us,* 58.

24. Nicky Silver, *Raised in Captivity* (New York: Dramatists Play Service, 1995).

25. Nicky Silver, *Beautiful Child,* directed by Terry Kinney. Vineyard Theatre, New York. 21 February 2004.

26. Nicky Silver, *The Agony and the Agony,* directed by Terry Kinney, Vineyard Theatre, New York, 9 December 2006.

27. George C. Wolfe, *The Colored Museum* (New York: Grove Press, 1988). All page references in parentheses refer to this edition. Wolfe would later succeed Joseph Papp as the artistic director of the Public Theatre, in addition to winning accolades as the director of *Jelly's Last Jam, Angels in America, Bring in da Noise/Bring in da Funk, Topdog/Underdog, Caroline or Change,* and other major works of new American theater.

28. In both the off-Broadway production and the PBS *Great Performances* telecast, Miss Roj was played by Reggie Montgomery. Montgomery, who frequently worked at the Public Theatre under the direction of Wolfe, later went on to portray the gay African American author and civil rights activist James Baldwin in two different plays.

29. Mark Dery, "Black to the Future," in *Flame Wars: The Discourse of Cyberculture* (Durham, NC: Duke University Press, 1994).

30. Ken McLeod, "Space Oddities: Aliens, Futurism, and Meaning in Popular Music," *Popular Music* 22, no. 3 (2003): 342.

31. David Bowie, *The Rise and Fall of Ziggy Stardust and the Spiders from Mars* (RCA, 1972). For a contemporaneous analysis of Bowie's pose as a gay alien, see Michael Watts,

"Oh You Pretty Thing," *Melody Maker,* 22 January 1972, reprinted in Elizabeth Thomson and David Gutman, eds., *The Bowie Companion* (New York: Da Capo, 1996), 47–51.

32. Todd Haynes's 1998 film *Velvet Goldmine,* a gay fantasia on Bowiesque themes, imagines extraterrestrial origins for fabulous queerness from Oscar Wilde to glam rock. Dana Luciano, in discussing the space alien homosexual in *Velvet Goldmine,* has described "the combined suffering and exultation marking the queer's relation to outcast or alien status." Dana Luciano, "Nostalgia for an Age Yet to Come: *Velvet Goldmine*'s Queer Archive," in *Queer Times, Queer Becomings,* ed. E. L. McCallum and Mikko Tahkanen (Albany: State University of New York Press, 2011), 145.

33. For a thorough discussion of the legend of Tiresias and the powers of androgyny, see Marjorie Garber, *Bisexuality and the Eroticism of Everyday Life* (New York: Routledge, 2000).

34. Craig Lucas, *The Dying Gaul,* in *What I Meant Was: New Plays and Selected One-Acts* (New York: Theatre Communications Group, 1999), 1–78. All page references in parentheses refer to this edition. *The Dying Gaul* premiered in New York at the Vineyard Theatre, under the direction of Mark Brokaw, in 1998. The play received its Los Angeles premiere at the Elephant Theatre in 2008.

35. Craig Lucas, "Afterword" to *The Dying Gaul,* in *What I Meant Was: New Plays and Selected One-Acts* (New York: Theatre Communications Group, 1999), 77.

36. Note also the symbolic meaning of Robert's last name—Isaacson—since Isaac's son is Jacob, who wrestled with the angel.

37. Note also how the play, self-reflexively and ironically, alerts the audience to its position in the discourse of homicidal homosexuals. In the very first scene, Robert critiques "the faggy portrayal of the killer" in the film *The Silence of the Lambs* (12).

38. Lucas, "Afterword," 78. Lucas also wrote about his experiences of grief and rage in the personal essay "Postcard from Grief" written for *The Advocate,* reprinted in *Gay Men at the Millennium,* ed. Michael Lowenthal (New York: Tarcher/Putnam, 1997).

Chapter 7

1. David Schmid, *Natural Born Celebrities: Serial Killers in American Culture* (Chicago: University of Chicago Press, 2006), 7.

2. Ibid., 8.

3. Diana Fuss, "Oral Incorporations: *The Silence of the Lambs,*" in *Identification Papers* (New York: Routledge, 1995), 95.

4. Philip Jenkins, *Using Murder: The Social Construction of Serial Homicide* (New York: Aldine de Gruyter, 1994), 184.

5. Joyce Carol Oates, "Three American Gothics," in *Where I've Been and Where I'm Going* (New York: Plume, 1999), 233.

6. Schmid, *Natural Born Celebrities,* 225. On the attribution of Dahmer's crimes to homosexuality, see p. 216.

7. Ibid., 228.

8. Vito Russo, *The Celluloid Closet,* rev. ed. (New York: Harper & Row, 1987); Suzanna Danuta Walters, *All the Rage: The Story of Gay Visibility in America* (Chicago: University of Chicago Press, 2003).

9. Judith Halberstam, for one, defends *The Silence of the Lambs* as an antihomophobic horror film in *Skin Shows: Gothic Horror and the Technology of Monsters* (Durham, NC: Duke University Press, 1995), 161–77.

10. I would argue that such audiences can already be actively involved in deconstructing Hollywood's homophobic texts. A lesbian viewer can create a resistant position that ironically roots for Sharon Stone's killer in *Basic Instinct,* and a gay man can campily quote Jame Gumb's lines ("It places the lotion in the basket!") from *The Silence of the Lambs,* both identifying with and mocking the Hollywood construction of the monstrous queer. The stage production of *Silence! The Musical,* which began as a 2011 fringe hit and then played an extended run off-Broadway, recreates Demme's film as a low-budget camp spectacle, complete with a chorus of singing sheep. When seen in a theatrical style that makes *all* performances of gender and sexuality rather ridiculous, the perversion of Jame Gumb is actually "normalized."

11. The facts of Dahmer's case are recounted in many sources, ranging from the sensational to the scholarly. A sampling includes: Donald Davis, *The Jeffrey Dahmer Story: An American Nightmare* (New York: St. Martin's, 1991); Anne E. Schwartz, *The Man Who Could Not Kill Enough: The Secret Murders of Milwaukee's Jeffrey Dahmer* (Secaucus, NJ: Carol Publishing, 1992); and Richard Tithecott, *Of Men and Monsters: Jeffrey Dahmer and the Construction of the Serial Killer* (Madison: University of Wisconsin Press, 1997).

12. Glenn Collins, "Theatrical Director's Calling Card: Sex and Death," *New York Times,* 24 February 1992, 15.

13. Reza Abdoh, *The Law of Remains,* in *Plays for the End of the Century,* ed. Bonnie Marranca (Baltimore: Johns Hopkins University Press, 1996), 9–94. All page references in parentheses refer to this edition. For more on Abdoh's aesthetic and productions, see Daniel Mufson, ed., *Reza Abdoh* (Baltimore: Johns Hopkins University Press, 1999).

14. Stephen Holden, "Theater in Review: *The Law of Remains,*" *New York Times,* 26 February 1992, 19.

15. The name Snarling perhaps echoes Candy Darling, the transsexual Warhol superstar who died in 1974, as well as punk rock monikers such as Johnny Rotten and Sid Vicious.

16. Holden, "Theater in Review," 19.

17. Alisa Solomon, "AIDSmerica," *Village Voice,* 10 March 1992, 95.

18. Around the same time as Abdoh's production, the depiction of the serial killer as celebrity could be seen in Neil Gaiman's acclaimed comic book series, *The Sandman.* In the volume entitled *The Doll's House* (New York: DC Comics, 1990), Gaiman introduces the Corinthian, a handsome man who happens to have teeth where his eyes should be and murders boys so he can eat their eyeballs. The Corinthian attends a "convention" of serial killers, where he is treated as a superstar, with fans asking for his autograph. The Corinthian is a nightmare created—and ultimately destroyed—by Morpheus, the King of Dreams and hero of the series.

19. Derf Backderf, *My Friend Dahmer* (New York: Abrams ComicArts, 2012), 129-42.

20. The trope of Dahmer as performer is also seen in *Jeffrey Dahmer Live!*, a solo cabaret written and performed by Avner Kam at the New York International Fringe Festival in 2011. Kam portrays Dahmer in prison, wearing an orange jumpsuit, directly addressing the audience and singing songs about the important events in his life. The perfor-

mance creates a tension between form and content, mocking the ingratiating charm typically attributed to cabaret performers by juxtaposing it with Dahmer's repulsive acts.

21. Solomon, "AIDSmerica," 95; Holden, "Theater in Review," 19; Collins, "Theatrical Director's Calling Card," 15.

22. Jim Grimsley, *Dream Boy* (Chapel Hill: Algonquin Books, 1995). Grimsley has also been a writer in residence at Atlanta's 7 Stages Theatre, which premiered many of his plays. See Jim Grimsley, *Mr. Universe and Other Plays* (Chapel Hill, NC: Algonquin Books, 1998).

23. Jim Grimsley, *Fascination,* unpublished manuscript, 2003. Parenthetical citations refer to this manuscript.

24. Jonathan Abarbanal, "Theater: *Fascination,*" *Windy City Times,* 14 May 2003, http://www.windycitymediagroup.com/lgbt/THEATER-Fascination/2636.html.

25. Tony Adler, "Performing Arts Review: *Fascination,*" *Chicago Reader,* 15 May 2003, http://www.chicagoreader.com/chicago/fascination/Content?oid=912077.

26. Chris Jones, "Gay Serial Killer Fails to Fascinate," *Chicago Tribune,* 8 May 2003, 3.

27. Joyce Carol Oates, *Zombie* (New York: Dutton, 1995); Joyce Carol Oates, *Zombie,* adapted by Bill Connington, Theatre Row Studio, New York, 24 April 2009.

28. Joyce Carol Oates, "I Had No Other Thrill or Happiness: The Literature of Serial Killers," in *Where I've Been and Where I'm Going* (New York: Plume, 1999), 255.

29. Ibid., 258.

30. Sigmund Freud, *The Uncanny,* trans. David McLintock (New York: Penguin Books, 2003).

31. Dennis Cooper, *Jerk* (San Francisco: Artspace Books, 1993). All page references in parentheses refer to this edition. The theatrical version, which follows the text of Cooper's original story quite closely, has toured to various locations and was staged at Performance Space 122 in New York City, as part of the Under the Radar Festival, in January 2010. In 2011 Vienne published a book of photographs, which included an audio CD of Capdevielle performing *Jerk.* Gisèle Vienne, Dennis Cooper, and Peter Rehberg, *Jerk/Through Their Tears* (Paris: Editions Dis Voir, 2011).

32. Dean Corll, nicknamed "The Candy Man," murdered twenty-eight teenage boys between 1970 and 1973 in Houston. David Brooks and Elmer Wayne Henley served as accomplices who helped lure the boys to Corll's home. Henley murdered Corll, and Brooks and Henley are currently serving life sentences. See Jack Olsen, *The Man with the Candy: The Story of the Houston Mass Murders* (New York: Simon and Schuster, 1974).

33. Oates, "Three American Gothics," 234.

34. Ibid., 235.

35. Brian Masters, *Killing for Company: The Story of a Man Addicted to Murder* (New York: Dell, 1994), 298.

36. Lynda Hart, *Fatal Women: Lesbian Sexuality and the Mark of Aggression* (Princeton, NJ: Princeton University Press, 1994), 136.

37. Ibid., 141.

38. In addition, the case inspired the 1992 television movie *Overkill: The Aileen Wuornos Story,* starring Jean Smart as Aileen, and an opera entitled *Wuornos,* by Carla Lucero, which debuted in San Francisco in 2001 as part of a Queer Arts festival.

39. Carson Kreitzer, *Self Defense, or Death of Some Salesmen,* in *Women Playwrights:*

The Best Plays of 2002, ed. D. L. Lepidus (Hanover, NH: Smith and Kraus, 2003). All page references in parentheses refer to this edition.

40. *Self Defense* was also produced by the Actor's Gang in Los Angeles and the Steppenwolf Garage in Chicago in 2004.

41. *Monster*, directed and written by Patty Jenkins (Media 8 Entertainment, 2003).

42. Schmid, *Natural Born Celebrities*, 235.

43. The character Bob in *Beyond Therapy* (1981) is a would-be gay murderer who pretends to kill people with a starter's pistol. First he shoots his therapist because she repeatedly calls him a "cocksucker," and then he shoots Bruce, his male lover, who wants to leave him for a woman. While acknowledging the genuine pain caused by homophobia and emotional abandonment, Durang's satire questions the psychotherapeutic benefits of attempting to achieve emotional catharsis through pretend acts of violence.

44. Christopher Durang, *Betty's Summer Vacation* (New York: Dramatists Play Service, 2000). All page references in parentheses refer to this edition. The Obie committee gave the Playwrights Horizons production awards for playwriting, directing (Nicholas Martin), set design (Thomas Lynch), and acting (Kristine Nielsen in the role of Mrs. Siezmagraff).

45. Note, however, that—in the style of ancient Greek tragedy—acts of bloody violence do not actually occur onstage. They happen offstage and then are reported by the characters.

Afterword

1. Jasbir K. Puar, *Terrorist Assemblages: Homonationalism in Queer Times* (Durham, NC, Duke University Press, 2007), xii.

Bibliography

Plays

Abdoh, Reza. *The Law of Remains.* In *Plays for the End of the Century,* edited by Bonnie Marranca, 9–94. Baltimore: Johns Hopkins University Press, 1996.

Aguirre-Sacasa, Roberto. *Golden Age.* Kraine Theatre, New York, 15 April 2005.

Barry, Bob. *Murder among Friends.* New York: Samuel French, 1976.

Bell, Hunter, Jon Kaplan, and Al Kaplan. *Silence! The Musical.* Elektra Theatre, New York, 10 August 2012.

Bizet, Georges, Henri Meilhac, and Ludovic Halévy. *Carmen: Opera Guide 13.* Translated by Nell Moody and John Moody. London: John Calder Press in association with the English National Opera, 1982..

Bornstein, Kate. *Strangers in Paradox.* Staged reading at La MaMa Theatre, New York, 12 June 2004.

Busch, Charles. *Judith of Bethulia.* Theatre for a New City, New York, 19 April 2012.

Busch, Charles. *Psycho Beach Party.* In *The Tale of the Allergist's Wife and Other Plays,* 37-105. New York: Grove Press, 2001.

Busch, Charles. *Shanghai Moon.* New York: Samuel French, 2000.

Busch, Charles. *Vampire Lesbians of Sodom.* In *The Tale of the Allergist's Wife and Other Plays,* 1-35. New York: Grove Press, 2001.

Christie, Agatha. *The Mousetrap and Other Plays.* New York: Bantam, 1981.

Cooper, Dennis. *Jerk.* Adapted by Gisèle Vienne. Performance Space 122, New York, 14 January 2010.

Dolginoff, Stephen. *Thrill Me: The Leopold and Loeb Musical.* Abingdon Theatre, New York, 19 July 2003.

Durang, Christopher. *Betty's Summer Vacation.* New York: Dramatists Play Service, 1999.

Durang, Christopher. *Beyond Therapy.* In *Christopher Durang Explains It All for You: Six Plays,* 215–97. New York: Grove Weidenfeld, 1983.

Euripides. *The Bacchae.* In *Euripides V.* Translated by William Arrowsmith, edited by David Greene and Richard Lattimore, 141-220. Chicago: University of Chicago Press, 1959.

Farrington, Reid. *Gin & "It."* Wexner Center for the Arts, Columbus, Ohio, 7 March 2010.

Five Lesbian Brothers. *The Secretaries.* In *The Five Lesbian Brothers: Four Plays,* 117-91. New York: Theatre Communications Group, 2000.

Five Lesbian Brothers. *Voyage to Lesbos.* In *The Five Lesbian Brothers: Four Plays,* 1-37. New York: Theatre Communications Group, 2000.

Gilbert, Sky. *Rope Enough.* Toronto: Playwrights Canada Press, 2005.

Grimsley, Jim. *Fascination.* Unpublished manuscript, 2003.

Grimsley, Jim. *Mr. Universe and Other Plays.* Chapel Hill, NC: Algonquin Books, 1998.

Hamilton, Patrick. *Angel Street (Gaslight).* New York: Samuel French, 1942.

Hamilton, Patrick. *Rope: A Play.* London: Constable, 1929.

Henning, Daniel. *Dickie & Babe: The Truth About Leopold & Loeb.* Blank Theatre Company, Los Angeles, February 2008.

Holmes, Rupert. *Accomplice.* New York: Samuel French, 1991.

Hughes, Holly. *The Well of Horniness.* In *Out Front: Contemporary Gay and Lesbian Plays,* edited by Don Shewey, 221–51. New York: Grove Press, 1988.

Hussey, Maurice, ed. "The Fall of Lucifer." In *The Chester Mystery Plays,* 3–10. New York: Theatre Arts Books, 1957.

Jackson, Erik. *Carrie.* Performance Space 122, New York. 13 December 2006.

Jones, LeRoi (Amiri Baraka). *The Baptism and The Toilet.* New York: Grove Press, 1966.

Kam, Avner. *Jeffrey Dahmer Live!* International Fringe Festival, New York, 20 August 2011.

Kreitzer, Carson. *Self Defense, or Death of Some Salesmen,* in *Women Playwrights: The Best Plays of 2002,* edited by D. L. Lepidus, 273–326. Hanover, NH: Smith and Kraus, 2003.

Levin, Ira. *Deathtrap.* New York: Dramatists Play Service, 1979.

Levin, Meyer. *Compulsion: A Play.* New York: Simon and Schuster, 1959.

Logan, John. *Never the Sinner: The Leopold and Loeb Story.* Woodstock, NY: Overlook Press, 1999.

Lucas, Craig. *The Dying Gaul.* In *What I Meant Was: New Plays and Selected One-Acts,* 1–75. New York: Theatre Communications Group, 1999.

Ludlam, Charles. *The Complete Plays of Charles Ludlam.* New York: Harper & Row, 1989.

McNally, Terrence. *The Lisbon Traviata* (1985). In *Out Front: Contemporary Gay and Lesbian Plays,* ed. Don Shewey, 355–418. New York: Grove Press, 1988.

McNally, Terrence. *The Lisbon Traviata* (1989 revision). New York: Dramatists Play Service, 1990.

McNally, Terrence. *The Lisbon Traviata* (1990 revision). New York: Dramatists Play Service, 1992.

McNally, Terrence. *Master Class.* New York: Dramatists Play Service, 1995.

Meade, Laural. *Leopold and Loeb: A Goddamn Laff Riot.* Videotape of live performance, Los Angeles, 2003.

Moon, Gerald. *Corpse!* London: Samuel French, 1985.

Oates, Joyce Carol. *Zombie.* Adapted by Bill Connington. Theatre Row Studio, New York, 24 April 2009.

O'Brien, Richard. *The Rocky Horror Show.* New York: Samuel French, 2010.

Shaffer, Anthony. *Sleuth.* London: Marion Boyers, 1971.

Silver, Nicky. *The Agony and the Agony.* Directed by Terry Kinney. Vineyard Theatre, New York, 9 December 2006.

Silver, Nicky. *Beautiful Child.* Directed by Terry Kinney. Vineyard Theatre, New York, 21 February 2004.

Silver, Nicky. *Fat Men in Skirts.* In *Etiquette and Vitriol: The Food Chain and Other Plays,* 217–300. New York: Theatre Communications Group, 1996.

Silver, Nicky. *Free Will & Wanton Lust. In Etiquette and Vitriol: The Food Chain and Other Plays,* 151–216. New York: Theatre Communications Group, 1996.

Silver, Nicky. *Pterodactyls. In Etiquette and Vitriol: The Food Chain and Other Plays,* 69–150. New York: Theatre Communications Group, 1996.

Silver, Nicky. *Raised in Captivity.* New York: Dramatists Play Service, 1995.

Split Britches. *Lesbians Who Kill.* In *Split Britches: Lesbian Practice/Lesbian Performance.* Edited by Sue-Ellen Case, 185-223. New York: Routledge, 1996.

Vienne, Gisèle, Dennis Cooper, and Peter Rehberg. *Jerk/Through Their Tears.* Paris: Editions Dis Voir, 2011.

West, Mae. *The Drag.* In *Three Plays by Mae West,* edited by Lillian Schlissel, 95-140. New York: Routledge, 1997.

Wolfe, George C. *The Colored Museum.* New York: Grove Press, 1988.

Yew, Chay. *Two Plays: Porcelain and A Language of Their Own.* New York: Grove Press, 1997.

Films and Recordings

Basic Instinct. Directed by Paul Verhoeven, screenplay by Joe Eszterhas. Tri-Star Pictures, 1992.

Bowie, David. *The Rise and Fall of Ziggy Stardust and the Spiders from Mars.* RCA, 1972.

The Cheat. Directed by Cecil B. DeMille, screenplay by Hector Turnbull and Jeanie Macpherson. Kino Video 2002.

Compulsion. Directed by Richard Fleischer, screenplay by Richard Murphy, from the novel and play by Meyer Levin. Twentieth Century Fox, 1959.

Cruising. Directed and written by William Friedkin, from the novel by Gerald Walker. United Artists, 1980.

Deathtrap. Directed by Sidney Lumet, screenplay by Jay Presson Allen, from the play by Ira Levin. Warner Bros., 1982.

Les Diaboliques. Directed and written by Henri-Georges Clouzot, from the novel by Pierre Boileau and Thomas Narcejac. Filmsonor, 1955.

Die! Mommie! Die! Directed by Mark Rucker, screenplay by Charles Busch. Aviator Films, 2003.

The Dying Gaul. Directed and written by Craig Lucas. Sony Pictures, 2006.

Funny Games. Directed and written by Michael Haneke. Kino on Video, 2006.

Funny Games. Directed and written by Michael Haneke. Warner Home Video, 2008.

Monster. Directed and written by Patty Jenkins. Media 8 Entertainment, 2003.

Murder by Numbers. Directed by Barbet Schroeder, screenplay by Tony Gayton. Castle Rock Entertainment/Warner Bros., 2002.

Pink Flamingoes. Directed and written by John Waters. Dreamland, 1972.

Psycho Beach Party. Directed by Robert Lee King, screenplay by Charles Busch. Strand Releasing, 2000.

The Rocky Horror Picture Show. Directed by Jim Sharman, screenplay by Richard O'Brien. Twentieth Century Fox, 1975.
Rope. Directed by Alfred Hitchcock, screenplay by Arthur Laurents, from the play by Patrick Hamilton. Warner Bros., 1948.
Rope. Directed and written by Kendall Sinn, from the play by Patrick Hamilton. Gunn Park Entertainment, 2002.
The Silence of the Lambs. Directed by Jonathan Demme, screenplay by Ted Tally, from the novel by Thomas Harris. Orion Pictures, 1991.
Swoon. Directed and written by Tom Kalin. American Playhouse/Fine Line, 1992.

Books, Articles, and Other Sources

Alford, C. Fred. *What Evil Means to Us.* Ithaca, NY: Cornell University Press, 1997.
Anonymous Queers. "Queers Read This: I Hate Straights." Reprinted in *The Columbia Reader on Lesbian and Gay Men in Media, Society, and Politics,* edited by Larry Gross and James D. Woods, 588–94. New York: Columbia University Press, 1999.
Auerbach, Nina. *Our Vampires, Ourselves.* Chicago: University of Chicago Press, 1995.
Backderf, Derf. *My Friend Dahmer.* New York: Abrams ComicArts, 2012.
Barthes, Roland. "The Death of the Author." In *Image-Music-Text.* Translated by Stephen Heath, 142–48. New York: Hill and Wang, 1978.
Bataille, Georges. *Erotism: Death and Sensuality.* Translated by Mary Dalwood. San Francisco: City Lights Books, 1986.
Benshoff, Harry M. *Monsters in the Closet: Homosexuality and the Horror Film.* Manchester: Manchester University Press, 1997.
Bersani, Leo. *Homos.* Cambridge, MA: Harvard University Press, 1995.
"Bisexual Chic: Anyone Goes." *Newsweek,* 27 May 1974.
Bok, Sissela. *Mayhem: Violence as Public Entertainment.* Reading, MA: Perseus Books, 1998.
Bornstein, Kate. *Gender Outlaw: On Men, Women, and the Rest of Us.* New York: Routledge, 1994.
Botto, Louis. "A Night at the Opera." *Playbill,* November 1989.
"Brady Bunch's Dad's Secret Gay Life: The Shocking Untold Story." *National Enquirer,* 3 June 1992.
Brecht, Stefan. *Queer Theatre.* London: Methuen, 1986.
Bronski, Michael. "Closet Drama." *Boston Phoenix,* 15 November 2001.
Bronski, Michael. *Culture Clash: The Making of Gay Sensibility.* Boston: South End Press, 1984.
Bryer, Jackson R., ed. *The Playwright's Art: Conversations with Contemporary American Dramatists.* New Brunswick, NJ: Rutgers University Press, 1995.
Bullough, Vern. *Science in the Bedroom: A History of Sex Research.* New York: Basic Books, 1994.
Bumiller, Elisabeth. "Under Fire, Conservative Withdraws from AIDS Council." *New York Times,* 28 January 2003.
Busch, Charles. "Notes on *Myrtle Pope, The Story of A Woman Possessed.*" www.charles-busch.com/Myrtle%20Pope.htm.

Busch, Francis X. *Prisoners at the Bar: Notable American Trials.* Indianapolis: Bobbs-Merrill, 1952.

Cameron, Paul. "Violence and Homosexuality." Family Research Institute, 1993. http://www.familyresearchinst.org/2009/02/violence-and-homosexuality/.

Carlson, Marvin. *Deathtraps: The Postmodern Comedy Thriller.* Bloomington: Indiana University Press, 1993.

Carlson, Marvin. *Theatre Semiotics: Signs of Life.* Bloomington: Indiana University Press, 1990.

Carter, David. *Stonewall: The Riots That Sparked the Gay Revolution.* New York: St. Martin's Griffin, 2005.

Cavell, Stanley. "The Avoidance of Love." In *Disowning Knowledge in Six Plays of Shakespeare,* 39–124. New York: Cambridge University Press, 1987.

Chauncey, George. *Gay New York: Gender, Urban Culture, and the Making of the Gay Male World, 1890–1940.* New York: Basic Books, 1994.

Chester, Craig. *Why the Long Face? The Adventures of a Truly Independent Actor.* New York: St. Martin's, 2003.

Clément, Catherine. *Opera: The Undoing of Women.* Minneapolis: University of Minnesota Press, 1988.

Clum, John M. *He's All Man: Learning Masculinity, Gayness, and Love from American Movies.* New York: Palgrave, 2002.

Clum, John M., ed. *Staging Gay Lives: An Anthology of Contemporary Gay Theater.* Boulder, CO: Westview Press, 1996.

Clum, John M. *Still Acting Gay: Male Homosexuality in Modern Drama.* New York: St. Martin's Griffin, 2000.

Collins, Glenn. "Theatrical Director's Calling Card: Sex and Death." *New York Times,* 24 February 1992.

Cooper, Dennis. *Jerk.* San Francisco: Artspace Books, 1993.

Curtin, Kaier. *"We Can Always Call Them Bulgarians": The Emergence of Lesbians and Gay Men on the American Stage.* Boston: Alyson Publications, 1987.

Davis, Donald. *The Jeffrey Dahmer Story: An American Nightmare.* New York: St. Martin's, 1991.

Davy, Kate. "From *Lady Dick* to Ladylike: The Work of Holly Hughes." In *Acting Out,* edited by Lynda Hart and Peggy Phelan, 55–84. Ann Arbor: University of Michigan Press, 1993.

Davy, Kate. *Lady Dicks and Lesbian Brothers: Staging the Unimaginable at the WOW Café Theatre.* Ann Arbor: University of Michigan Press, 2011.

Denizet-Lewis, Benoit. "Double Lives on the Down Low." *New York Times Magazine,* 3 August 2003.

Dery, Mark. "Black to the Future." In *Flame Wars: The Discourse of Cyberculture,* 179–222. Durham, NC: Duke University Press, 1994.

Dickson, Caitlin. "Fringe Factor: Should Oral Sex Be a Crime?" *Daily Beast,* 21 July 2013. http://www.thedailybeast.com/articles/2013/07/21/fringe-factor-should-oral-sex-be-a-crime.html.

Dolan, Jill. *The Feminist Spectator as Critic.* Ann Arbor: University of Michigan Press, 1991.

Dolan, Jill. *Theatre and Sexuality.* New York: Palgrave Macmillan, 2010.

Duberman, Martin. *Stonewall.* New York: Plume, 1994.

Duggan, Lisa. *Sapphic Slashers: Sex, Violence, and American Modernity.* Durham, NC: Duke University Press, 2000.

Eagleton, Terry. *Literary Theory: An Introduction.* Minneapolis: University of Minnesota Press, 1983.

Edelman, Lee. *No Future: Queer Theory and the Death Drive.* Durham, NC: Duke University Press, 2004.

Eng, David. *Racial Castration: Managing Masculinity in Asian America.* Durham, NC: Duke University Press, 2001.

Evans, David, and Scott Michaels. *Rocky Horror: From Concept to Cult.* London: Sanctuary Publishing, 2002.

Fass, Paula S. "Making and Remaking an Event: The Leopold and Loeb Case in American Culture." *Journal of American History* 80, no. 3 (December 1993): 919–51.

Ferguson, Roderick A. "Of Our Normative Strivings: African American Studies and the Histories of Sexuality." *Social Text* 23, nos. 3–4 (October 2005): 85–100.

Fine, Ruth. "Oklahoma Rep. Sally Kern Says Gays Are a National Threat, Worse Than Terrorism." *LGBT Weekly,* 12 September 2011. http://lgbtweekly.com/2011/09/12/oklahoma-rep-sally-kern-says-gays-are-a-national-threat-worse-than-terrorism/.

Fisher, James, ed. *"We Will Be Citizens": New Essays on Gay and Lesbian Theatre.* Jefferson, NC: McFarland, 2008.

Foucault, Michel. *The History of Sexuality. Vol. 1: An Introduction.* Translated by Robert Hurley. New York: Vintage Books, 1990.

Freud, Sigmund. "Letter to an American Mother." In *Come Out Fighting: A Century of Essential Writing on Gay and Lesbian Liberation,* edited by Chris Bull, 18. New York: Thunder's Mouth Press, 2001.

Freud, Sigmund. *Three Essays on the Theory of Sexuality.* New York: Basic Books Classics, 2000.

Freud, Sigmund. *The Uncanny.* Translated by David McLintock. New York: Penguin Books, 2003.

Fuss, Diana. "Oral Incorporations: *The Silence of the Lambs.*" In *Identification Papers,* 83–106. New York: Routledge, 1995.

Gaiman, Neil. *The Sandman: The Doll's House.* New York: DC Comics, 1990.

Garber, Marjorie. *Bisexuality and the Eroticism of Everyday Life.* New York: Routledge, 2000.

"Gay Secret That Made Snipers Kill." *National Enquirer,* 12 November 2002.

Geis, Gilbert, and Leigh B. Bienen. *Crimes of the Century: From Leopold and Loeb to O. J. Simpson.* Boston: Northeastern University Press, 1998.

Gilman, Sander. *The Jew's Body.* New York: Routledge, 1991.

Goldstein, Richard. "What Gay Friendly Republicans?" *Village Voice,* 4 June 2003.

Granger, Farley. *Include Me Out: My Life from Goldwyn to Broadway.* New York: St. Martin's Griffin, 2008.

Griffin, Sean. *Tinker Belles and Evil Queens: The Walt Disney Company from the Inside Out.* New York: New York University Press, 2000.

Grimsley, Jim. *Dream Boy.* Chapel Hill, NC: Algonquin Books, 1995.

Gross, Larry P. *Up from Invisibility: Gay Men, Lesbians, and the Media in America.* New York: Columbia University Press, 2001.

Gross, Larry, and James D. Woods, eds. *The Columbia Reader on Lesbian and Gay Men in Media, Society, and Politics.* New York: Columbia University Press, 1999.

Halberstam, Judith. *Skin Shows: Gothic Horror and the Technology of Monsters.* Durham, NC: Duke University Press, 1995.

Halperin, David M. *How to Do the History of Homosexuality.* Chicago: University of Chicago Press, 2002.

Halttunen, Karen. *Murder Most Foul: The Killer and the American Gothic Imagination.* Cambridge, MA: Harvard University Press, 1998.

Hamilton, Marybeth. *When I'm Bad, I'm Better: Mae West, Sex, and American Entertainment.* New York: Harper Collins, 1995.

Harris, John F. "God Gave U.S. 'What We Deserve,' Falwell Says." *Washington Post,* 14 September 2001. http://www.washingtonpost.com/wp-dyn/articles/A28620-2001Sep14.html.

Hart, Lynda. *Fatal Women: Lesbian Sexuality and the Mark of Aggression.* Princeton, NJ: Princeton University Press, 1994.

Hart, Lynda, and Peggy Phelan, eds. *Acting Out.* Ann Arbor: University of Michigan Press, 1993.

Hartinger, Brent. "Ask the Flying Monkey." After Elton (blog), 19 August 2008. http://www.afterelton.com/askmonkey/08-19-08?page=0%2C1.

Hayward, Susan. "Literary Adaptations of the 1950s: *Therese Raquin* (1953) and *Les Diaboliques* (1955)." *Studies in French Cinema* 3, no. 1 (2003): 5–14.

Helfer, Richard. "Mae West on Stage: Themes and Persona." PhD diss., City University of New York, 1990.

Henry, William, III. "*Deathtrap:* A Comedy with Screams Becomes Broadway's Longest-Running Thriller." *New York Sunday News,* 29 March 1981.

Higdon, Hal. *The Crime of the Century: The Leopold and Loeb Case.* New York: G. P. Putnam's Sons, 1975.

Ingebretsen, Edward J. *At Stake: Monsters and the Rhetoric of Fear in Public Culture.* Chicago: University of Chicago Press, 2001.

Itaborahy, Lucas Paoli, and Jingshu Zhu. "State-Sponsored Homophobia." International Lesbian, Gay, Bisexual, Trans, and Intersex Association, May 2013. http://old.ilga.org/Statehomophobia/ILGA_State_Sponsored_Homophobia_2013.pdf.

Jacobs, Arthur, and Stanley Sadie. *The Limelight Book of Opera.* New York: Limelight Editions, 1985.

James, Christopher. "Denying Complexity: The Dismissal and Appropriation of Bisexuality in Queer, Lesbian, and Gay Theory." In *Queer Studies: A Lesbian, Gay, Bisexual, and Transgender Anthology,* edited by Brett Beemyn and Mickey Eliason, 217–40. New York: New York University Press, 1996.

Jenkins, Philip. *Using Murder: The Social Construction of Serial Homicide.* New York: Aldine de Gruyter, 1994.

Jervis, Joe. "Scott Lively Again Takes Credit for Russia's Ban on Homosexual Propaganda." *Joe.My.God* (blog), 22 July 2013. http://joemygod.blogspot.com/2013/07/scott-lively-again-takes-credit-for.html.

Katz, Jonathan Ned. *Gay American History.* New York: Thomas Y. Crowell, 1976.

Katz, Jonathan Ned. *The Invention of Heterosexuality.* New York: Plume, 1995.

Kaufman, David. *Ridiculous! The Theatrical Life and Times of Charles Ludlam.* New York: Applause Theatre & Cinema Books, 2002.

Kennedy, Hubert. *Ulrichs: The Life and Works of Karl Heinrich Ulrichs, Pioneer of the Modern Gay Movement.* Boston: Alyson Publications, 1988.

"Killer's Secret Gay Life." *Globe,* 7 May 2007.

Klein, Fritz. *The Bisexual Option: A Concept of One Hundred Percent Intimacy.* Excerpted in *Bisexuality: A Critical Reader,* edited by Merl Storr, 38–48. London: Routledge, 1999.

Koestenbaum, Wayne. *The Queen's Throat: Opera, Homosexuality, and the Mystery of Desire.* New York: Da Capo, 2001.

Laurents, Arthur. *Original Story By: A Memoir of Broadway and Hollywood.* New York: Applause Books, 2001.

Levin, Ira. *Rosemary's Baby.* New York: Random House, 1967.

Levin, Ira. *The Stepford Wives.* New York: Random House, 1972.

Lucas, Craig. "Afterword" to *The Dying Gaul.* In *What I Meant Was: New Plays and Selected One-Acts,* 77–78. New York: Theatre Communications Group, 1999.

Lucas, Craig. "Postcard from Grief." Reprinted in *Gay Men at the Millennium,* edited by Michael Lowenthal, 146–48. New York: Tarcher/Putnam, 1997.

Luciano, Dana. "Nostalgia for an Age Yet to Come: *Velvet Goldmine*'s Queer Archive." In *Queer Times, Queer Becomings,* edited by E. L. McCallum and Mikko Tahkanen, 121–55. Albany: State University of New York Press, 2011.

Ludlam, Charles. *Ridiculous Theatre, Scourge of Human Folly: The Essays and Opinions of Charles Ludlam.* Edited by Steven Samuels. New York: Theatre Communications Group, 1992.

Machtan, Lothar. *The Hidden Hitler.* New York: Basic Books, 2001.

Mackenzie, Frederick A. *Twentieth Century Crimes.* Boston: Little, Brown, 1927.

Martin, Carol, ed. *A Sourcebook of Feminist Theatre and Performance.* New York: Routledge, 1996.

Masters, Brian. *Killing for Company: The Story of a Man Addicted to Murder.* New York: Dell, 1994.

McLeod, Ken. "Space Oddities: Aliens, Futurism, and Meaning in Popular Music." *Popular Music* 22, no. 3 (2003): 337–55.

Medhurst, Andy. "Camp." In *Lesbian and Gay Studies: A Critical Introduction,* edited by Andy Medhurst and Sally R. Munt, 274–93. London: Cassell, 1997.

Miller, D. A. "Anal Rope." Reprinted in *Inside/Out,* edited by Diana Fuss, 119–41. New York: Routledge, 1991.

Miller, Neil. *Sex-Crime Panic: A Journey to the Paranoid Heart of the 1950s.* Los Angeles: Alyson Books, 2002.

Mufson, Daniel, ed. *Reza Abdoh.* Baltimore: Johns Hopkins University Press, 1999.

Mustian, Jim. "Gays in Baton Rouge Arrested under Invalid Sodomy Law." *Advocate,* 28 July 2013. http://theadvocate.com/home/6580728–125/gays-in-baton-rouge-arrested.

National Museum and Archive of Lesbian and Gay History. *The Gay Almanac.* New York: Berkley Books, 1996.

"The New Bisexuals." *Time,* 13 May 1974.

Nietzsche, Friedrich. *On the Genealogy of Morals.* Translated by W. Kaufmann and R. J. Hollingdale. New York: Vintage, 1969.

Oates, Joyce Carol. "I Had No Other Thrill or Happiness: The Literature of Serial Killers." In *Where I've Been and Where I'm Going,* 243–66. New York: Plume, 1999.

Oates, Joyce Carol. "Three American Gothics." In *Where I've Been and Where I'm Going,* 232–42. New York: Plume, 1999.

Oates, Joyce Carol. *Zombie.* New York: Dutton, 1995.

O'Haire, Robert. Interview with Kabuki Starshine. Originally published in *Juicy Zine,* Winter 1994. Reprinted at Blacklips. www.blacklips.org/interview/interv.html.

Olsen, Jack. *The Man with the Candy: The Story of the Houston Mass Murders.* New York: Simon and Schuster, 1974.

Pereira, John W. *Opening Nights: 25 Years of the Manhattan Theatre Club.* New York: Peter Lang, 1996.

Poison Eve. "Blacklips: Its Life and Its Many, Many Deaths." Blacklips. www.blacklips.org/essay/essay.html.

Puar, Jasbir K. *Terrorist Assemblages: Homonationalism in Queer Times.* Durham, NC: Duke University Press, 2007.

Robin, Corey. "The Way We Live Now: Closet-Case Studies." *New York Times Magazine,* 16 December 2001.

Román, David. *Acts of Intervention: Performance, Gay Culture, and AIDS.* Bloomington: Indiana University Press, 1998.

Ross, Marlon B. "Beyond the Closet as a Raceless Paradigm." In *Black Queer Studies: A Critical Anthology,* edited by E. Patrick Johnson and Mae G. Henderson, 161–89. Durham, NC: Duke University Press, 2005.

Russo, Vito. *The Celluloid Closet.* Rev. ed. New York: Harper & Row, 1987.

Savran, David. *Communists, Cowboys, and Queers: The Politics of Masculinity in the Work of Arthur Miller and Tennessee Williams.* Minneapolis: University of Minnesota Press, 1992.

Savran, David. *The Playwright's Voice: American Dramatists on Memory, Writing, and the Politics of Culture.* New York: Theatre Communications Group, 1999.

Savran, David. *A Queer Sort of Materialism: Recontextualizing American Theatre.* Ann Arbor: University of Michigan Press, 2003.

Schildcrout, Jordan. "Drama and the New Sexualities." In *The Oxford Handbook of American Drama,* 455–69. New York: Oxford University Press, 2014.

Schildcrout, Jordan. "Performance Review: *Carrie.*" *Theater Journal* 59, no. 3 (October 2007): 519–20.

Schmid, David. *Natural Born Celebrities: Serial Killers in American Culture.* Chicago: University of Chicago Press, 2006.

Schwartz, Anne E. *The Man Who Could Not Kill Enough: The Secret Murders of Milwaukee's Jeffrey Dahmer.* Secaucus, NJ: Carol Publishing, 1992.

Sedgwick, Eve Kosofsky. *The Epistemology of the Closet.* Berkeley: University of California Press, 1990.

Sedgwick, Eve Kosofsky. *Tendencies.* Durham, NC: Duke University Press, 1993.

Shewey, Don. *Out Front: Contemporary Gay and Lesbian Plays.* New York: Grove Press, 1988.

Sinfield, Alan. *Out on Stage: Lesbian and Gay Theatre in the Twentieth Century.* New Haven, CT: Yale University Press, 1999.
Sisley, Emily L. "Notes on Lesbian Theatre." *The Drama Review* 25, no. 1 (1981): 47–56. Reprinted in *A Sourcebook of Feminist Theatre and Performance,* edited by Carol Martin, 52–60. New York: Routledge, 1996.
Solomon, Alisa. "Great Sparkles of Lust: Homophobia and the Antitheatrical Tradition." In *The Queerest Art: Essays on Lesbian and Gay Theatre,* edited by Alisa Solomon and Framji Minwalla, 9–20. New York: New York University Press, 2002.
Solomon, Alisa. "The WOW Café." *The Drama Review* 29, no. 1 (1985): 92–101. Reprinted in *A Sourcebook of Feminist Theatre and Performance,* edited by Carol Martin, 42–51. New York: Routledge, 1996.
Sontag, Susan. *Against Interpretation and Other Essays.* New York: Farrar, Straus & Giroux, 1966.
Sontag, Susan. *AIDS and Its Metaphors.* New York: Farrar, Straus & Giroux, 1989.
Storr, Merl. *Bisexuality: A Critical Reader.* London: Routledge, 1999.
"A Theatregoer's Notebook." *Playbill,* May 1982.
Tithecott, Richard. *Of Men and Monsters: Jeffrey Dahmer and the Construction of the Serial Killer.* Madison: University of Wisconsin Press, 1997.
Walters, Suzanna Danuta. *All the Rage: The Story of Gay Visibility in America.* Chicago: University of Chicago Press, 2003.
Warner, Sara. "Rage Slaves: The Commodification of Affect in the Five Lesbian Brothers' *The Secretaries.*" *Journal of Dramatic Theory and Criticism* 23, no.1 (Fall 2008): 21–45.
Waters, John. "Introduction to an Introduction—1996." In *Trash Trio: Three Screenplays by John Waters* v–vi. New York: Thunder's Mouth Press, 1996.
Watts, Jill. *Mae West: An Icon in Black and White.* New York: Oxford University Press, 2001.
Watts, Michael. "Oh You Pretty Thing." *Melody Maker,* 22 January 1972. Reprinted in *The Bowie Companion,* edited by Elizabeth Thomson and David Gutman, 47–51. New York: Da Capo, 1996.
Wilde, Oscar. "The Decay of Lying." In *The Complete Works of Oscar Wilde,* 970–92. New York: Harper & Row, 1989.
Williams, Mary Elizabeth. "Pastor: Blame Gays for Hurricane Sandy." *Salon,* 29 October 2012. http://www.salon.com/2012/10/29/pastor_blame_gays_for_hurricane_sandy/.
Wood, Robin. "The Murderous Gays: Hitchcock's Homophobia." Reprinted in *Out in Culture: Gay, Lesbian, and Queer Essays on Popular Culture,* edited by Corey K. Creekmur and Alexander Doty, 197–215. Durham, NC: Duke University Press, 1995.

Reviews

Abarbanal, Jonathan. "Theater: *Fascination.*" *Windy City Times,* 14 May 2003. http://www.windycitymediagroup.com/lgbt/THEATER-Fascination/2636.html.
Adler, Tony. "Performing Arts Review: *Fascination.*" *Chicago Reader,* 15 May 2003. http://www.chicagoreader.com/chicago/fascination/Content?oid=912077.
Anonymous. Review: *The Lisbon Traviata. Variety,* 3 July 1985.
Armistead, Claire. Review: *Porcelain. Guardian,* 13 August 1992.
Barnes, Clive. "Fat Lady Sings New Tune." *New York Post,* 1 November 1989.

Barnes, Clive. "McNally's Guide to Opera." *New York Post,* 18 June 1985.
Barnes, Clive. "Operatic Obsession." *New York Post,* 7 June 1989.
Bruckner, D. J. R. "Leopold and Loeb as Everymen." *New York Times,* 2 December 1997.
Carr, C. "The Lady Is a Dick: The Dyke Noir Theatre of Holly Hughes." *Village Voice,* 19 May 1987.
De Jongh, Nicholas. Review: *Porcelain. Evening Standard,* 6 August 1992.
Denford, Antonia. Review: *Porcelain. City Limits,* 28 May 1992.
Drake, Sylvie. "*Traviata*: McNally's Tragic Torch Song." *Los Angeles Times,* 30 November 1990.
Eder, Richard. Review: *Deathtrap. New York Times,* 27 February 1978.
Feingold, Michael. Review: *The Lisbon Traviata. Village Voice,* 13 June 1989.
Gill, Brendan. Review: *Murder among Friends. New Yorker,* 12 January 1976.
Gottfried, Martin. "They Called It Murder, but It's Just Hot Air." *New York Post,* 29 December 1975.
Gussow, Mel. "Agony and Ecstasy of an Opera Addiction." *New York Times,* 7 June 1989.
Gussow, Mel. "*Lisbon Traviata:* Tale of Two Opera Fans." *New York Times,* 14 June 1985.
Gussow, Mel. "A New, Nonviolent Ending for *Lisbon Traviata:* A Lesson Learned, Life Isn't Opera." *New York Times,* 1 November 1989.
Hammond, John. Review: *The Lisbon Traviata. New York Native,* 26 June 1989.
Holden, Stephen. "Theater in Review: *The Law of Remains.*" *New York Times,* 26 February 1992.
Horvath, John. Review: *The Lisbon Traviata. Show Business,* 21 June 1989.
Jones, Chris. "Gay Serial Killer Fails to Fascinate." *Chicago Tribune,* 8 May 2003.
Jones, Chris. Review: Road—*Deathtrap. Variety,* 14 October 1996.
Kissel, Howard. "*Traviata:* A Magnificent Obsession." *Daily News,* 1 November 1989.
Klein, Alvin. "*Deathtrap* Can't Get Away with Murder." *New York Times,* 5 March 2000.
Kramer, Mimi. "The Manhattan Traviata." *New Yorker,* 19 June 1989.
Langdon-Davies, Jane. Review: *Porcelain. What's On,* 20 May 1992.
Littell, Robert. "The New Play." *World News,* 20 September 1929.
Loynd, Ray. "Getting to the Heart of *Lisbon Traviata.*" *Los Angeles Times,* 28 November 1990.
Maslin, Janet. "Film Review: *Swoon.*" *New York Times,* 27 March 1992.
Munk, Erika. "Death and Transfiguration." *Village Voice,* 20 March 1978.
Nachman, Gerald. "Slicing and Dicing the Divas." *San Francisco Chronicle,* 27 September 1990.
Patterson, John S. Review: *The Lisbon Traviata. New York Native,* 15 July 1985.
Shenton, Mark. "Reviews: *Deathtrap.*" *The Stage,* 8 September 2010. http://www.thestage.co.uk/reviews/review.php/29533/deathtrap.
Simon, John. "Anti-Romances." *New York,* 19 June 1989.
Simon, John. Review: *The Lisbon Traviata. New York,* 15 July 1985.
Simon, John. Review: *The Lisbon Traviata. New York,* 13 November 1989.
Solomon, Alisa. "AIDSmerica." *Village Voice,* 10 March 1992.
Stone, Laurie. "Sand Blast." *Village Voice,* 28 July 1987.
Winer, Laurie. Review: *The Lisbon Traviata. Wall Street Journal,* 9 June 1989.
Winer, Linda. Review: *The Lisbon Traviata. Newsday,* 1 November 1989.
Winn, Steven. "Unsettling Extremes in *Lisbon:* Comedy Turns to Tragedy in Tale of Gay Opera Fans." *San Francisco Chronicle,* 23 September 1990.

Index